THE BOARDROOM JOURNEY

THE BOARDROOM JOURNEY

PRACTICAL GUIDANCE FOR WOMEN TO SECURE A SEAT AT THE TABLE

DR. KEITH D. DORSEY

WILEY

Published by John Wiley & Sons, Inc., Hoboken, New Jersey.
Published simultaneously in Canada.

For general information on our other products and services or for technical support, please contact our Customer Care Department within the United States at (800) 762-2974, outside the United States at (317) 572-3993 or fax (317) 572-4002.

Wiley also publishes its books in a variety of electronic formats. Some content that appears in print may not be available in electronic formats. For more information about Wiley products, visit our web site at www.wiley.com.

Library of Congress Cataloging-in-Publication Data is Available:

ISBN 9781394331789 (Cloth)
ISBN 9781394331796 (ePub)
ISBN 9781394331802 (ePDF)

Cover Design: Jon Boylan
Cover Image: © Dabarti/Adobe Stock
Author Photo: Courtesy of the author

SKY10100158_031325

To early career women like Lauren, who take bold first steps to shape the future of business: dream big and start now.

To mid-career women like Denise, who balance ambition and resilience to carve their unique paths: embrace the journey and grow stronger with each step.

To late-career women like Michelle, whose expertise and determination inspire and transform boardrooms: know that your contributions leave a lasting impact.

To post-career women like Sharon, whose legacy empowers the next generation: pass the torch, and let your wisdom empower those who lead.

To the mentors, sponsors, and allies standing beside them in solidarity, championing that diversity and meritocracy can coexist: united in purpose, we drive excellence together.

To the organizations and networks dedicated to helping women secure board seats: keep driving meaningful change in corporate leadership and governance—our journey continues.

To all: let's move forward together on this inspiring path.

CONTENTS

CONTENTS

FOREWORD

Embracing diversity and inclusion or delivering strong business performance is not a choice. You can and should have both. The cultural conversation right now is largely ignoring the most obvious point: two things can be true. In a global economy, creating a product or service that resonates with the largest possible base of consumers is an absolute imperative.

The most effective approach for a business to connect with the community it serves is to have its workforce and board of directors reflect its consumers. Delighting the community becomes part of a company's ethos when it lives and breathes the same wants, needs, and desires.

At e.l.f. Beauty, our team is 74% women, 76% Gen Z/millennials, and 44% diverse, largely mirroring our consumers. We believe this gives us a competitive advantage in our speed and quality of decision-making.

Leaders, especially at the board of directors or C-suite levels, condition and reinforce the muscle to understand where the community is and what it is thinking. They not only set the tone but also it's their own perspectives that set the strategy for the future. Life lessons can be the greatest asset in that blueprint. Building governance on this sets up a business to be agile, spot opportunity, and enhance credibility and connection its community.

Growing up in suburban Washington, DC, I had the invaluable experience of helping my immigrant family run our motel business. That taught me the importance of treating people with respect and shaped my framework for approaching business. At e.l.f. Beauty, we believe in the power of inclusivity and stand by the notion that having top talent and unique voices make us stronger in every way.

The relationship between being purpose-led and results-driven is complementary, not contradictory. Businesses and boards have a tremendous opportunity to reap the benefits of diversity of thought, which have been left on the table for years. If, as business leaders, our goal is to maximize returns for shareholders, we must take seriously our responsibility to have a best-in-class brain trust surrounding us.

At e.l.f., we've never had a DEI department, targets, or quotas. We haven't needed them. Positivity, inclusivity, and accessibility are the principles on which we built the company and have seamlessly woven through the entire fabric of our organization. It is who we are, what we are all about and what shapes our highly engaged workplace environment, including our board.

Strong boards shape what's next. They drive innovation, growth, and expansion, and, hopefully, long-term success. That's the equation for productive financial performance. The people who sit in these highest seats of power should be there because they have incredible expertise *and* experience so they can navigate opportunities and challenges with clear, steady, and informed guidance. An inclusive approach, in my opinion, is the most effective way to build a board that leads to improved outcomes and reduced risk.

Since taking e.l.f. public in 2016, I have been very intentional in finding complementary talents to enhance the future of a company with incredible whitespace ahead of it. The knowledge doesn't come from one sector, one geography, one gender, or one generation. A diverse team encourages every individual to leverage their strengths and contribute to a sum that is greater than its parts. The power is in the collective.

Getting to this point, where e.l.f.'s board of directors is 78% women and 44% diverse, wasn't hard, but required purposeful action. I consider myself lucky to have a highly inclusive network that represents the leading voices in business. Not every CEO, and certainly not every potential board member, has that lever to pull.

We must all help carve a path for the next generation of board members that are influenced by what they know and how they learned it versus who or where they learned it from. Board readiness is an art and science that not enough people have access to. I applaud what Keith advocates in *The Boardroom Journey* to equip women with the tools they need to gain exposure and skills—especially those concerning governance and competence in business continuity that grow a business to the next level. Let's be honest: that's what we all want.

In 2025, we shouldn't be starting board journeys from scratch. A guide like this book provides a road map so we create a broad and diverse pool of exceptional director candidates to fuel the best and brightest companies. I encourage all the leaders of today and tomorrow to prioritize normalized board diversity and development, improved market understanding and decisions, productive conflict, enhanced management accountability, and, perhaps most important, board participation. Your value and your influence are directly related to being an active participant in the conversation.

Each one of us has a responsibility to our investors, teams, and customers to strengthen our companies' performance and the communities around us. By earning a seat at the boardroom table, your potential impacts have the possibility of outsized impact.

—Tarang Amin

PREFACE

Every great journey starts with a single step.

—Maya Angelou

In the early stages of conducting research for my doctoral dissertation, I found myself continually distracted. I realize this is not uncommon for doctoral students. But rather than reading what I sat down to read, I repeatedly found myself engrossed in articles, books, and studies related to the composition and dynamics of corporate boards. I came to realize that this behavior wasn't merely a distraction. Instead, it reflected a deeper passion and an urgent issue I felt compelled to address.

The more I delved into the subject, the more apparent the disparities and challenges faced by women and other underrepresented groups in boardrooms became. I vividly recall one particular evening when I was supposed to be researching my original dissertation topic. Instead, I was reading a compelling study on the effects of gender diversity on corporate governance. The insights were too powerful to ignore, and I spent hours jotting down notes and brainstorming ways to address these issues comprehensively. The consistent pull toward this topic led me to realize that my original dissertation topic could wait, but the need for actionable guidance on increasing boardroom diversity could not. I switched my dissertation topic, and the idea for this book soon began to take shape.

During my own evolution, a complex backdrop of divisiveness and upheaval surrounding diversity, equity, and inclusion also was unfolding. We moved from an era of negligible corporate board diversity to a period marred by corporate scandals, social unrest, and consequent demands for diversity and inclusion. Movements, organizations, and legislative acts were launched. Real improvement followed. Diversity initiatives shone the light on the incredible talent that exists around the world, and boards began learning how to find and recruit this talent.

Alongside these changes, other movements and organizations have dedicated themselves to increasing women's representation in executive roles. Lean In, launched in 2013 by Sheryl Sandberg, ignites conversations about women's leadership and highlights the gender gap in corporate leadership. Organizations like the Athena Alliance work to equip women leaders through executive coaching, mentorship, and networking opportunities. Chief, an exclusive network designed for women in leadership roles, offers a community where female executives can support one another while also preparing for corporate board roles.

e.l.f. Beauty launched its bold campaign Change the Boardgame in May 2024, which grabbed attention with its memorable slogan "So many Dicks, so few of everyone else." Pointing out that public corporate boards in the United States have more men named Dick (e.g., Richard, Rich, Rick) than entire groups of underrepresented people, this cheeky but powerful campaign calls for direct action in diversifying boards and achieving gender equity in leadership roles.

These are important contributions and, yet, we have turned another corner: as I finished this manuscript in 2024, a seismic backlash emerged to question the goals and methods of diversity initiatives, slowing the pace of our progress.

This tumultuous backdrop only strengthened my resolve to contribute meaningfully to the conversation by revealing and emphasizing the fact that meritocracy and diversity can and do coexist. For example, the many individuals I interviewed in this book have had incredible careers and have provided equally impressive value to their boards. To this end, I offer the concept of Optimal Diversity™, which refers to ensuring that observable/demographic diversity is coupled with diversity of thought. This approach emphasizes not only what we see but also the diverse experiences, perspectives, and cognitive approaches that individuals bring to the table. It is only by assembling an optimally diverse board that we can confidently say we are serving our boards, organizations, communities, and various stakeholders to our best capabilities.

My key objective through this book is to equip women with the tools they need to be seen and known as they work toward securing corporate board seats and, in doing so, dispel the myth that there aren't enough qualified women to serve on corporate boards. First, I demystify the boardroom and the process of securing a seat at the corporate table by offering a proactive, strategic road map for women at every career stage. Insights, strategies, actionable steps, and real-life examples are provided to illuminate readers' journeys.

Second, I want to spark a broader conversation about Optimal Diversity, revealing that meritocracy and diversity are not opposing aims but instead are symbiotic and share a common goal. I do this to help close the gaps created by well-intentioned but often superficial boardroom diversity initiatives, such as diversity quotas or one-off training programs that focus on meeting immediate targets but frequently result in tokenism, where diversity is pursued for appearance's sake rather than for its intrinsic competitive value.

Producing this manuscript required extensive and meticulous research. I conducted countless conversations, panel discussions, and interviews with female executives, board members, and industry experts around the globe to gather firsthand insights and connect the many dots that make up the puzzle of Optimal Diversity. These conversations were supplemented by a thorough review of existing literature and research on board diversity, governance, and leadership. My approach was holistic, integrating quantitative and qualitative data to provide a breadth and depth of perspectives. Producing this manuscript involved not just reading, thinking, and writing but also iterative feedback sessions with my peers, mentors, and a dedicated editorial team.

This book would not have been possible without the support and involvement of many individuals. Thanks go to my dissertation chair, Dr. Corinne Hyde, who first gave me the vision that I could turn my passion into a book, and to my dissertation committee member, Dr. Sharoni Little, who echoed that such a book was needed. I am indebted to the hundreds of existing and aspiring board members who shared their insights through formal interviews and informal conversations, and specifically to the women who generously shared their stories of struggle and triumph in the making of this book. Your stories have been a constant source of inspiration and motivation. I will never forget a conversation with one senior executive who, despite her achievements, expressed doubts about her readiness for board service. Her story reinforced the need for this book and reminded me of the importance of self-belief and perseverance.

Thanks also go to my colleagues, family, and friends, who gave me grace when I missed many events and one-on-one time in service of writing this book. Their words of encouragement sustained me as I spent countless days and nights reviewing and revising chapters, navigating moments of doubt that eventually gave way to the satisfaction of seeing the manuscript take shape. In this process, editorial support from Dr. Karen Koepp was instrumental in bringing this book to fruition in my uniquely "bilingual" dialect of executive and academic speech. Her dialogue, insights, and feedback, and unwavering belief in the project, helped me balance reflection with progress.

For readers, I suggest approaching this book not as a one-time read, but as a guide to be revisited throughout your career. Each chapter is designed to provide insights and action steps that can be worked through and implemented for your development. The effort you dedicate to these exercises will have a powerful effect on your search. Use this book as a resource to plan your path, reflect on your progress, and stay motivated. Whether you are just starting out, are already on your way to board service, or are on your path to gain your next seat, this book offers something for every stage of your journey.

In conclusion, the landscape of boardroom diversity has seen some progress, but there is still a long way to go. We have moved from a time when boardrooms were almost exclusively male to an era where diversity is at least part of the conversation. Looking ahead, I envision a future when optimally diverse boards are the norm. This book is a step and a call to action toward that future, challenging you to dream bigger, to push through barriers, and to claim your place at the table.

To Your Journey,

Dr. Keith D. Dorsey

ABOUT THIS BOOK

This book is a comprehensive guide designed to empower women at every career stage to secure a seat at the corporate boardroom table. It navigates the complex journey of board service with practical, actionable advice and real-life examples. Throughout this book, we follow four women on their journey to the boardroom. Each woman represents a different life and career stage; consequently, readers will be able to find examples and inspiration from their stories.

The book begins by outlining the urgent need for greater boardroom diversity and setting the stage for the journey ahead. In Part I, Surveying the Landscape, readers are introduced to the corporate board environment, its significance, and the current state of diversity. Readers also learn how to identify their personal motivations for seeking board service and define their board service goals. The final chapter in this section offers tools for self-assessment so readers can determine their readiness for board roles.

In Part II, Gearing Up for the Trek, readers are introduced to five types of capital they need to develop and leverage to secure a seat at the corporate board table. These capitals include cultural capital, the strength and drive we acquire during our formative years as a result of our family, friends, experiences, successes, and challenges; director capital, the personality traits and working style, training, experience, and knowledge specific to filling the role of a director on the board;

human capital, the sum of our education, knowledge, skills, personal attributes, and experience to generate a given set of outcomes; social capital, the sum of structural, cognitive, and relational resources available to us via our social networks; and Commitment Capital™, the combination of human, social, and other resources we use to execute and complete a specific task. The final chapter in this section discusses how to integrate the various forms of capital to create a compelling board readiness story and candidacy.

In Part III, Navigating the Journey, readers are encouraged to optimize their chances of success in reaching the boardroom by employing strategies for overcoming opposition and skepticism as well as assembling a support team of mentors, sponsors, and allies. The final chapter in this section describes how readers can fail-proof their journeys to bolster their resilience and long-term success.

The book concludes with a look ahead at what's next for readers, a review of various resources that can help them along the way, and a return to our four protagonists to find out where they are now.

By addressing both observable demographic diversity and the often hidden sources of diversity within all board members, this book advocates for Optimal Diversity as a means to enhance corporate governance and performance.

CHAPTER ONE

INTRODUCTION

To get something you never had, you have to do
something you never did.
  —Denzel Washington, University of Pennsylvania Commencement
  Address, May 16, 2011

t was an exciting time, indeed. The stock market was booming, and nearly everyone from the working poor to the well-heeled were in it to win it. Shareholders of all stripes piled on as initial public offerings were released. Stock prices soared, money flowed, and times were good.

But like most good things, it wasn't to last. Less than a year later, prices started dropping. One after another, investors were forced to liquidate their positions, triggering a spate of bankruptcies. As similar bubbles started popping around the world, share prices continued to fall. The wealth of many was decimated and significant global economic damage was evident.

Then came the ugly truth. The company that had started it all (and the companies that followed suit) had defrauded the public and their shareholders by misrepresenting their prospects, inflating their stock prices, and encouraging speculative trading. It was corporate scandal writ large, all made possible by insufficient governance.

Does this story sound familiar? Probably. Can you name the company in question? Probably not.

The reason it is difficult to recognize this as England's 1720 South Sea Bubble[1] (named after the public-private partnership titled the South Sea Company) is because problems of inadequate corporate management and governance are far too common. The subsequent three hundred years have been riddled with such events, including corporate accounting scandals; national financial crises; environmental disasters; and ethical, social, and health care crises. Many of these outcomes can be traced back to mismanagement, unethical behavior, and excessive risk-taking, resulting in severe impacts for the organizations in question, in addition to serious economic and social consequences for organizational stakeholders and the public. The quest to prevent and mitigate such events has heightened efforts to improve how we regulate, manage, and oversee the corporations on which we and our global economy rely.

THE PUSH TO IMPROVE GOVERNANCE

The mandate is simple: corporate governance must improve to ensure effective and responsible business operation, risk mitigation, business continuity, and success. That is how boards protect shareholders' interests.

1. **Protection of shareholder interests.** Strong corporate governance guarantees that management behaves in the shareholders' best interests and gives them access to information and a say in business decisions. By promoting a more sustainable approach to business and balancing management's objectives with the company's long-term health, better corporate governance can also aid in the shift in emphasis from short-term gains to long-term value generation.

2. **Accountability and appropriate risk-taking.** Sound corporate governance fosters accountability from organization leaders. Executives and board members are held accountable for their activities by establishing clear

procedures for decision-making and reporting. This kind of accountability aids in the prevention of mismanagement, fraud, and unethical activity. Sound company governance also promotes effective risk identification and management, which lower the possibility of monetary and reputational problems.

3. **Sustainability.** Good corporate governance promotes moral and conscientious business practices, including attention to the social and environmental effects of business operations. Robust governance frameworks also have the potential to foster organizational creativity and flexibility balanced with effective decision-making procedures and cultural practices that honor the company's original concept. These in turn can support a company's long-term viability and strengthen the company's competitiveness and brand.

Achieving these aims helps preserve customer and public trust, attract investors, and uphold the organization's role as social actor. These outcomes are critical because the success of any corporation depends on the trust of its stakeholders—including the public and its suppliers, employees, and customers. To further safeguard public interest, corporate governance must hold itself to relevant regulations. Companies who disregard these regulations risk legal repercussions as well as reputational harm.

Furthermore, both institutional and individual investors are more inclined to invest in companies that have sound governance, as such practices improve the company's reputation and help reduce costs. Top talent also tends to gravitate toward employers who value sound governance in the form of transparency, ethical behavior, and responsible decision-making.

One board member I interviewed as part of my research for this book explained that improving governance was her driving motivation to become an independent director. She shared:

> When I dealt with boards, I realized that a lot of board members are detached from business and ecosystem. They're career board members. It's almost like becoming inbred. The way to fight it is to make sure that the other large enterprises take the necessary step to save themselves and have impact on the ecosystem so that we don't end up with only three companies in the world.

THE CASE FOR GENDER AND ETHNIC DIVERSITY ON CORPORATE BOARDS

Although poor governance has a long global history, the push for diversity on boards did not begin in earnest until the early 2000s as corporate scandals and questionable business tactics grew rampant. Psychologist and Stanford professor Philip Zimbardo, who created the 1971 watershed Stanford prison experiment and later produced a range of works examining why good people do bad things observed, "Most of the evil of the world comes about not out of evil motives, but somebody saying 'get with the program, be a team player,'"[2] ultimately resulting in uncritical adherence to group norms. Boards tend to be relatively homogeneous compared to the stakeholders they serve, and researchers suggest that this lack of diversity is the reason for poor corporate governance and missed opportunities. Researchers have found that homogeneous boards lack cognitive diversity and are less likely to promote strategies that differ from historical norms and industry competitors.[3] In turn, board diversity is believed to be an antidote to the risk of playing well together that instead turns into the slippery slope of groupthink.

Combined with increased risks such as cybercrime and an accelerating pace of change and industry disruption, boards began turning to "refreshment practices," meaning strategies boards use to periodically evaluate and update their composition, bringing in new members with relevant skills, expertise, and perspectives to ensure they had the human capital they needed to fulfill their mandates and navigate the complex demands they faced. These pressures led businesses, institutional investors, stock exchange indexes, government leaders, and other policymakers to argue for increased gender and ethnic diversity in the boardroom.

The focus on board diversity has been accompanied by a rash of gender diversity research and a somewhat less vigorous exploration of board diversity based on race and ethnicity.[4] These studies have revealed that not only does board diversity make ethical sense[5] but also several practical benefits follow an increase of women and people of color on corporate boards[6]:

- **Normalizes board diversity and development.** Research suggests that having at least one-third of the board directors be female creates a critical mass that normalizes diversity.[7] These studies additionally found that such boards are more likely to commit to creating board development practices that enhance the board's operational and strategic control, enhancing organizational performance and innovation.[8]
- **Improves board participation.** Attendance at periodic board meetings is essential because directors carry out their board duties during these meetings. Studies show that women directors have better board meeting attendance, prepare better for meetings, engage more actively, and require more robust discussion compared to their male counterparts.[9] These same studies indicate that male directors' attendance, preparation, and participation improve in response to their female colleagues' behavior, thus improving board decision-making and performance.[10]
- **Improves market understanding and decisions.** Women and ethnically diverse directors help the board gain a broader understanding of the marketplace, its stakeholders, and complex issues. These fresh perspectives aid in correcting informational biases during problem-solving, leading to improved decisions, oversight, and organizational bottom lines.[11]
- **Creates productive conflict.** Although more homogeneous boards tend to be more cohesive and have less debate and conflict,[12] these debates have a high likelihood of being productive, as women directors have been found to have enhanced collaboration skills, heightened sensitivity toward others, and increased ability to resolve task-related and interpersonal disagreements.[13] Without conflict negotiation skills on the board, however,

heterogeneous boards risk losing their diversity advantage if there is destructive dialogue or an excessive focus on consensus-building.[14]

- **Enhances management accountability.** Women and people of color are more likely to have encountered discrimination in their careers, potentially heightening their awareness to inequity and other unethical behavior.[15] Accordingly, studies suggest that these directors demand more management accountability, are more challenging monitors of executive teams, and are less apt to excuse financial misreporting, inadequate executive performance, and excessive chief executive pay.[16] Care must be taken, however, to ensure that productive challenge does not turn into over-monitoring, which builds distrust between management and the board, slows down decision-making, increases agency costs, and delays the achievement of strategic growth objectives.[17]

Many of the directors I speak with deeply understand these benefits. One of these explained to me:

I do spend a lot of time on conservative boards explaining the business value of diversity. I compiled a list of the top 10 studies from the most conservative outlets like *Wall Street Journal* to show the business benefit of diversity and how companies can make more money. Investors see that this makes sense and, frankly, customers do too. There's a lot more attention to companies that have leadership that lacks diversity, and that will hurt them.

Several noteworthy examples prove this director's point. Accenture, which ranks among the companies with the most diverse boards, stated that its director diversity enables it to incorporate more viewpoints, leading to enhanced global competitiveness. However, Uber faced challenges related to lack of board diversity and inadequate oversight, which critics say contributed to a toxic culture, poor decision-making, and numerous scandals. Furthermore, the longer board homogeneity is allowed to persist, the more vulnerable the board is to overlooking risks, signposts, and critical moments when executives' decisions need to be challenged rather than simply approved. These benefits reveal that increasing the number of women and people of color on boards simply makes good business sense. So where do we stand today?

BOARD DIVERSITY BY THE NUMBERS

Since the 1990s, researchers studying board composition primarily focused on gender over other diversity categories. Scholars speculated that as board diversity increased, white women would be preferentially selected for sponsorship due the biases of similarity attraction and white male directors being more likely to select women from a similar racial group. Accordingly, ethnic minority women would be the least represented group on corporate boards because of the intersectional multiplying effect of being both female (gender diverse) and ethnically diverse.[18]

These speculations appear to bear out in the statistics. In Deloitte's 7th edition of their Missing Pieces report,[19] which tracks board diversity in America's largest and most prominent public companies, researchers characterized the progress of diversity as "uneven." They found that in 2022, women and individuals (of all genders) from underrepresented racial and ethnic groups held an unprecedented 44.7% of Fortune 500 board seats (up from 26.7% in 2012). However, women from underrepresented racial and ethnic groups occupied only 7.8% of board seats, and women of all racial and ethnic backgrounds held 30.4% of seats across Fortune 500 companies. Although these are impressive gains over 10 years compared to 3.2% of seats and 16.6% of seats in 2012, respectively, a stark lack of parity remains, given that women comprise 50.5% of the Fortune 500 working population (see Table 1.1). The researchers predict that board diversity for Fortune 500 companies will reach parity with the general population for African American and Asian men and women by 2030 and for women of all ethnic and racial backgrounds by 2040. However, the researchers do not predict ever reaching parity for Latino individuals for the forecasted period (up to 2060).

These statistics suggest that although gender diversity is improving on boards, white women's representation is increasing faster than that of ethnic minority women. Perhaps more shockingly, the 2020 PwC Annual Corporate Directors Survey revealed that 47% of board directors said gender diversity is very important, whereas only 34% of directors said it was important to have racial diversity on their board.[20]

Table 1.1   Fortune 500 Board Seats by Gender and Ethnicity.

Demographic	2012	2022	Percentage of Working Population in 2022
All underrepresented racial and ethnic groups	13.3%	22.2%	40.6%
All women	16.6%	30.4%	50.5%
Women from underrepresented racial and ethnic groups	3.2%	7.8%	—
White women and individuals from underrepresented racial and ethnic groups	26.7%	44.7%	—

SOURCE: Deloitte (2022).

Becoming a board director myself and noticing the advantages diverse boards had over more homogenous boards motivated me to dedicate my doctoral studies to investigating board composition more deeply. What I learned convinced me that further research and action was needed to understand how the intersection of multiple identities could help reveal the disadvantages ethnic minority women directors accrue and what could be done to broaden the pathway to the boardroom for all women. That is the purpose of this book. But first, I want to share a little more about me.

MY STORY

My board service story traces all the way back to my early childhood in the late 1960s Washington, DC, although few, if any, at that time could have predicted the journey that culminated in writing this book. In my family, a high school diploma was a terminal degree and the career pathway for men was the military. I followed suit and enlisted in the Air Force the summer before my senior year of high school. I left for basic training just weeks after high school graduation. I rose in the ranks as quickly as I could, but my lack of patience for seniority-based advancement ultimately prompted me to seek a civilian career in business in my early 20s.

I went on to forge a 30-plus year track record of supporting businesses from small firms to large multinational companies achieve exponential sales growth and shareholder value. I held executive roles in sales and served as a coach and consultant. I specialized in helping businesses navigate significant periods of change by uncovering root causes, crafting strategic growth plans, and attracting, developing, coaching, engaging, and retaining key talent. As of this writing, I am transitioning from managing partner at a global executive search firm to The Boardroom Journey, my own firm dedicated to helping aspiring and existing board members find their next seat via accountability-based coaching and helping boards achieve optimal outcomes.

My path to board service was far less straightforward—and, if I'm honest, it was accidental. I served on my first board, which was for the Pepperdine University Graziadio Business School, in 2016 but still didn't begin to comprehend the potential opportunities and responsibilities of board service until two years later when I received my first invitation to serve on a private company board. My full-time role did not permit me to accept the seat, but the seed had been planted.

Only months later, a corporate reorganization dramatically changed the course of my career. Rather than accept another role in the company, I chose early retirement and dove headfirst into governance. I joined the National Association of Corporate Directors (NACD), swiftly completed their Governance Fellowship program, and was among the first 100 members to earn NACD's "Directorship Certified" designation. Additionally, I am a member of the Executive Leadership Council, and a graduate of Santa Clara University's Black Corporate Board Readiness program. As of this writing, I hold board seats at a private technology and third-party administration company, a major university's business school, a municipality's financial advisory commission, and a well-known trail association nonprofit. Previously, I served on the board of a firm that provides recruitment process outsourcing and talent acquisition services.

Although I didn't make it back to college until my 40s, I ultimately completed the journey, earning a bachelor's, master's, and finally an actual terminal degree in the form of a Doctor of Education (EdD) in organizational change and leadership from the University of Southern California. By that time, I was passionate about the role boards play in business and was convinced that effective board performance requires careful attention to *who* is on the board. I dedicated my doctoral dissertation to examining the pathways Black women executives take to secure corporate board seats.

Since then, I write, research, and speak extensively to help create signposts that illuminate and broaden the otherwise tangled pathway to the boardroom. I do this so that those individuals with the fortitude and passion to serve can reach this important destination. This book is my latest contribution to that effort.

As the adage goes, hindsight is 20/20. Given my nontraditional path to board service, I have ample hindsight and a dedication to improving corporate governance by equipping the talented and passionate individuals who can elevate our boards and organizations. By following the pathways of four women of different ages, career stages, backgrounds, and ethnicities, my hope is that you will begin to see how you, too, can chart your own pathway to board service.

MEET THE WOMEN

Although the mindset, strategies, and tactics presented in this book can be useful for wide audiences, this book specifically focuses on women, who are needed now more than ever before on corporate boards. By blending research, practical tips, and compelling stories, this book provides the information, inspiration, and practical techniques for securing board member positions. Throughout the book, we will follow the stories of four women: Lauren, 25; Denise, 40; Michele, 55; and Sharon, 62. The stories of these women were inspired by a variety of talented professionals and board members I have been fortunate to meet in my career, research, and board service journey. However, any similarity to actual persons, living or dead, is purely coincidental.

> **Lauren** is an Asian American 25-year-old single college graduate. She grew up in the mid-Atlantic United States and attended a public state university. She was intrigued by her business classes and knew since her junior year of college that she wanted to pursue a career in sales. This fell a bit outside her parents' hopes for her to be in medicine, as Lauren's mom is a pharmaceutical sales representative for a major pharmaceutical firm and her dad is a physician. Lauren's career inspiration was sparked by her dad's oldest brother, a chief financial officer who serves on several boards. She had always been intrigued by the stories he would casually share about

flying here or there for board meetings. Lauren accepted an entry-level sales position for a Fortune 1,000 company at age 22 and was tapped for a middle management position only three years later due to her sales prowess, willingness to help colleagues, and her selfless leadership on the team. She made certain that those around her were as successful as she was. When she was tapped for her first management role, her uncle started advising her about the things she should consider in shaping her career. Lauren found a willing mentor in her uncle, as his own children are in the medical and legal professions. Lauren's uncle took her under his wing and is now helping her craft her career to position herself for a board position.

Denise is a Latina 40-year-old married mother of two teenagers. She grew up in Texas and earned her bachelor's at a public state university before earning a law degree at age 25. She completed two years at a small law firm specializing on energy and environmental law, and then took four years off to have her children. At age 31, she joined a boutique firm dedicated to environmental, social, and governance (ESG) consulting in the energy sector. She moved up the ranks from consultant to strategic advisor and was awarded a partner position at age 39. She never considered board service until she was asked to join the board of a prominent gymnastics not-for-profit organization due to her 13-year-old daughter's participation in competitive gymnastics.

Michele is a married 55-year-old African American empty nester. She has one child in college and one who recently graduated. Michele grew up in the Bay Area and earned her bachelor of business administration at an Ivy League institution before being hired into the management training track at a Fortune 500 company. She gained a breadth of experience and business knowledge over her four years there thanks to the multiple six- to nine-month cross-functional rotations she completed. She then earned an Ivy League master of business administration before joining a Big 4 consulting firm where she gained extensive global experience focused on IT transformation. After four years, she returned to the Bay Area where she joined the ranks of various Fortune 500 tech firms as she moved through progressive leadership roles, beginning with manager of IT, then director, then vice president, and senior vice president. For the past five years, she has held the executive vice president of technology role at a Fortune 500 tech company. Board service didn't cross her mind until two of her C-suite colleagues secured board seats. This intrigued her, but she filed it under "things to do when I have time." Two events soon catalyzed her entry into the boardroom: the signing of California Senate Bill 826 in 2018, which instituted board gender diversity legislation, and the social unrest of summer 2020. The groundswell for gender and racial equity that followed led to Michele being tapped for a board seat.

Sharon is a divorced 62-year-old white mother of three children. Sharon grew up in Michigan and earned her bachelor of science in electrical engineering at age 22 from a public state university. She worked for five years at an automotive manufacturer before becoming a stay-at-home mom. When she divorced at age 37, staying home with her children was no longer viable and she joined the ranks of her father's $45 million original equipment manufacturer family-owned business. She gained a breadth and depth of experience as she rotated throughout the company and took over the chief executive role at age 50 when her father stepped down. After 12 years, she retired, handing the chief executive role to her 50-year-old brother. Although she had served on the internal board during her time as chief executive, she had never served on any other board, nor had she even thought about it until she realized she had few plans for her retirement besides some vague intentions to "spend some time with the grandkids" and "read that book everyone is talking about."

In this book, we will follow these women as they survey the corporate board landscape, assess and grow the competencies they need to secure a board seat, and manage themselves and their mindsets through the arduous journey ahead. Each of these women are beginning at a different starting point, yet each has value to add and the potential to secure a seat. Their journeys will be different in their length and details. However, all will face challenges, and all will need careful self-reflection, planning, and self-management to navigate these challenges. My hope is that you can see aspects of yourself in their stories, learn with them and through them, and enjoy the journey along the way.

HOW THIS BOOK IS ORGANIZED

This book guides you through the process of finding your route to meaningful board service. First, we get oriented to the board landscape and the benefits of holding a board position. Then, we learn the process of self-evaluation and mobilization for the journey. Finally, we gain tools and tactics for managing ourselves along the way in order to achieve the best possible board service results. In each chapter, we also revisit our protagonists to see how they are navigating each step of the journey and gain practical action steps to implement on the journey.

> **Part I: Surveying the Landscape.** We begin in Chapter 2 with an overview of the boardroom, including what a board of directors is and what they do. We also discuss the types of boards that exist, who serves on these boards, and the approach we need to take to be valuable board members—which can be different than the approach we take as executives. In Chapter 3, we tackle why people want to be board members and invite you to explore your own why for doing so. Chapter 4 guides you in making some initial decisions about your intended board service destination, and Chapter 5 provides a process for you to gauge your fitness level for making the journey.

> **Part II: Gearing Up for the Trek.** In Part II, we gain a structured process of gearing up for your journey by outlining the principles and practices for gauging and enhancing the competencies you will need to secure a board seat and serve on a board. We talk about these competencies as five types of capital: cultural capital (Chapter 6), director capital (Chapter 7), human capital (Chapter 8), social capital (Chapter 9), and Commitment Capital (Chapter 10). We end Part II with practical guidance on how to leverage your capital portfolio (Chapter 11).

> **Part III: Navigating the Journey.** As the saying goes, the best laid plans often go awry. For this reason, we discuss the need and provide tools and techniques for managing yourself, your mindset, and your career in Part III. We begin with discussing how to neutralize naysayers (whether

yourself or others) in Chapter 12. In Chapter 13, we review the individuals critical to your success—your support team, including your role models, mentors, allies, sponsors, and accountability partners. Finally, in Chapter 14, we review how to fail-proof your journey by navigating glass cliff opportunities and setting and monitoring your pace.

In Chapter 15, the book concludes by bringing it all home with a final set of guidance, actionable steps, and tools. Throughout this book, pay attention to not only your journey but also the journeys of our four protagonists as they seek to secure their first, second, third, or fourth board seats. Pay attention to what they do and learn. Pay attention to what their sponsors and mentors say. You will need these words of wisdom, and you may find yourself providing these words of wisdom to others along their own journeys.

I also encourage you to implement the action steps you learn and to begin the active process of charting your course. As a board member, you will have no shortage of homework in preparation for meetings. This book and the action steps contained within can help you get in the practice of learning and doing homework now.

PART I

SURVEYING THE LANDSCAPE

We begin with an overview of the boardroom, including what a board of directors is and what they do. We also discuss the types of boards that exist, who serves on board, and the approach we need to take to be valuable board members—which can be different than the approach we take as executives. We also tackle why people want to be board members and invite you to explore your own reasons for pursuing this goal. Finally, we guide you in making some initial decisions about your intended board service destination and outline a process for you to gauge your fitness level for making the journey.

CHAPTER TWO

WELCOME TO THE BOARDROOM

There are things known and things unknown, and in between are the doors.

—Jim Morrison

M any executives—even those who have been invited to serve on a board—lack understanding of the history, role, and work of a board of directors. This chapter provides an overview of these issues to prepare you to evaluate and enhance your readiness for board service. In this chapter, we discuss the history and definition of boards of directors, the work that boards do, the types of boards that exist, and the roles directors play.

WHAT IS A BOARD OF DIRECTORS?

The creation of board governance as the standard for corporations is traced to roots in the Muscovy Trading Company (founded 1555), the Levant Company (founded 1592), and the East India Company (founded 1600), among others. The law generally believed to be the first statute outlining the rules of incorporation for US corporations was New York's 1811 Act, which mandated that "the stock, property and concerns of such company shall be managed and conducted by trustees, who, except those for the first year, shall be elected at such time and place as shall be directed by the by laws of the said company."[1]

Today, businesses, nonprofit organizations, and even government agencies all may have boards of directors. The board of directors is a group of individuals from inside the company (called executive directors) and outside the company (called nonexecutive or independent directors) who are tasked with oversight of the company's activities, including appointing the chief executive officer (CEO) of the organization and approving its overall strategic direction.

This board-centered model is the accepted standard in US corporation law and the most common model of corporate governance practiced around the world.[2] Although the world of governance can be highly idiosyncratic from company to company, three fundamental concepts distinguish this governance paradigm from management and oversight in other business forms:

- **Role of shareholders.** Shareholders own the business and choose the directors who will run it. Directors typically are offered one- to three-year terms. Shareholder involvement will look different depending on whether the company is publicly or privately held. In a public company, shareholders are the investors who buy stocks in the company. During the proxy season/ annual board meeting, these investors can vote on the elected board members who were vetted and selected by the board's nomination and governance committee.

  In a private company, the shareholders often comprise a small group of investors. In these situations, the board members are usually chosen by the board itself or by the nominations and governance committee, if one exists. Shareholders then vote on the proposed director selections. In other business forms (e.g., partnerships), the partners own and manage the business or agree on who will manage the business.

- **Decision-making practices.** In companies with boards, decisions of certain types or magnitude require board approval. These board decisions are made by a group of peers operating in concert through a process of voting and majority rule. The concept of the group is very important according to corporate law rule—specifically, directors have no authority to act individually. This means that directors gain their authority only through group action exercised during board meetings. By contrast, in businesses without boards, decisions typically are made by a single person (in smaller or simpler organizational structures) or by hierarchical groups (in larger or more complex organizations).

- **Selection and supervision of CEO.** The ultimate authority for choosing and managing the CEO rests with the board.[a] Some company's bylaws also require directors to assist the CEO in selecting the rest of the C-suite.

The powers, duties, and responsibilities of the board of directors are determined by government regulations and the organization's own constitution and bylaws. These authorities may specify the number of members of the board, how they are to be chosen, and how often they are to meet.

For example, the board of the Federal Home Loan Bank of Des Moines operates under a cooperative structure in which its member institutions are its shareholders. Decision-making is collective and emphasizes regulatory compliance and stakeholder interests. There is a significant focus on governance and ensuring that the decisions align with the cooperative's mission and regulatory requirements. The CEO selection process is rigorous and involves a competitive process with self-nomination being a possible route. Supervision of the CEO is thorough and involves close alignment with the board's strategic vision and regulatory expectations.

---

[a] In private companies led by founder CEOs, the CEO first selects the directors, who then manage the CEO.

To provide some contrast, Premera Blue Cross is a more conventional public company setup in which its shareholders play a significant role in influencing the board's decisions through their voting rights and other traditional means of corporate governance. The board focuses on strategic oversight and governance with a blend of independent directors bringing diverse perspectives. The practices include standard corporate governance mechanisms with a strong emphasis on fiduciary responsibilities. CEO selection is typically influenced by the board's nominating and governance committee, ensuring that the selected individual aligns with the company's strategic objectives and performance metrics. Supervision includes regular performance reviews and strategic alignment checks.

These examples illustrate the diversity in corporate board structures and practices, highlighting how the role of shareholders, decision-making processes, and CEO oversight can vary significantly between organizations.

WHAT BOARDS DO

The primary task of corporate boards is to provide governance of the firm by monitoring the management team on behalf of the company's shareholders. Boards do this through three activities:

- **Oversight.** Making sure the management team does not pursue its own interest at the expense of shareholders' interests, such as monitoring compliance with regulatory requirements. The board's oversight function is to put measures in place so the management team does not pursue its own interest at the expense of shareholders' interests. This practice establishes board independence so it functions in the best interest of shareholders.
- **Management.** Providing guidance regarding strategic changes in the organization, including hiring and firing the firm's top executive and setting their compensation; collaborating with the management team to design and form the corporate strategy; serving as the governing agency to sanction and oversee the company's strategic course; approving mergers, acquisitions, divestitures, and significant purchases; and providing advice on complex transactions. Under the management component of corporate

governance, the directors get involved in hiring and firing the firm's top executives and setting their compensation. Directors additionally collaborate with the management team to design and form the corporate strategy and serve as the governing agency to sanction and oversee its strategic course. The board also gets involved in approving mergers, acquisitions, divestitures, and significant purchases. The CEO often consults with various board members to seek advice on complex transactions.

- **Service.** Acting as executive advisors for the chief executive and the rest of the management team for decision-making and offering alternative viewpoints. Importantly, independent directors can approach complex situations from an outsider's perspective and offer alternative viewpoints. Outside directors also can help boards increase the legitimacy and trust of the firms they serve by providing additional awareness of risk and competence in decision-making.

TYPES OF BOARDS

Although all boards are tasked with oversight, management, and service responsibilities, the amount and nature of these activities vary from board to board. Accordingly, your experience, competencies, and interests may be a great fit for one board but not for another board. Table 2.1 helps illustrate the differences among the various kinds of boards in existence.

Not-for-profit boards serve legally established tax-exempt organizations of any size.[3] These organizations are run by volunteers and can be called "recreational organizations." These organizations do not have a business goal of earning revenue, and any money earned through business activities or donations is allocated to running the organization rather than generating a profit for any owners. Board members for these organizations tend to be individuals who are dedicated to the mission of the organization and who have business development skills, networking skills, connections to potential donors, and personal funds to make annual donations to the organization. Due to the need for and focus on fundraising, these boards tend to be larger than other types of boards. Although board members

Table 2.1   Features and Needs of Boards of Directors.

Type of board	Company description and objectives	Board activities	What the board needs
NONPROFITS AND NOT-FOR-PROFITS			
Not-for-profit board	Legally established nonprofit of any size run by volunteers and do not have a business goal of earning revenue	↔ Oversight ↓ Management ↓ Service	Individuals with business development skills, networking skills, connections to potential donors, and personal funds to make annual donations to the organization
Nonprofit board	Legally established nonprofit of any size formed explicitly to benefit the public good. Nonprofits are run like a business with the aim generating revenue and earning profits that do not support any single member.	↑ Oversight ↑ Management ↔ Service	Individuals with connections to potential donors and who can offer needed knowledge and skills to act as advisors to the executive director/CEO as they seek to exercise prudent financial management and achieve a sustainable future
PRIVATE ORGANIZATIONS			
Startup private boards	Founder CEOs who are functional specialists and want to scale their private business	↔ Oversight ↑ Management ↑ Service	Individuals with connections to funding who have done what the company is now trying to do, who are capable of providing strategic advice, and who can provide monitoring and governance to support the organization's growth
Family-owned private boards	Small to large private businesses looking to scale	↔ Oversight ↓ Management ↑ Service	Individuals with connections to funding and who have done what the company is now trying to do, those capable of providing strategic advice, and those capable of providing monitoring and governance to support the organization's growth

(Continued)

Table 2.1   (Continued)

Type of board	Company description and objectives	Board activities	What the board needs
Mutual company private board	Small to large business owned by customers or policyholders, commonly found in insurance and some banking organizations	↑ Oversight ↓ Management ↓ Service	Individuals capable of providing strategic advice as well as monitoring and governance to support the organization's growth
Private equity– or venture capital– funded private boards	Small to medium private businesses looking to scale	↔ Oversight ↓ Management ↑ Service	Individuals capable of providing strategic advice as well as monitoring and governance to support the organization's growth and those who have done what the company is now trying to do
PUBLIC ORGANIZATIONS			
Small cap public corporate boards	A public company with total market capitalization of less than $1 billion focused on growth	↑ Oversight ↑ Management ↑ Service	Individuals capable of providing strategic advice as well as monitoring and governance to support the organization's growth
Mid- to large cap public corporate boards	A public company with total market capitalization of $1 billion or more focused on reputation	↑ Oversight ↑ Management ↓ Service	Well-recognized executives and board members capable of providing the monitoring and governance necessary to protect the organization's reputation

↑ - high levels of this activity; ↓ - low levels of this activity; ↔ - moderate levels of this activity;

provide moderate oversight capacity, they provide lower levels of management and service. Serving on this type of board tends to produce a sense of accomplishment in supporting the organization's vision, mission, and values and can expand the directors' social capital and network, which may help lead to other board service opportunities.

Nonprofit boards serve legally established tax-exempt organizations of any size that are formed explicitly to further a social cause and provide a public benefit.[4] Nonprofit organizations include hospitals, universities, national charities, and foundations. Nonprofits are run like a business and try to earn a profit, although profits are reinvested in the business rather than used to produce profits for owners or any single member. Nonprofit boards are tasked with providing oversight, advisory, and management of the nonprofit's executive director or president. Experience on nonprofit boards can produce transferable knowledge, skills, and experience that can be applied to private and public boards. As one director I interviewed expressed, "The only difference between nonprofit and for-profit board service is the 'non.'" She explained, "The lessons you learn in board governance are so key. You learn about budgetary matters, and you learn to speak with confidence; you learn how to set agenda and just governance." Limited attention is given in subsequent chapters of this book about securing a seat on nonprofit boards. This book primarily focuses on preparing oneself best to secure a private or public corporate board seat.

Private boards oversee organizations owned by startup founders, executive management, families, customers or policyholders, private equity firms, or venture capital firms. In startup firms, early-stage companies often have three to five seats, which are held by the startup's CEO and financial investors, as well as independent directors (usually peer CEOs), and the company's legal counsel. In private businesses owned by private equity or venture capital firms, the directors primarily consist of internal executives (e.g., founder/CEO, CFO) and investors. In these companies, board members are particularly vital for providing advice related to skill gaps in the company.

Another type of private company is a mutual company, which its policyholders or customers own. Its profits are shared with its policyholders or customers. The policyholders or customers select the board members and could even be policyholders. Most board members have industry experience. The experience gained from serving on the board of a mutual company is directly transferrable to serving on a private or public corporate board.

Some private companies are very large family-owned businesses (e.g., Cargill, Chik Fil-A, Amway). Their boards resemble and operate like public company boards. In these companies, the family or groups of families control at least 50% of the voting shares, and the remaining board seats typically are occupied by friends or associates of the family for smaller family-owned businesses.

The boards of public organizations are staffed by internal executives as well as independent directors from outside the organization. Compared to private organizations, public organizations serve a larger and more diverse collection of shareholders, tend to have a stronger focus on short-term profits, and are susceptible to shareholder activism.

Reflecting on my research for this book, the directors I interviewed described very different kinds of experiences, depending on the kind of board they served. Each type of board directorship offers unique challenges and opportunities, influenced by the nature of the organization and its objectives. Public board directors face higher regulatory scrutiny, greater stakeholder accountability, and deal with more complex and large-scale operations. Several directors described the multiyear and highly complex process of helping take their companies public. Private board directors tend to enjoy greater flexibility, focus on growth and innovation, and often have closer working relationships with the company's leadership. One director described her role in this way: "I'm interested in teaching and coaching and advising and being the right sounding board. I love building. I love being involved with strategic thinking. So I decided to offer that by being a board director to other companies." Meanwhile, nonprofit board directors tend to be mission-driven, focus on fundraising and advocacy, and typically work with a diverse group of board members. One director I interviewed explained, "So I'm on a very large nonprofit organization board that is the largest community foundation in the world. Many people on those larger boards are also on corporate boards. So you get to meet other people and they get to see you in action. It's great for your corporate board career."

TYPES OF DIRECTORS

The specific makeup of the corporate board depends on the size, sector, and governance structure of the company. Several types of directors may occupy positions on a corporate board.

One or more seats of any corporate board are occupied by inside directors, also called executive directors. These are members of the management team, such as the CEO, CFO, and other senior executives who provide the board with insights into the company's daily operations to help the board make effective decisions. Voting rights typically are retained only by the CEO and occasionally the CFO. The company's general counsel also may occupy a board seat to carry out the secretary function but generally does not have a fiduciary or voting role.[b]

Within a private company owned by a private equity or venture capital firm, one or more additional seats are occupied by investor directors. The number of seats taken by the investing firm is negotiated as part of the acquisition deal, with managing partners and partners of investment firms often being assigned board seats in the companies within their portfolio. Investor directors help ensure the investing firm's oversight over its investments. This was the case for one director I interviewed, whose term ended when the board sold the company to a private equity, who then filled two seats with its own people.

Although the executives who run the company and those who fund the company's operations may be obvious choices for the board, another critical addition to a corporate board is the outside director, also called a nonexecutive or independent director. These individuals have no close financial or personal ties to the company, its shareholders, or its management. These directors' outsider status enables them to provide an objective viewpoint and sense of assurance that the board will make choices that optimize the interests of all shareholders. Historically, outside directors have been active or retired CEOs and CFOs from other companies. More recently, given the rise of cybercrime, accounting scandals, environmental concerns, and other issues, boards have looked beyond these

---

[b] Despite these limitations, legal professionals holding a secretary role on an internal board receive excellent preparation for future independent director roles on external boards.

traditional posts to include chief technology officers, chief operating officers, chief human resources officers, and senior leaders with deep functional expertise. Many independent directors bring a wealth of knowledge and experience, especially if they serve on several boards.

Several directors I interviewed had gained extensive experience serving on multiple boards. One such individual served on a large private insurance company and several smaller innovative companies, which enabled her to bring valuable insights to each board. Her role involved learning from the agility and innovation of younger companies and applying those lessons to more mature organizations. In turn, the practices she gained from the larger organizations aided the smaller organizations in maturing their operations. Her ability to transfer knowledge and innovative practices from one board to another provided each company with a broader perspective and new strategies for growth and agility. This cross-pollination of ideas and best practices enriched the governance and strategic direction of all the companies she was involved with, demonstrating the unique value of directors who serve on multiple boards.

Stock exchange listing standards mandate the inclusion of outside directors on public boards. Accordingly, the balance of inside and outside directors is steadily increasing. The NACD reported in its Inside the Public Company Boardroom study, that only 15% of boards in the Russell 3,000 had compositions in which 90% of board members were independent directors in 2020. This figure increased to 17% in 2021 and 18% in 2022.[5] By contrast, only one-third of private company boards were found to have independent directors in a 2021 survey by Bolster.[6] The presence of independent directors can bring critical insights and prevent potential missteps by providing a necessary check on the board's decisions. Without independent directors, boards may miss out on important perspectives that could protect the company's long-term interests. One director I spoke with shared her experience as an independent director of being the only board member to vote no on a significant decision, which later proved to be the correct stance. This story highlights the importance of having independent directors who can provide alternative viewpoints and act in the best interest of the company without being swayed by groupthink or internal pressures. The lack of more independent directors can lead to poor decision-making and oversight, as the board may not fully consider all perspectives and potential risks.

Another important contributor to effective governance is played by board advisors. These individuals are not directors and, therefore, do not have fiduciary responsibilities, voting rights, or influence over decision-making. However, they do act as on-call experts for the board and management team. The insights provided align with the advisor's unique background and expertise, typically relating to legal, financial, technology, or business-related concerns. Filling an advisor role can be a precursor to board service.

One individual I interviewed initially served as an outside general counsel advising an education company on legal matters. After working closely with the company and its leadership, she advocated for a more involved role on the board, leveraging her advisory experience to transition into an independent director position. She explained, "After working for them for a few years I actually went to the CEO and I said I would like to be on your board. You need me on your board. I'm the voice of your customer, and you don't have that on your board."

The Mental Shift from Executive to Board Member

Switching from the role of successful executive to board member requires a substantial shift in mindset and competencies. To do so, you must first deliberately turn off what has likely become an autopilot modus operandi of corporate executive. Next, you must take on the role of board director—and this may require the development of certain competencies that grow over time, just as your career competencies took time to develop.

Although some tasks and traits may be familiar to you—such as understanding and articulating the company's big picture and strategic outlook, participating in strategy formulation, and aiding in shifting and sustaining a strategy-supportive organization culture—some may be less familiar. For example, although you may be used to being the "big dog" and all decisions go through you in your organization, being on a board requires a collaborative and collegial approach so that the directors see each other as peers and believe that the best decisions will be made *together*. This transition is not always easy. As one director observed, "Oftentimes, CEOs don't translate well to directors because they want to 'do,' but because I'm on my third phase of life, I'm not interested in doing. I'm interested in teaching and coaching and advising and being the right sounding board." Another director agreed, "The worst thing is a board member who tries to micromanage and doesn't understand their role. I've seen it before, and it just disrupts everything. It's important to remember that we're there to provide guidance and oversight, not to run the company." As these directors emphasized, it is critical for board members to avoid micromanagement and allow for effective governance and company operations.

In other words, serving on a board requires a humble and hands-off attitude—typically encapsulated in the adage: "Noses in, fingers OUT!" or "heads in, hands out." As a board member, you oversee and advise the organization leaders, but you must leave the *doing* to them. Deloitte researchers emphasized in their Director's Alert that board members should ask questions that "are purposeful and legitimately probe and advance the strategy without grandstanding or attempting to 'one up' management."[7] This means that as a director, you must refine your skills in offering fresh insights that influence executives' perceptions while remaining unattached to whether those insights will be adopted and implemented. Several directors I spoke with offered stories in which the management team chose not to implement the board's recommendations. In some cases, these decisions worked out, and others led to learning opportunities and the need for damage control. One director shared, "We had advised them to diversify their product line, but the management team decided to focus on their core offerings. While it worked out in the short term, they eventually had to revisit our advice as market demands shifted."

I provide these stories to emphasize that this kind of hands-off approach is no easy feat! Making these shifts requires self-awareness, alertness, agility, tolerance for ambiguity, the ability to collaborate with others, and sensitivity to valid strategies and cultures already in place within the organization. Inventiveness, curiosity, and intuition also are invaluable traits to have as a director. The reward for embracing the shift is reaching the point of trusting your peers and their advisory capabilities as well as entrusting the organization's executive team to lead the organization. Moreover, only when the shift from executive to director is accomplished can it become possible to fulfill the three duties of a director.

Three Duties of a Director

Three responsibilities serve as the cornerstone of a directors' duties—both individually and collectively—to guarantee that the board functions in the organization's and its stakeholders' best interests. Although these objectives may vary slightly based on the rules and regulations relevant to the jurisdiction in which the company operates, the basic duties are as follows:

1. **Duty of care.** Directors act as the organization's guardians and must manage its affairs with the same level of caution and due diligence that a reasonable and responsible individual would employ. Doing so means staying actively involved in board activities by meaningfully participating in meetings, becoming knowledgeable about the organization's operations, understanding and reviewing the company's financial documents and strategic reports, developing an orientation for both long- and short-term thinking, posing critical questions, comprehending hazards, and deliberately gauging which risks are acceptable. One director I interviewed described this responsibility as "being vigilant and proactive. We constantly review policies and procedures, ensuring that we're not just compliant but also forward-thinking in our governance practices." Another director explained, "We engage in detailed strategic planning sessions. We evaluate every aspect of our long-term strategy to ensure it serves the best interests of the company and its stakeholders."

2. **Duty of loyalty.** Directors are required to behave in the organization's best interests, even if that means passing up a chance that might benefit them personally. Directors are prohibited from receiving excessive pay, financial benefits, or other benefits as a result of the organization's operations or from serving on its board. Ensuring they are adhering to the organization's conflict of interest policy includes disclosing and avoiding any potential conflicts of interest, such as declaring any earnings, any ties to family members, or any commercial dealings between the organization and themselves, their business interests, family members, or other pertinent associations. Even the appearance that a director is profiting at the organization's expense should be avoided. To do so, directors with potential

conflicts of interest should abstain from discussions and decisions pertaining to the proposed transaction in which their objectivity could be jeopardized. One director I interviewed explained, "Board members must always prioritize the company's interests above their own and avoid any situations that could lead to a conflict of interest. This is fundamental to maintaining trust and integrity on the board."

3. **Duty of obedience.** Directors enact the duty of obedience by ensuring that the organization abides by its articles and bylaws, by all applicable laws, and by all reporting requirements. The organization's directors should attest that it is striving to achieve its goals and objectives while abiding by all legal requirements and filing all necessary reports. To assess whether the organization is abiding by its bylaws and carrying out its declared purpose, each board member should be conversant with the group's formal organizing documents, such as the articles, bylaws, and applications for exemption.

Directors need to be aware of how these responsibilities influence and direct their behavior and performance standards. For example, every director must ensure they understand financial statements and investment market reports and be aware of the laws that affect the organization. Board members cannot simply depend on outside counsel or third-party advisors to carry out these duties and compliance-related tasks.

Before accepting a director seat or joining a committee, you must carefully consider the requirements, expectations, and skill sets it entails to make sure you are equipped with the knowledge and experience to effectively and faithfully execute your duties. Failing to do so may attract lawsuits from shareholders and other stakeholders.

Director Roles

The organization's bylaws and governance rules often specify the precise duties and obligations of board members as well as the specifications of the board. Accordingly, the roles on a board of directors can vary depending on the size, type, and nature of the organization. Some standard roles on a board of directors include the following:

Chair. The chair role ideally is held by an independent director, although the CEO may occupy this role in certain situations. The chairperson's responsibilities include leading board meetings, setting the agenda, and ensuring that the board operates effectively. The chairperson often acts as a liaison between the board and executive management. In some cases, the board president may be a separate role and carry a different set of responsibilities from the chairperson. The president may lead the board when the chairperson is not available, or they may have specific responsibilities related to board governance. A vice chair or vice president also may be designated to assist the chairperson or president and may assume their responsibilities in their absence. This role often involves supporting the overall leadership and governance of the board.

Lead director. When the CEO acts as chair, a lead director (usually a more tenured board member) must be designated to run the executive session portion of the board meeting when the CEO is excused so that the remaining board members can discuss the CEO's performance.

Secretary. The secretary is responsible for maintaining accurate records of board meetings, including minutes and official documents. They may also handle communications, correspondence, and governance-related documentation. The secretary role commonly is occupied by the firm's general counsel. If so, this individual has no voting rights or influence over the board's decisions.

Committee chairs. Committee chairs play leadership roles on the board by overseeing one or more specific committees, typically, after having served on the committee as a member. Chairs lead their committee's meetings, facilitate the committee's communication with the full board, collaborate with stakeholders, and ensure compliance with laws and regulations. Committee chairs are responsible for strategic planning within their scope of their committee, engage with company management, and present recommendations to the board. They contribute to effective governance by fostering a positive committee environment, overseeing committee activities, and ensuring ethical conduct and compliance.

Committee members. Committee members on a board of directors actively participate in committee meetings, contribute their expertise, and engage in discussions to address specific issues within the committee's focus. They review relevant information, collaborate with the committee chair, and may work on special projects or tasks. Members stay informed about industry trends, maintain confidentiality, and provide feedback on proposals. Overall, committee members play a crucial role in enhancing the board's ability to make informed decisions and address specific areas of governance. If the board has committees, every board member is selected to serve on one to three committees. The selections are largely based on the board's needs; however, board members' interests and human capital also are considered during committee assignments.

For example, a director I will call Najma has an extensive background serving on various board committees, bringing her expertise and insights to ensure effective governance and strategic direction. Her involvement often focuses on critical areas such as audit, governance, and risk management, and she leverages her experience to contribute significantly to the board's oversight functions. She explained:

> My background has been really valuable in serving on the audit committee, where I focus on ensuring that our financial reporting is accurate and transparent. We delve into the details of financial statements, risk assessments, and compliance with regulatory requirements. It's about making sure that everything is in order and that we are mitigating any potential risks that could impact the company.

Najma's role on the audit committee involves a meticulous review of financial reports and a strong emphasis on compliance and risk management. Her contributions help the board maintain a clear and accurate financial picture of the company, ensuring that all regulatory requirements are met and potential risks are proactively addressed. Furthermore, her dedication to her committee work exemplifies the importance of having experienced and knowledgeable directors on board committees, where their expertise can guide the company toward sound financial and strategic decisions. Her efforts in the audit committee highlight her commitment to upholding the highest standards of governance and accountability.

It's important to note that the specific roles and titles can vary among organizations. Some smaller organizations may have fewer roles, and larger corporations may have additional specialized roles on their boards. Additionally, not all boards include every role mentioned here, and some roles may be combined, depending on the organization's needs and structure.

Board Committees

The number and nature of committees on a board are influenced by the size of the board, the organization's bylaws, and regulatory framework governing the organization. Small boards may have no committees and larger boards may have several. Although there are many possible variations, commonly occurring committees on corporate boards include the following:

> **Audit committee.** Oversees financial reporting and disclosure, ensures compliance with legal and regulatory requirements, and manages relationships with external auditors and reviews internal controls. This committee is crucial for ensuring financial transparency and accountability.

> **Nominations and governance (nom-gov) committee.** Manages the process for nominating board members, oversees board self-assessments and evaluations, and develops and monitors corporate governance policies and practices. The nom-gov committee is responsible for overseeing the board's composition, structure, and effectiveness. This includes nominating new directors, conducting board evaluations, and recommending changes to governance policies.

> **Compensation committee.** Oversees executive and board compensation; develops and reviews policies on salary, bonuses, and other benefits; and ensures compensation practices are aligned with organizational goals and shareholder interests. The compensation committee plays a crucial role in promoting a fair and transparent executive compensation system that aligns with the company's strategic objectives and enhances

shareholder value. The committee's decisions also can have a significant impact on the organization's ability to attract, retain, and motivate key executives.

Finance committee. Oversees the financial strategy, including budgeting and financial planning; manages significant financial transactions, like mergers and acquisitions; and reviews financial performance and capital expenditures. The finance committee ensures the organization's financial health and sustainability through careful oversight of its financial activities, ranging from dividend policies to capital structure, investment portfolios, risk management, and financial reporting.

Risk management committee. Identifies, assesses, and manages risks facing the organization; develops crisis management and emergency response plans; and ensures the organization has a proactive approach to risk management. The risk management committee plays a vital role in safeguarding the organization against potential technological, geopolitical, and market threats. The committee also ensures the organization's compliance with industry regulations, legal requirements, and internal policies, and evaluates the adequacy of the organization's insurance coverage.

Corporate social responsibility or sustainability committee: Oversees policies related to social responsibility and sustainability, including charitable contributions and community engagement programs, monitoring the impact of the company's operations on the environment and society, and ensuring alignment with ethical standards and stakeholder expectations. This committee is crucial in promoting and measuring the company's commitment to ethical business practices and social responsibility, with particular attention to aligning with stakeholders' concerns.

Strategic planning committee. Focuses on long-term goals, aligns plans with the organization's mission, and guides its future direction. It conducts market analysis, evaluates mergers and partnerships, fosters innovation, develops and monitors performance metrics, ensures optimal resource allocation, and assesses the competitive landscape to inform strategic decisions.

WHERE THEIR STORIES BEGIN

Lauren had been aware (albeit via a vague teenage awareness) of corporate boards since high school. At that time, her ears perked up when she heard her uncle mention having to excuse a company's CEO and search for a new chief executive. She remembered thinking with awe, "A CEO can be *fired*? CEOs have *bosses!*?" The seeds of her interest in board service had been planted. Along the way, as she learned about corporate scandals in college and, more recently, witnessed social unrest and the corporate responses and regulatory acts that followed, she and her uncle had many spirited discussions about corporate and board responsibility. Although she still has much to learn about boards, their practices, and what it takes to become a board member, Lauren's early career success and access to her uncle, a capable mentor, places her in an excellent position to fill her knowledge gaps.

Denise had little to no exposure to corporate boards through her upbringing, academics, or legal career. Her first exposure to board service occurred seemingly accidentally when she was invited to join the board of a gymnastics not-for-profit organization. She was intrigued by the invitation and agreed to observe a board meeting. Before that meeting, she really had only a fuzzy idea of what a board was, as she pictured older white male retirees chatting around a table at a hunting lodge. She was pleasantly surprised to see the diversity of genders, ages, and ethnicities at the meeting. She also was surprised at the vibrant dynamic and thought it felt more like a club than a board. She ultimately agreed to join the board and pay the associated fee; however, she remained no more aware of the nature and work of corporate boards.

Michele had been so busy moving into progressive leadership roles that board service had never crossed her mind (aside from the activities related to the internal board responsibilities associated with her professional roles). This changed several years ago when two members of her C-suite separately mentioned securing board seats. Although she did not fully know what this meant, she was intrigued and resolved, "When I have time, I plan on researching and beginning to do something about this." Before she found time to do that, California Senate Bill 826 was enacted, and the social unrest of 2020 erupted. She was tapped that fall for two boards: one private equity–owned private board and one large cap public board. Emboldened by her strong background and service to internal boards, she accepted. With that, she jumped headfirst into the world of corporate board service.

Sharon served on her company's internal board for 12 years as CEO. Although independent directors served on her board, she herself had never served on any other board and never gave it any thought. It was only when the freedom of retirement lost its luster that she realized she wanted to serve on corporate boards as part of her post-career strategy.

Although all four women vary in age, background, and experience, all are new to corporate board service, and all have much to learn. The remaining chapters will continue to follow these women as they increase their qualifications and ability to serve.

ACTION ITEMS

Take a moment to reflect on your current understanding and readiness for board service using the following questions:

1. What is your level of understanding, experience, and skill related to board service?
2. What type(s) of boards are you most interested in serving? Which do you think you are most qualified to serve?
3. What questions do you have about boards and serving on boards?

Periodically return to your answers to these questions as you progress through this book so you can see how your understanding is evolving and what new insights and questions are emerging.

SUMMARY

Boards have played critical roles for more than four hundred years in providing oversight, management, and advisory services to the companies they govern. Carrying out these roles requires the engaged but hands-off involvement of a range of internal and external stakeholders. Although understanding the history, roles, and work of boards is important, it is only the beginning of the journey. In Chapter 3, we explore why you might want to serve on a board.

CHAPTER THREE

FIND YOUR WHY

To live is to choose. But to choose well, you must know who you are and what you stand for, where you want to go and why you want to get there.

—Kofi Anan

There are many reasons for becoming an independent director, including gaining insights to bring back to your own organization; acquiring transferable board and committee experience; gaining a sense of accomplishment in supporting the organization's vision, mission, and values; expanding your social network; and even compensation. However, board service is a substantial commitment, beginning with the effort to simply find and secure a seat. Therefore, it is critical for you to more deeply understand why you may want to serve on a board. This chapter reviews the concepts and underlying theories of why and provides steps for discovering your why.

THE THEORY AND NATURE OF WHY

A wide range of researchers from various disciplines and theoretical orientations have attempted to investigate and explain why purpose is so central to being human. Of the many possible theories, one that aligns especially well with my understanding of the boardroom journey was developed by German American child psychoanalyst Erik Erikson in the mid-20th century. Erikson studied under Anna Freud before publishing his own view of how we develop as humans both psychologically and socially, culminating in his stages of psychological development.[1]

Erikson believed that, rather than being driven by wild animalistic urges, we are driven by our ego and desire to progress our "self." In turn, we navigate and develop as human beings through a series of identity crises. What most struck me when learning about Erikson's work was Stage 7, when we become concerned with creating and nurturing things that will outlast us. Although that can occur through having children, it also includes giving back from our accumulated life and work experience so that others may benefit from and build on it.

Our interest and efforts to contribute to the future generation of individuals, organizations, and institutions is symbiotic in nature: although the future generation receives mentoring and guidance, we gain the sense of being capable allies, mentors, sponsors, and leaders. For me, a central activity of my post-career is giving back my expertise and guidance through serving on boards of directors. I found that many of the directors I have interviewed over the years express a similar desire to share the wisdom, perspective, skills, and knowledge that only they have, and that other leaders and companies vitally need. In exchange, they gain a sense of impact, fulfillment, and possibly even ongoing income. One executive and director I interviewed explained her reasoning to pursue board service:

> But then I figured, "What am I going to do for the rest of my life? I have too much energy. *I have too much energy.*" I was part of the National Association

of Corporate Directors, so I started attending some of their sessions about how to get a board seat.

Purpose is important not only in the established adulthood stage when we are starting to think about legacy, as Erikson proposed. Instead, finding meaning throughout life is critical because passing through many stages of early to middle and later adulthood naturally involves significant identity adjustment as we relinquish certain roles in exchange for others—such as shifting from individual to contributor to manager, or from executive to retiree.

Similarly, British American author Simon Sinek greatly popularized the need to find our why beginning with his book and TED Talk on the topic in 2009.[2] According to Sinek, getting grounded in our why can give us a distinct advantage over others seeking the same position or market opportunity because rooting ourselves in our very own "reason for being" transforms our ability to inspire ourselves and others, and multiplies our capacity to achieve our goals.

Applied to the focus of this book, Sinek's model suggests that our why consists of our reason for wanting a board seat, including values that drive this desire and the loftier objectives or causes we are seeking to achieve through board service. This driving purpose and set of values, in turn, motivate the specific behaviors that are unique to us and that we enact to secure a board seat. Moreover, these behaviors produce the observable results of our efforts.

Sinek explained that most individuals and organizations communicate from the outside in, beginning with explaining *what* they do, going on to describe *how* they do it, and very infrequently addressing *why* they do what they do. He contends that companies and leaders who break this tendency are those who are genuinely inspiring and successful. To inspire individuals and help them connect with their deeper sense of purpose, he argues that people and organizations should *begin* with why and only then work their way down to the how and the what. Sinek further argued that by beginning with why, leaders may inspire greater passion and drive from their teams and clients as well as develop stronger, more devoted followings. The business and leadership communities have embraced this idea as a means of motivating and guiding their organizations with purpose. *Why* similarly is a good starting place for planning your board journey.

HOW TO FIND YOUR WHY

As simple as starting with why may sound, actually figuring out your why can be difficult. Parker Palmer, in *Let Your Life Speak*, emphasized that finding purpose involves deeply listening to our lives and trying to understand what they are truly about—separate from what we might like our lives to be about. If we fail to do that, he warns, our lives (including our careers and post-careers) will fall short of what they could be.

If you are reading this book and contemplating how to secure your first (or subsequent) board seat, you have likely participated in or even led your company through at least one visioning session. Turn these skills on yourself to try crafting your own vision, mission, and values so you can figure out your why, your legacy, and your post-career. Several exercises are helpful to that end.

The first exercise involves the fundamental step of self-reflection. Review your life experiences, work pursuits, and pivotal decisions. Pay particular attention to those experiences that most enhanced your sense of energy, passion, and fulfillment.

Once you have identified those experiences, find the common threads behind what truly matters to you, what best uses your strengths and talents, and what reflects the legacy you want to leave.

These common threads become working hypotheses about the elements of your purpose or driving sense of why. When you have those, share them with those who know you well and who can step beyond their own biases and agendas for your life. Their perspectives may offer you validation as well as additional insights about the core motivations guiding your life.

With a clearer understanding of your why, compare your current personal and professional activities and consider whether they stand up to the test. When you realize that certain activities do not align with your why, take steps to either modify them to close the gap or even taper off these activities. After reading my articles in *Forbes* on designing a meaningful post-career of board service,[3] a director

I knew contacted me to let me know that gaining clarity about her own why helped her realize that she did not want to renew one of her terms as board member. She explained:

> I realized that this board and even this type of board just didn't match with my values and what most motivated my board service. Before tuning into my why, I knew I hadn't been enjoying it for some time, but I didn't have words to explain it. Without that clarity, I couldn't just walk away. Now I can walk away from that one, knowing that surrendering my spot creates the opportunity for another whose why *does* align with what that board needs. It also means that I am available for a different opportunity that aligns with my own values. Moving forward, I want to make sure that everything I do aligns with what matters to me.

The final step in finding your why is remembering that it may evolve over the course of your life and career. These are not "one-and-done" exercises but instead should be revisited periodically, especially after particularly pivotal achievements or life events.

When I meet with aspiring directors, whether they are seeking their first, second, or fifteenth seat, I always ask what energizes them and what brings them joy. This is critical when trying to narrow down what type of board they want to be on—and if they genuinely want a board seat at all. Too many people I meet with tell me, "I don't care, Keith. I just want to be on a paid board."

That is the wrong answer. It's the wrong answer for the board, and it's the wrong answer for them.

You must know your why, even if it doesn't make sense to others immediately. As long as you know your why and can communicate that convincingly, you can demonstrate your value to the board. One executive and seasoned board member with strong manufacturing experience demonstrated the power of why when she shared her experience being interviewed for a seat on the board of a mutual insurance company. She explained:

> The company president asked me, "Why would you want to be on this board? You don't have a mutual insurance or financial service background."

I responded, "The only way I can answer this is to make it personal. One work day, I woke up at 3:30 a.m. to catch an early morning flight. I started getting ready and walked into the bathroom. I found my husband there. He had unexpectedly passed away in the night. This was a terrible shock for my family; yet, the only thing that changed in my kids' lives was, sadly, losing their father. They still had a roof over their heads, food on the table, and clothes on their backs. Why? Because of fiscal responsibility. Insurance is one vehicle for fiscal responsibility. Sitting here as a board member, I would be thinking about every other single mother or single father out there, thinking about whether they have the means to be fiscally responsible and ensure they are protected in the event of some unfortunate occurrence. In short, I am deeply passionate about insurance."

All the president could do after my answer was gulp.

As this story shows, your why may be rooted in expected or unexpected aspects or events of your life. Before outlining your path to board service, take the time to figure out not only where you want to go but why you want to get there.

THE WHYS OF OUR FOUR PATHMAKERS

When Lauren took the time to reflect on her own driving motivation for board service, she recalled the stories her uncle would tell her about the senior leadership events he attended and what he did as a board member. She also remembered her sense of astonishment in eighth grade when she learned that her uncle was part of the hiring committee to select the next CEO of a company. Before that, she had thought that CEOs were the Big Bosses, with no one above them. Finding out that her very own uncle was above them simply blew her mind. When she learned even more of the story—that the outgoing CEO was the original founder of the company, and her uncle was helping find a new CEO who could take the company through all the transformations it needed to go public and be on the stock exchange, was almost more than she could comprehend at that age. Her uncle quickly gained a celebrity status in her mind that never tarnished. Reflecting on these experiences helped Lauren realize that becoming a professional qualified to participate in these pivotal activities was very meaningful to her . . . and she couldn't deny that the level of influence had its appeal as well.

Although the other women could not recall developmental experiences quite as pivotal that motivated their interest in board service, they still were able to identify their own reasons. Denise admitted that her reasons were both intrinsically and competitively motivated. She recalled, "In my professional roles, I have always felt a sense of satisfaction when I contribute my ideas and see clients valuing and benefiting from them. The idea of being able to do that as a board member is compelling." She additionally confessed:

> At the last meeting of the not-for-profit gymnastics board I'm on, I learned through casual conversation that several of the other board members serve on nonprofit and corporate boards. I've seen how we all participate, and I actually think I contribute a little better than those other members do. So, if they can be on corporate boards, I can too. Since then, I've had this persistent feeling that I've been missing out.

When Michele reflected on her professional experiences, she recalled her Big 4 consulting experiences where she was able to share her insights and expertise with companies that vitally needed it to transform their operations. Her experience of sharing frameworks, insights, and expertise and then seeing these have real-world impacts that culminated in improved organizational performance was powerfully rewarding for her. She then recognized why she felt so engaged in the board meetings for the private equity–owned private firm: she was enlisted to provide advice to support the organization's growth and strategic objectives. This aligned very well with what has brought her the most joy throughout her career.

Joining her father's company and eventually becoming CEO had not been in Sharon's career plans initially, although she was grateful for the opportunity when divorce took her on a different life path. Because Sharon had initially intended to be a stay-at-home mom, she also had anticipated a rather traditional retirement of spending time with her grandkids, pursuing hobbies she hadn't had time for, and traveling more. It didn't take long, however, for the disorientation of weekdays blurring into weekends blurring into weekdays to leave her feeling restless. She realized she missed being relevant, having influence, and contributing her expertise to those who could apply and benefit from it. She wanted to remain connected to organizational life in some way.

ACTION ITEMS

Try the following exercises to reflect on your why:

1. Review your life experiences, work pursuits, and pivotal decisions, paying particular attention to those experiences that most enhanced your sense of energy, passion, and fulfillment. It is helpful to document these in some way, whether in a list or as a life map.

2. Reflect on those experiences, noting what they revealed about what truly matters to you, what strengths and talents you used, and what you found meaningful about it.

3. Look across the experiences and what they revealed to identify the common themes that emerged most frequently. Formulate these as statements of your core values, your top strengths, and your desired impacts.

4. Share what you found with a few trusted contacts to gather any additional observations and insights they may have about you and your why.

SUMMARY

Finding and securing a board seat and fulfilling your duties as a board member requires significant focus and effort. Because this is not a casual or easy pursuit, it is critical to understand why you want to do it. If your purpose includes using your unique experiences and strengths to benefit others in small and large ways, sitting on corporate boards may be for you. As a corporate board director, you are expected to offer your extensive expertise and experience through the insights you share and thought-provoking questions you ask. The organizations you serve can then apply your wisdom to achieve their objectives, mitigate risk, and, ideally, disrupt themselves and seek new strategic frontiers. This can create a powerful sense of purpose for many board members as they participate in creating a powerful and self-regenerating legacy. At the same time, these are not the only valid reasons for seeking a board seat. Finding your why is a deeply personal and ongoing journey that takes time, introspection, attention, and self-discovery. Your why can be a source of inspiration and guidance, helping you lead a more purposeful and fulfilling life. Once you know your why, it is time to select a general destination, which is the focus of Chapter 4.

CHAPTER FOUR

SELECT A DESTINATION

If you don't know where you want to go, then it doesn't matter which path you take.

— Lewis Carroll, *Alice in Wonderland*

N ow that you have learned about the importance of boards (Chapter 1), what boards are (Chapter 2), and why you want to seek a board seat (Chapter 3), it is time to figure out roughly what kind of organizations and boards you would like to serve as an independent director. In this chapter, we discuss selecting a general destination for your board journey.

THE IMPORTANCE OF THE DESTINATION

Beginning the journey to a board seat is not unlike Alice's trip to Wonderland. Like Alice falling down a rabbit hole and discovering herself in an alternate universe, the idea of a board seat often doesn't even cross our minds as busy executives until we stumble into this alternate universe due to an unexpected invitation to board service or hearing about someone else's experience. However, wanting a seat and knowing how to land a seat are two different things. And in a world where many kinds of boards and board seats exist, it can be very difficult to chart a path.

Finding herself in this similar predicament, Alice in Lewis Carroll's story was relieved to see the Cheshire Cat lazing in a tree, whom she promptly asked which way she should go.

> "That depends a good deal on where you want to get to," said the Cat.
> "I don't much care where—" said Alice.
> "Then it doesn't matter which way you go," said the Cat.
> "—so long as I get somewhere," Alice added as an explanation.
> "Oh, you're sure to do that," said the Cat, "if you only walk long enough."

When we take a similar approach to board service, we end up spending precious time and resources on experiences that fail to benefit ourselves and the boards and companies we are trying to serve. Or worse, we end up accepting a two- to three-year term serving on a board and only then discover that we don't enjoy it, aren't prepared for it, or don't do it well. We then are left to grind our teeth through the remainder of our term or face the adverse professional and social consequences of resigning early from our post.

Furthermore, setting a destination for our journey is important from the perspective of motivation and goal setting. For example, goal-setting theory,[1] initially developed by US psychologist Edwin Locke, focuses on the relationship between specific challenging goals on one hand and individual performance and motivation on the other. Locke and his colleagues found through their research that we tend to tackle, persist toward, and achieve goals that are clear, difficult but attainable, and personally meaningful. The aim of this book is to help you understand why you want to pursue board service, to gain clarity on specifically what types of boards are appropriate for you, and to provide the steps and tools to make the effort neither too easy nor too challenging. Although you generally cannot decide in advance that you will secure a board seat on a specific company's board, it is helpful to understand the options and then to select a general destination.

REVIEWING THE OPTIONS

Organizations across the globe, in all industries and of various sizes and situations, need good governance. As an aspiring director, it is important to think about the variety of board service options available as you begin to contemplate which types of seats you may be most interested in and suited for.

The question boils down to this: what is the right fit for you? When I sit down with senior leaders seeking a first or an additional seat, I always ask what they are looking for. One aspiring director had told me, "I want to be with a high-growth company. I would go crazy in a stable environment. If it's too stable, I may try to break it just so I can fix it again." Another executive was seeking a private firm that wants to go public because she had ample pre-initial public offering (IPO) to IPO experience. Yet another desired to serve firms whose growth strategy focused on mergers and acquisitions (M&A) transactions. The point is, there is no right or wrong answer—only the answer that matches your background and strengths. If your background and qualifications don't match the firm's intended pathway, the chances of you securing a board seat there is slim—and if you get a board seat, the experience will not be favorable for you, the board, or the firm because you will not be able to add much value. This section reviews various factors to consider when contemplating and selecting a general goal for your board journey.

Organization Sector

In Chapter 2, we reviewed the basic types of boards you may find yourself on over the course of your career in board service. Board type is one of several ways to think about the options you have as an aspiring director. Although you can review that chapter for the details, the basic options are as follows:

> **Not-for-profit and nonprofit sector.** Nonprofit organizations assemble boards of two basic types: fundraising/charity boards and fiduciary boards. Fundraising boards seek members with business development skills, networking skills, connections to potential donors, and personal funds to make annual donations to the organization. Your primary takeaways as a

board member are the sense of accomplishment in supporting the non-profit and expanding your social network. Fiduciary nonprofit boards exercise the oversight and management characteristic of corporate boards and have the objective of supporting the nonprofit in exercising prudent financial management and achieving a sustainable future. Accordingly, fiduciary boards seek members who have connections to potential donors and who can offer needed knowledge and skills to act as advisors to the executive director/CEO. Your takeaways as a board member include preparation for corporate boards, gaining transferable board and committee experience, and expanding your social network.

Private sector. Private sector organizations, including startups, family-owned businesses, mutual companies, and private equity (PE)– and venture capital (VC)–funded companies, are not required to have boards, although many do. These businesses seek board members who can provide oversight and strategic guidance, who have connections to funding, and who have done what the company is now trying to do. Organizations funded by PE or VC firms additionally seek board members who can provide monitoring and governance to support the organization's growth. Your takeaways as a private company director include an expanded social network and transferable board and committee experience. Startups and family-owned companies typically offer equity or stock options and investor-funded firms may offer cash compensation plus stock options and/or restricted stock units (RSUs).

Public sector. By law, all public sector organizations must have a board. Public small cap firms seek directors capable of providing strategic advice as well as monitoring and governance to support the organization's growth, whereas mid- to large cap firms tend to seek well-recognized executives and board members capable of providing the monitoring and governance necessary to protect the organization's reputation. Public board service includes roles held as an inside director as well as an independent director. Public board service helps expand your social network, gives you transferable board and committee experience, leads to quarterly compensation plus stock options and/or RSUs, and makes it easier to secure future public board seats.

Ownership Structure

A firm's ownership structure substantially influences its strategic orientation, culture, operations, growth goals and trajectories, and more. Some of the factors that vary depending on whether the firm is publicly traded or privately owned (and by whom) include the following:

Long-term versus short-term focus. Public companies have become notorious for focusing on short-term profits and market growth, whereas some privately owned companies tend to be have a longer-term focus. In particular, successful family-owned businesses must take a long-term view that simultaneously delivers strong organizational performance and keeps the family engaged and equipped to lead the business for generations.[2] This long-term view could mean prioritizing preparation of the next generation over quarterly returns, even if the market consistently outperforms them.

As an independent director, it is important to determine what your preferred focus is so that you are aligned with the board and the company. For example, if you are a Fortune 500 executive accustomed to living and breathing quarterly returns and cutting expenses for the purpose of showing growth, you may be happier on a public board. If you join the family-owned company board, you may be facing a three-year battle with the executives and fellow board members until your term ends—unless you are prepared to surrender your Fortune 500 growth mentality and align yourself with the aims of the organization. Bernice, one director I interviewed, is all too familiar with these challenges, gaining firsthand experience of the complexities of different board environments within a single company as it transitioned from private to public and then back to private. She shared, "I was on the board of a company that was private VC backed. We took that company public, and I was lead independent director at that time. That transition involved rigorous regulatory compliance, increased scrutiny from shareholders, and a heightened need for transparency. We sold it after a couple of years and took it private again. The transition back to private presented its own set of challenges, including restructuring the board's focus and adjusting to a different set of stakeholder expectations."

Shareholder communication. Public organizations typically have a larger and more diverse shareholder base. As a result, communication strategies and practices may need to be more sophisticated to effectively engage with this broad range of shareholders. By contrast, more tightly held organizations such as those owned by PE or VC firms may have fewer investors and more direct communication channels with shareholders, allowing for more personalized engagement. In my research with directors, I uncovered many differing accounts of how shareholder communication varies across boards. For example, public boards have stringent requirements for communication with shareholders. They must provide regular financial reports, hold annual general meetings, and issue press releases about significant events. Effective communication helps build trust and accountability across the public company's diverse stakeholders, helping them feel informed and confident about the company's direction. However, the high level of visibility can also attract shareholder activism. If shareholders feel their concerns are not being addressed, they may push for changes in governance or strategy.

Communication in private boards is often more direct and less formal. Private companies typically have fewer shareholders, making it easier to maintain direct lines of communication. Communication with shareholders often centers on growth, innovation, and strategic direction without the need for the same level of public disclosure as public companies. This direct communication fosters close relationships between the board and shareholders, and the lack of regulatory requirements allows for more flexibility and quicker responses to shareholder concerns and market opportunities, enabling more agile decision-making. Meanwhile, communication with stakeholders in nonprofits often focuses on the organization's mission, impact, and funding needs. Transparency about how funds are used and the outcomes achieved is crucial for building trust and fostering a sense of community and shared purpose among stakeholders.

Shareholder activism. Public organizations are susceptible to various forms of stakeholder activism, such as when shareholders purchase substantial amounts of company stock and then use this as leverage to advocate for changes in corporate policies or practices—for example, by proposing resolutions at shareholder meetings, engaging in dialogue with company management, or even taking legal action. In recent years, shareholder activism has centered on advocating for more sustainable and socially responsible business practices, resolutions pertaining to climate change, and progress and transparency related to creating diverse and inclusive workplaces. Janine, one director I spoke with, shared her experience with shareholder activism while serving on the board of a company. She explained:

We had a situation where shareholders were very vocal about their dissatisfaction with the company's direction. They were pushing for changes that we, as a board, were not entirely aligned with. The activism forced us to reevaluate some of our strategies and to engage more directly with our shareholder base to understand their concerns and to communicate our long-term vision more effectively.

As Janine explained, shareholder activism becomes a challenge because if forces directors to balance the demands of the activists with what they believe is in the best interest of the company. She summarized, "In some cases, this meant making difficult compromises."

Balance of oversight, management, and service. Ownership structure can dramatically affect the nature of your contribution as a director. Startup firms may require significant management and service from board members as they seek additional funding rounds, grow their executive teams, enter new markets, and navigate M&A deals.

Firms owned by PE or VC investors prioritize service from their board members and prefer agreement rather than challenge from independent directors regarding oversight and management issues. In such firms, you would be valued for the industry knowledge and advice you bring as an independent director (although VC firms also tend to call on their own bench of industry experts to weigh in on emergent issues). A challenge some independent directors experience when serving on these boards is that the investing firm's goals sometimes seem to affect the investor director's objectivity. One independent director explained it this way:

> It seems like the investor board member who works for that PE or VC firm has an independent director on their right shoulder and an investor director on their left shoulder, like the angel and the devil. When they should be thinking with their independent director hat, it's sometimes hard to ignore the investment side of things. So then you have the investor director who just wants whatever is going to give them the return they're looking for or, worse, a liquidity event in the next year when everyone else on the board knows we shouldn't even consider it for another 24 to 36 months. But they want their money out, and they don't care.

Family-owned businesses tend to emphasize service, while minimizing oversight and management from their independent directors. Accordingly, they try to surround themselves with people who will agree with rather than challenge their wishes and may even avoid having a board with independent directors altogether. Often, it is the need for outside advice, expertise, and skill that prompts these businesses to issue an invitation in the first place. These companies do not want board members who will vote out their CEO, make decisions that affect leadership within the next generation, or otherwise play a heavy hand in management matters. Some family businesses may even avoid having a board with independent directors altogether. Often, it is the need for outside advice, expertise, and skill that prompts them to issue an invitation for a director in the first place.

In public firms, the presence and diversity of shareholders means that oversight and management are emphasized on the board as a means of ensuring satisfactory quarterly returns. Additionally, small cap firms tend to be focused on growth, meaning that service is important within these boards as a means for gaining strategic guidance and advice to help the organization anticipate and navigate the associated challenges. In this way, the nature of board service on public boards vary compared to service on private boards, and serving on small cap boards can look different than serving on mid-sized or large cap boards.

Industry Characteristics

In addition to the basic board options presented by organization sector and ownership structure, you may be suited to serve in certain industries more than others due to your interests or your ability to help organizations navigate the challenges and opportunities posed by industry life cycles, dynamics, and other conditions. Elements to consider when evaluating industries include the following:

Regulatory environment. Different industries may be subject to varying degrees of regulation. For example, highly regulated industries such as finance, pharmaceuticals, transportation, health care, life sciences, and energy, may have more stringent governance requirements than less regulated sectors. Companies in regulated industries often need to comply with specific governance standards and reporting requirements set by regulatory bodies. In turn, achieving compliance with various regulations may require dedicated resources, specialized expertise, extensive internal control systems, and more comprehensive auditing processes to ensure transparency and accountability.

Risk management. Corporate governance mechanisms need to address the unique risks associated with the industry. Industries with higher levels of risk, such as technology or biotechnology, may require more robust risk management practices. Boards of directors in high-risk industries may need to have expertise in risk assessment and management.

Market competition. Intense competition in certain industries may push companies to adopt governance practices that promote innovation, efficiency, and strategic decision-making. In highly competitive industries, the pressure to perform well can influence governance structures to ensure quick and effective decision-making.

Ownership structure. Industry conditions can influence the ownership structure of companies. For example, family-owned businesses are prevalent in the food, retail, hotel, and real estate industries,[3] whereas PE- and VC-owned companies have become more common in technology and energy sectors.[4] Ownership structure affects companies' governance frameworks and dynamics, influencing the primary activities and contributions of directors, as well as the qualifications boards are seeking in their directors.

Stakeholder expectations. Stakeholders of corporate governance include shareholders, directors, executives, employees, customers, suppliers, creditors, regulators, communities, NGOs, competitors, and the media. These diverse groups have varying interests and expectations in the company's operations, decisions, and performance, and the board plays a central role in balancing these concerns. Stakeholder activism, in particular, has become a growing concern in technology, industrials, and health care sectors.[5] In response, boards in these industries face heightened pressure to adjust their governance practices to address these concerns and align with stakeholder expectations.

Technological disruption. Industries undergoing rapid technological change may require boards and executives to have a deep understanding of emerging technologies and their impact on the business. Accordingly, governance structures may need to be adaptable to address the challenges and opportunities presented by technological disruption. Although few industries remain untouched by digital transformation, industries may vary in the degree to which they are affected.

Life cycle. Industrial sectors have a life cycle and development path, from birth to youth to maturity and decline. At the birth of the industry, the number of firms and production levels are typically low. These numbers increase exponentially throughout the industry's youth (growth stage) and then start to decline in the maturity stage as companies exit. During industry birth and youth, the focus is on product innovation by small, new firms. In mature industries, large firms tend to dominate and focus on standardization and process innovation. Market shares are highly volatile during industry birth and youth, becoming more precisely defined in later stages. Governance in younger industries, in turn, may have a stronger focus on service and strategic guidance, whereas governance in mature industries may feature a stronger focus on oversight. Board members play critical roles in guiding the organization through these industry life stages by facilitating deliberate discussion, risk management, forecasting, decision making, planning, and implementation. Board members also can help facilitate and guide decisions about whether to exit early or persist through industry decline.

In addition to the factors described here, you may simply have a particular interest in one industry versus another. For example, you might have a deep personal commitment to environmental sustainability and, therefore, have an interest in green energy companies or nonprofits dedicated to ecological protection. Alternately, your driving sense of purpose in life may center on the value of supporting activities for personal and community well-being and, therefore, may be inclined to serve on sports-related boards. This was the case for Nadia, whose decision to serve on the board of one venture was significantly influenced by the industry's focus on technological innovation and its alignment with her professional background and interests. Her experience on the board was enriched by the industry's dynamic nature, which required constant adaptation and forward-thinking strategies. She explained, "Being part of the technology sector and working with this company has been an incredible journey. The fast-paced nature of this industry means that we're always on our toes, adapting to new trends and innovations. This alignment with my expertise in technology and innovation made my decision to join the board an easy one."

Organization Size

Organization size also may influence the nature, balance of activities, and composition of the board. In general, small organizations require stronger advisory and guidance as they navigate new strategic challenges and resource constraints. Larger organizations often face greater scrutiny, requiring more sophisticated governance structures, whereas smaller organizations may focus on flexibility in their governance approach. Specific aspects of governance affected by organization size include the following:

> **Board structure, dynamics, and size.** Larger organizations may have more highly structured and larger boards of directors and more independent directors to adequately represent shareholder interests. Decision-making

processes also may be more formalized and structured using committees, subcommittees, and layers of management to ensure effective decision making across various functions. Smaller organizations may have more informal decision-making processes, potentially involving a more hands-on approach by top executives. For example, a small private organization may have a four-member board with only two independent directors and no committees. In the public sector, Bank of America ($241.61 billion market cap) has 14 board members[6] and four committees compared to WeBuy Global's ($120.72 million market cap) five-member board and three committees.[7]

Nature of risks, liabilities, and challenges. The scale and nature of challenges may vary with organization size. Larger organizations tend to be slower to change than their smaller, more agile counterparts. However, large firms also may have more resources to weather the inevitable turbulence of doing business, whereas smaller organizations may be thrown into decline or even death by black swan events. A final key difference based on organization size is the scope of duties carried out by any one individual. Hearkening back to my military days, I associate working for or serving on the board of a large organization to being stationed on base. In both situations, you and your colleagues each have a narrowly defined role. By contrast, working for or serving on the board of a small organization is like being stationed on a ship. In these situations, a relatively small number of individuals are responsible for handling whatever arises. This means that every person needs to be ready and willing to wear multiple hats and switch them as needed.

Leadership concerns. Leadership concerns, the layers of leadership, organizational reporting structures, and executive compensation often differ based on the size of the organization. Larger organizations tend to have more extensive structures and larger executive compensation plans, whereas smaller organizations tend to feature flatter structures and smaller packages but steeper challenges related to succession planning and leadership continuity.

Resource allocation. Larger organizations may have more resources available to invest in governance-related functions, such as compliance departments, internal audit teams, and governance technology. By contrast, small organizations can be subject to a "liability of smallness," meaning they generally have access to fewer resources, less capital and less ability to raise capital, less leverage to secure desired talent and ability to develop it, and fewer sources of competitive advantage in the marketplace.

Given these various differences, it is critical to determine your own preferences before selecting a destination. In one case, a small organization had recruited a star Fortune 500 executive to serve on their board. It was optimism and excitement on all sides until the first session when it became apparent that this new director was unaware that everyone had to roll up their sleeves to get things done. In her professional role, she had a large team under her, and she excelled in setting a vision and then mobilizing and empowering them to act. It didn't take long for everyone to realize that this director was a poor fit for the board.

Organizational Life Cycle

Yet another factor of organizations that affects governance is the life cycle the company is in. Organizational life cycles span from inception and early growth to maturity and, potentially, decline. As David K. Hurst[8] depicted (see Figure 4.1), organizations begin with emergent entrepreneurial action and then require rational action in the form of strategic management to achieve growth. To avoid unsustainable growth, constraint is required in the form of conservation and prudent decision-making. Crisis and decline is inevitable in the life of an organization. Although this can spark confusion, if transformational leadership is present, the organization reenters the phase of rational action that restores performance and returns it to a phase of emergent action—this time, in the form of creativity and choice, leading once again to entrepreneurial action.

Figure 4.1   Organizational Life Cycle.

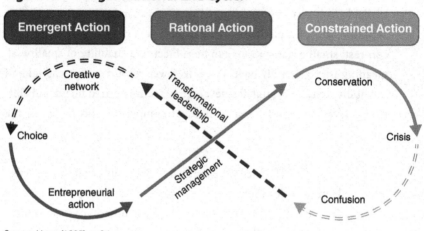

Source: Hurst (1995), p. 34.

Accordingly, the challenges, priorities, and governance structures that organizations face can differ significantly at different stages of their life cycle. A profile of the characteristics and dynamics at each organizational life stage are as follows:

Early stage. At inception and during its early life, organizations reflect an entrepreneurial focus and heavy founder influence. Key organizational objectives include innovation, product development, and market entry. Challenges can include a liability of newness, wherein they lack proven organizational routines and capabilities, established stakeholder relationships, access to resources, and market power and presence. In turn, corporate governance may be flexible and informal, emphasizing agility, rapid decision-making, and strategic advisory.

Growth stage. Organizations in a growth stage face challenges related to scaling operations, managing increased complexity, and expanding the workforce. As this occurs, corporate governance practices typically need to grow in sophistication and evolve to a higher level of professionalism to address these challenges. Such measures may include enrolling independent directors and implementing more formal processes.

Mature stage. At this stage, organizations focus on stability, market leadership, and global expansion. Accordingly, board members' focus turns to maintaining operational efficiency, managing risks, and ensuring ethical conduct. Shareholder relations may also take precedence, leading to the measures to address sustainability concerns and enhance transparency. Governance structures continue to become more complex, particularly as it concerns audit and compliance mechanisms.

Decline stage. Decline, defined as an involuntary, steady, and substantive decrease in the organization's resource base over at least two years, is a natural phase in the organization that can trigger generative responses of adaptability and renewal.[9] Organizations in decline may face financial challenges, restructuring efforts, leadership changes, or become vulnerable to shareholder activism. Governance is crucial in these situations to oversee the development and implementation of turnaround initiatives, risk management and crisis response mechanisms, updated organizational strategies, accountability measures, leadership transitions, and improved governance structures. In the event of liquidation or exit, the board must aid in the responsible, ethical, and legal closure of operations, settling of obligations, and optimization of shareholder value.

In summary, the organization life cycle significantly shapes corporate governance. The evolving needs and challenges at each stage necessitate adjustments in governance structures, processes, and priorities to foster organizational sustainability, resilience, and ethical conduct.

When you reflect on your career path, you may have cultivated unique insights and deep expertise in a particular corporate life cycle. For example, in my tenure as a sales executive in corporate America, I built my career as a turnaround specialist as I helped one regional division after another reverse the inertia of accelerating decline and become valuable, high-performing units. In turn, I look for opportunities to provide this strategic guidance through my board roles.

A GENERAL PATHWAY

In general, the place many aspiring board members begin is taking a seat on a not-for-profit board. There, they gain the social capital they need to gain access to a nonprofit board, where they can prepare for corporate board service by gaining transferable board and committee experience and continuing to expand their social capital and network. After that, based on their unique interests, experiences, and skill sets, they find their way onto a private or public board. On these boards, in addition to developing their competencies as board members and building social capital, they also may receive compensation for their service.

At the same time, there are exceptions. Take the case of Miriam, a retired CEO of a construction company who serves on several different boards. Her journey started more than 20 years ago when she was approached by the fundraising committee of a nonprofit board who asked if her company would build a dream home at cost, which they would then sell through a raffle. Miriam refused. She continued:

> The committee members apologized for taking my time. I quickly responded, "No, I want to do it. But we cannot accept any payment for it. We will donate the home in full." The committee members were shocked, protesting that this had never happened before. I explained, "Well, I have 50 subcontractors who work for my company, and we're like a big family. I know they'd love to be charitable." We went on to build three of these homes and raised about $3 million net for the organization, until state regulations prohibited raffles.
>
> At that point, the organization asked if I would chair committees for their large local functions. I agreed and did this for years. Then they invited me to join the nonprofit's board of directors because they had slated more than $1 billion of capital construction in the coming years.

While on the board, Miriam served on several committees, including audit, building (as chair), finance (as vice chair), and strategic planning. In these roles, she formed the building charter and created financial benchmarks. Fundraising grew over her tenure from several hundred million annually to several billion annually.

Miriam's experience demonstrates that nonprofits can be the source of significant and meaningful board experiences rather than a stop along the pathway of board service.

FOUR DESTINATIONS

As Lauren considered her experience and ability to contribute, she realized that she needed to start with nonprofit boards to gain some experience and build her network. She reflected on her interests and speculated that a community organization related to her passions, such as a museum, performing arts center, social services organization, or girl's empowerment program, would suit her personal interests and her needs to develop board-related experience and relationships. She set her general goal as a nonprofit board in one of these areas.

Denise, who already is serving on a not-for-profit board, decided to set her goal as a family-owned private board. She chose this because she lacked public company experience. Furthermore, her contacts at the National Association of Corporate Directors told her that board secretaries are generally the in-house counsel; attorneys are perceived as naysayers who drag out conversations and, thus, are rarely recruited as independent directors; and PE and VC firms fear lawyers. She also was told that boards increasingly are appreciating attorneys' risk mitigation skills, as long as they are well-rounded businesspeople.

Michele already had public company experience as an executive and board member. Noting her enjoyment of the board meetings for the PE-owned private firm and after discussion with friends and contacts at the Executive Leadership Council, she set a goal of finding two more seats in a growth-oriented private and/or small to mid-cap public board so she could continue providing strategic advice.

Sharon's tenure as chief executive of her father's company gave her extensive experience in family-owned businesses. Therefore, she set the goal of finding a seat on a family-owned company's board.

ACTION ITEMS

In my experience participating in board search efforts, many aspiring directors tell me they want to serve on a public board. However, when I ask why this is their goal, many are unable to answer. This rationale is insufficient. Joining a board is about serving stakeholders. Determining your pathway and destination requires self-reflection regarding your qualifications and goals. Contemplate the following questions to begin to narrow down a general destination for your own journey:

1. What professional and board experience do you have in each sector?
2. Review the responsibilities of each board type. Which type of board aligns most with your interests and ability to contribute?
3. Which organizational size and life stage do you enjoy most?
4. In what industries do you have relevant professional and board experience? What industries align with your personal interests?
5. Catalog your professional and board experiences in terms of organizational challenges and opportunities (e.g., chapter 11 filings, M&A, turnaround, rapid growth, transformation). Which have you most enjoyed helping organizations navigate?
6. Where have you spent the majority of your career?
7. Based on all of your self-reflections, where do you believe you would add the most value? Why?

SUMMARY

This chapter reviewed the ways that boards vary and provided some guidelines for figuring out what kind of organizations and boards you would like to serve as an independent director. By understanding how sector, industry, organization size, and organizational life cycle affect the nature and dynamics of governance, as well as the qualifications of the directors that boards seek, you can begin to get a clearer idea of where you may best fit. Although it is inadvisable and impractical to set a firm goal that "I want a seat on this specific board," it is reasonable at this point to set a general goal and even a dream list of companies. This clarity will help you figure out what appeals to you in board service. Now that you have selected your general destination, it is time to gauge your fitness level for the coming journey, which is covered in Chapter 5.

CHAPTER FIVE

GAUGE YOUR BOARD FITNESS

The most fundamental harm we can do to ourselves is to remain ignorant by not having the courage and the respect to look at ourselves honestly and gently.

—Pema Chödrön, *When Things Fall Apart*

N ow that you have selected an initial general destination for your board journey, it is time to soberly assess your readiness to seek a board seat. This chapter will explain why understanding your board fitness is important, offer a process for measuring your board fitness, and review some basic fitness guidelines based on studies of public and private independent directors. This chapter closes by describing two of our protagonists' efforts to evaluate their fitness levels and offering some practical action steps you can take.

THE IMPORTANCE OF FITNESS

It wasn't the hottest May in Chicago history, but it surely felt like it. It was 1998 and I was training for my first marathon. I was nearing the end of the training program I was following, and it was time for my 18-mile run. I started out strong, congratulating myself on the choice to shrink my training program from the initial six months I had planned to four months and finally to two months. Rather than the Marine Corps October marathon in Washington, DC, I reset my sights on Grandma's Marathon in Duluth, Minnesota.

I had never contemplated running a marathon. The way I found myself pounding the pavement that day was the result of a bet. Although I had never run more than 4 miles, one of my direct reports was an avid marathon runner. I noticed that despite 10 years in our company, she had never won our circle of excellence sales award. I promised her that if she won the award, I would run a marathon. That apparently was the motivation she needed and, before long, I found myself selecting a training program.

That morning in May, it was already a balmy 78°F—warm, but manageable. All of that changed about a quarter of the way into the run when it suddenly got hot—*really* hot. I could not gulp enough water or sweat enough to combat the intense heat.

Soon, other troubling signs began to appear. With each mile, my feet and legs grew heavier. A tension crept from my shoulders toward my neck, eventually gripping my head in an unyielding vise. My mouth grew sticky.

Then I ran out of water. I was still several miles from home.

I eventually stumbled my way back, completing the 18 miles with a new-found respect for the undertaking I had signed up for. A marathon was no joke, and hydration was serious business. I had come dangerously close to doing real damage to myself. I vowed to never again embark on something like that so unprepared or ill-equipped.

In the same way, it is important to assess your readiness and fitness level for the board journey ahead of you. This journey will be filled with challenges and opportunities you will need to vet, negotiate, and adapt to as you grow your capabilities, relationships, and experiences to support your board service goals. Career fulfillment coach Jelena Radonjic described career fitness as "your current state of fulfillment with your work/job, as well as your preparedness for change, based on your knowledge of your own values, strengths and priorities."[1] Building on this definition, understanding and optimizing your board fitness level cultivates a mindset where you begin doing the following:

Actively seek ongoing development and career advancement. Ongoing learning and skill development help you attract the progressive job opportunities and achieve the career advancement that leads to board seat invitations. A fitness mindset also will orient you toward ensuring that your professional life has purpose and direction and will get you in the habit of setting and achieving meaningful career goals. In turn, you will be in a better position to discern which career opportunities to pursue and which to avoid, thus, achieving a balance between focus and adaptability.

Nurture your reputation and relationships. Building a strong professional reputation is crucial for career success. Having a fitness mindset engages you in actively managing your personal and professional brand, your reputation, and your relationships. In turn, you more readily attract new opportunities, collaborations, support, mentorship, and sponsorship.

Remain agile and adaptable. The business and governance landscape continually evolve due to technological advancements, economic shifts, and changes in industries and job markets. These changes affect your career and your board service prospects. Having a clear understanding of your board fitness helps you remain adaptable and agile in response to these changes so that you remain relevant and competitive as professionals and directors.

Cultivate resilience and sustainability. Gauging and enhancing your board fitness helps you remain competitive and relevant as a board member, thereby, supporting your ongoing development and progression toward your career and board service goals. Furthermore, fitness enables you to bounce back from inevitable setbacks in one's career, thus, reducing the risk of stagnation, obsolescence, and finding yourself off track.

Enhance your well-being. Board fitness also encompasses the ability to maintain a healthy work-life balance, manage your energy, nurture your mental and physical well-being, align your professional goals with personally meaningful outcomes, and cultivate financial stability and security through effective career and board service planning. These various aspects help bolster your sense of fulfillment and accomplishment while reducing your risk of burnout and stress-related issues.

The directors I spoke with as part of the research for this book emphasized the importance of nurturing and protecting their own well-being. Yasmin discussed her commitment to self-care and the importance of maintaining her health despite a demanding career. She highlighted the need for balance and the ability to recharge to sustain long-term success, explaining, "I need to take care of myself physically and mentally to perform well in my roles. It's crucial to find that balance and make sure I'm recharging." Balance can be particularly important when serving on multiple boards, like Amanda discovered. She elaborated, "It's about finding the right balance and making sure that my professional and personal life are aligned. I've always made career decisions that support my financial goals and personal well-being." She discussed how her careful planning and strategic career decisions have helped her achieve financial stability and manage her commitments effectively. Similarly, Amira discussed her approach to career planning, emphasizing the importance of strategic decisions to ensure financial stability and security. Her careful planning has enabled her to pursue board roles that align with her long-term financial goals.

The directors who maintain long careers of board service also emphasized the importance of aligning their professional goals with their personal values in order to ensure their work is meaningful and fulfilling. Kim explained that this alignment has helped her maintain motivation and satisfaction in her roles: "I seek out roles and opportunities that resonate with my personal values and what I find meaningful. This has been key to staying motivated and finding satisfaction in my work." Others described the importance of activities outside of work and board service as leaving them with a grounded sense of well-being and purpose. For example, Danielle highlighted how her involvement in community service projects has helped her nurture her mental well-being. She finds that giving back to the community provides a sense of purpose and balance. She explained, "Being active in community service projects not only helps those in need but also provides me with a sense of purpose and mental well-being. It's a crucial part of my balance."

These examples demonstrate how directors actively manage various aspects of their lives to maintain balance, well-being, and financial stability, ensuring they can effectively fulfill their professional responsibilities while also taking care of their personal needs.

In summary, board fitness helps you maintain the skills, mindset, and resources you need to thrive in your career and board service journey, adapt to changes, and design a successful and fulfilling professional life. Proactively understanding and nurturing your board fitness also can help you understand which types of board are a good fit for you, where you can add the most value, and where your gaps are on each step of the journey. Sometimes, careful examination of your board fitness can help you avoid missteps, like the one that chief financial officer (CFO) and seasoned board member Tina experienced. She shared with me her experience when she realized that she was not a good fit for a particular board due to misalignment with the board's values and expectations. This realization came after understanding the board's dynamics and the kind of contribution they were looking for, which did not align with her professional goals and personal values. She explained:

> I thought my financial expertise would be highly valued. However, it became clear that the board was more focused on maintaining the status quo rather than driving innovation and growth. It was frustrating because I felt that my skills and experience were not being utilized effectively. After a few months, I had to make a tough decision to step down. I realized that staying on a board where I couldn't contribute meaningfully would not be beneficial for me or the company. It was a hard lesson, but it taught me the importance of aligning my values and skills with the board's expectations.

Fortunately, such experiences can be avoided through careful attention to board fitness. For example, Suki, another director I interviewed, described her meticulous approach to ensuring she fits well with the boards she serves on. She explained:

> When you're younger, there's a tendency to collect experiences of different kinds, and you head in different directions because you are just given the ability to serve, and the ability to serve sometimes is enough. But then later, as you get into a different stage of your career, you've had all the ability to serve that two or three lifetimes might afford. Then it becomes about how do you want to serve? And what do you want to be in service to? That's the big question. Now I say no to a lot of boards, because we all have limited amount of time. It's got to be something I believe in, or I'm not going to go down that path. It's very intentional.

Suki's careful and intentional approach to board selection, which focuses on alignment with personal values and the mission of the organization, demonstrates her commitment to ensuring she is a good fit for the boards she serves on. This approach helps her to contribute effectively and maintain a fulfilling board service experience. Now let's take a deeper look at how to measure your current board fitness level.

MEASURING BOARD FITNESS

Gauging your board fitness is hard but necessary work for you to chart an effective and efficient path to board service. Completing the following exercises will help you understand how you measure up compared to existing board members. These exercises also will provide a clearer picture of the competencies, experiences, and networks you need to develop to secure the board seat you would like. With this knowledge, you can begin to set clear, achievable, and appropriate goals that help you stay motivated, aligned with, and making progress toward your long-term vision. Here's how to gauge your board fitness:

R	A	T	E
Refine the Target	**Assess the Target**	**Test the Target**	**Examine Your Fit**
Select three boards	Gauge bench strength	Assess board's strategic fit	Weigh mutual benefits

Refine your target. Chapter 4 discussed selecting a general target for the board journey, which involved identifying the sectors, ownership structures, industries, and organization sizes and life stages you are most qualified for and interested in. In this first step, select three organizations that fit the characteristics you identified.

Assess the target. For each organization you identified, compile the names of each board member by consulting the organization's website. Public organizations are required to and most private organizations do publish the names of their board members. In the absence of this, you may also locate board members by using social media search functions based on the organization name and "board member." After compiling the directors' names for each board, examine and catalog the qualifications of current board members, including their skill sets, professional background, academic background, activities, and other competencies. This step will give you clarity about the bench strength and competencies of the organization's existing board.

Test the target. In this step, you will examine the organization's direction, challenges, and opportunities and make your own determination of how well the board is equipped to provide oversight, management, and service to the executive team. The first step in this effort is reviewing the organization's annual and quarterly reports, SEC filings, CEO talks and announcements, and other documentation that reveals the organization's financial state, strategic direction, and imminent opportunities and threats. Most organizations can be researched through their website and social media, and public organizations additionally can be researched using the SEC's EDGAR database.[2] Many frameworks are available to think about and catalog the results of your research, including strengths, weaknesses, opportunities, and threats (SWOTs) or McKinsey 7-S model, among many, many others. Regardless of the chosen framework, the aim is to identify the organization's goals, direction, and constellation of challenges and opportunities they are likely to encounter en route. Once you understand these, revisit what you learned about the board members' qualifications. By comparing the two, you are then able to identify the strengths and competency gaps you see on the board.

Examine your fit. Compare your background and qualifications to those of the organization's board members and assign three scores:

- **Member similarity (none, low, moderate, high).** How similar are you compared to existing board members? Identify the main gaps in your profile as well as your key strengths and differentiators.
- **Strategic value to board (none, weak, moderate, strong).** Compare your qualifications to the strengths and competency gaps you identified for the board. How much strategic value would your addition create for the board?
- **Personal value (none, low, moderate, high).** Based on the other board members you would work with and the experiences you would gain on this board, what personal value would participation provide to you in terms of your professional development and personal fulfillment?

Now that you have rated your board fitness for your general destination and three potential targets, you can determine what to do next (see Figure 5.1). If (1) you are at least moderately similar to other board members, (2) you offer at least some strategic value, and (3) serving on the board would offer at least some personal value to you, you may choose to begin your outreach to that board. If not, you may opt to either adjust your target or use what you have learned to outline a development plan for yourself.

Although service on a specific board is not something you can proactively seek, pursue, and apply for as you might do for a job, you can begin developing

Figure 5.1   Determining Next Steps.

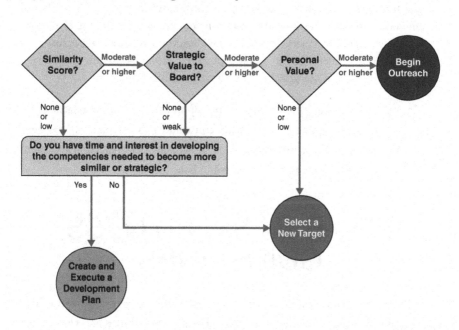

relationships with existing board members by connecting with them on social media, interacting with them at events hosted by board-related professional organizations, or seeking involvement on nonprofit boards they serve. Boards avoid placing directors they do not know; therefore, taking the time to get to know existing directors and, more important, allowing them to get to know you is critical.

Sami's journey to board service is an excellent example of how cultivating relationships with board members can pave the way for board appointments. When I spoke with her about her board journey, she emphasized the importance of networking, learning from others, and strategically positioning herself for opportunities. She actively sought advice, engaged with board members, and demonstrated her value, which eventually led to her being considered for board roles. She elaborated:

> I learned early on that building relationships and networking were critical. I made it a point to meet with board members, ask for their advice, and show genuine interest in their work. This not only helped me learn more about

what it takes to be an effective board member but also put me on their radar for future opportunities. One key moment was when I approached a board member after a conference. We had a long conversation about the challenges and rewards of board service. That connection was instrumental because they later recommended me for a board position. It was all about showing up, being present, and making those meaningful connections.

Sami's story illustrates how her proactive approach in building relationships with existing board members significantly contributed to her pathway to board service. By leveraging these connections and showcasing her dedication and capabilities, she successfully navigated her way into board roles.

SOME BASIC FITNESS GUIDELINES

In addition to measuring your board fitness using the exercises outlined in this chapter, several reports can give you a general idea of the competencies boards are seeking in prospective independent directors. KPMG reported in their Private Company Board Survey Insights that the top three contributions private boards sought in incoming independent directors were (1) offering advice, counsel, and a sounding board for company executives; (2) advising on strategy; and (3) offering an objective perspective to balance executives' and owners' views.[3] Private board priorities also can help you see how your interests and abilities measure up. KPMG reported that within the previous year, private boards increased their emphasis in two primary areas: (1) strategy, risk, disruption, and innovation and (2) risk management—especially as it concerns cybersecurity, data privacy, and related emerging risks. Looking ahead, private boards report needing to sharpen their focus and contributions related to (1) corporate strategy, including business development, partnerships, joint ventures, M&As; (2) talent management concerns; and (3) risk management.

Tentative fitness blueprints for aspiring public directors for companies in the S&P500 can be found in the Spencer Stuart Board Index.[4] The report indicated that the average age of new independent directors is 58, with only 11% being under age 50. In terms of professional backgrounds, global professional experience is ideal, and directors who are active or retired CEOs or who have a financial background (e.g., CFO, investment banker, public accounting executive) are most in demand.

Deloitte shared in their Missing Pieces report[5] based on Fortune 500 companies that public boards are taking more active roles in helping organizations navigate challenges related to economic uncertainty, shifting demographics and global workforce shifts, digitization, and high CEO turnover.

If you aspire to a board chair position, you additionally need to have strong competencies related to encouraging productive debate, managing conflict effectively, and promoting diversity, equity, and inclusion through all your board's processes.[6] For example, effective onboarding, integration, and education processes help new directors swiftly gain a sense of comfort and competency, thus, supporting them in becoming contributing members. Furthermore, although some standardization of processes is appropriate, such processes also need to be tailored to each new director through activities such as peer mentoring.

Your board journey can be thought of in three phases: getting the board ready (phase 1), navigating the board once you have a seat at the table (phase 2), and becoming a leader on the board (phase 3). Using this book as well as the findings and reports by KPMG, Spencer Stuart, Deloitte, EgonZehnder, and more can provide important insights for your board service journey. Not only do these findings provide a blueprint for what competencies these boards desire but also these findings enable you to consider your interest and fit with these roles.

TWO FITNESS EVALUATIONS

Lauren was excited. The idea of all she could do as a board member and the increased representation of women on corporate boards in recent years were thrilling. At the same time, she knew she needed to start by serving on a nonprofit board before she would have the experience, competencies, and connections to secure an opportunity on a corporate board. To begin the process of gauging her board fitness level, she began by looking up local museums, performing arts centers, and girl's empowerment programs, with the goal of finding one of each. After some review, she selected Girls on the Run Chesapeake, Columbia Center for the Theatrical Arts, and the Mitchell Art Museum. She then made a list of the executive director, board chair, and board members for each organization and explored how she could connect with each one on LinkedIn. She also prepared to select a different organization if the board had more than 15 members, as boards of this size were likely to be not-for-profit fundraising boards that offered limited opportunities to develop transferable board-related skills. She then catalogued each director's background to gain familiarity with their qualifications, compare their qualifications to her own, and consider how these directors would expand and complement her existing social network. Finally, she wrote a short message to the executive director and the chair of the nom-gov committee for each organization introducing herself, explaining her passion for the nonprofit's mission, and requesting to connect. After connecting, she requested a brief conversation to discuss their board experience, during which she inquired about the responsibilities and structure of the board, asked about her qualifications for the board, and asked what she could do to get on the board. The subsequent conversations helped expand her awareness of the steps she needed to take to secure a nonprofit board seat and, importantly, created others' awareness that she was available and interested in offering her service.

Denise already was serving on a not-for-profit board; therefore, she had set the goal of securing a spot on a family-owned private board. Her vast ESG-related experience precluded her from serving on any energy sector boards due to the conflict of interest it would create related to her employment. It then occurred to her to focus on industries where companies were facing regulatory or social pressure to expand their ESG strategies. After some reading, searching, and talking with contacts she made at an ESG event convened by Private Directors Association, waste management and logistics (e.g., trucking, freight, containers, warehousing) seemed like obvious fits because companies in these industries were seeking to remove unintended waste from their operations, create new revenue streams, reduce their carbon footprints, and focus on long-term innovation. Denise proceeded by selecting two family-owned waste management companies and two family-owned logistics companies. She then assessed the current board for each by examining the About section of each company's website, and then used the director bios and LinkedIn to catalog each board member's qualifications and background. After doing so, she gauged both her similarity with and differentiating factors relative to the board. She selected one director to reach out to on each board and wrote a short message to make a personal connection, explain her background, and request a 30-minute meeting to discuss the kinds of people who get on boards in their industry. She prepared for the conversation by assessing the organization's vision, mission, and strategic direction as well as its competitive and industry conditions using its website and tools such as Hoovers and Dun & Bradstreet. Based on her analysis, she considered the current board's SWOTs relative to supporting the organization and identified the board's capital and competency gaps. She then considered the ways that she could help fill those gaps. The ensuing conversations helped her gain more insights about how others perceived her background, and how directors in these industries secured their seats. She even found a potential mentor.

ACTION ITEMS

Having selected a general destination for your pathway to board service, it is now time to get more specific and clearer about your actual possibilities. Try the following steps to do so:

1. Based on the general destination you defined in Chapter 4, identify three organizations that fit your target sectors, ownership structures, industries, and organization sizes and life stages.
2. Compile the directors' names for each organization's board and compile individual and composite competency profiles for each board.
3. Collect financial and other relevant reports and documents for the organization. Based on your review of this organization, identify the board's key SWOTs.
4. Compare your analysis of the organization to your profile of its board and identify the board's gaps and SWOTs.

5. Compare your qualifications to the existing board and determine your similarity score.

6. Compare your qualifications to your analysis of the board's gaps, weaknesses, and threats and determine your strategic value to the board.

7. Review your analysis of the organization and the board and determine the personal value of serving on this board.

8. Based on the previous steps, decide whether to change your target, create your own development plan, or begin outreach to this board. The coming chapters will provide more insights and guidance on creating and implementing a development plan as well as reaching out to boards.

SUMMARY

Knowing your board fitness level helps you understand which boards are a good fit for you, where you can add the most value, where your gaps are, and which will best align with your own professional and personal goals. Gauging and optimizing your board fitness is essential to planning and navigating an effective and efficient path to your boardroom journey. By staying attuned to these aspects and taking proactive steps, you can better navigate the challenges and opportunities in the ever-evolving world of board service. In Part II of this book, we take a closer look at how you can develop your profile of competencies to best attract board service opportunities.

PART II

GEARING UP FOR THE TREK

I n this section, we gain a structured process of gearing up for your journey by outlining the principles and practices for gauging and enhancing the competencies you will need to secure a board seat and serve on a board. We talk about these competencies as five types of capital: cultural, director, human, social, and commitment. We end this section with practical guidance on how to leverage your capital portfolio.

CHAPTER SIX

CULTURAL CAPITAL

If you don't know where you've come from, you don't know where you're going.

—Maya Angelou

Cultural capital involves knowing your roots, your personal history, and where you are from. Although most people have never heard of this concept, it is a central part of my discussions with any aspiring or existing director seeking a seat at the table. I think of cultural capital as the source of strength and drive we acquire during our formative years as a result of our family, friends, experiences, successes, and challenges. For example, Rani, one director I interviewed as part of my research explained that she was one of many children and had lost her father early in her childhood. This plummeted her family into extreme hardship and poverty. When sharing her story with me, Rani explained that observing her mother's example instilled within her and her siblings a rock-solid work ethic: "We knew we just had to work hard. That's something that has helped me throughout my career." She learned from her mother's example that dedication to hard work could transform the most of dire circumstances.

Although your own story may differ from Rani's, you too have been profoundly shaped by your experiences, from your earliest formative ones to those gained up to the present day. These experiences form a unique and powerful type of capital that you must know and understand how to leverage in your board search. This chapter further explores this concept of cultural capital, explains why it is important, how it develops, and how it affects your board search. The chapter also provides guidelines for leveraging your cultural capital before closing with two of our protagonists' stories and action items for you to implement.

WHAT IS CULTURAL CAPITAL?

The concept of cultural capital was first introduced by French sociologist Pierre Bourdieu in the 1970s.[1] Bourdieu explained that our early experiences and ongoing socialization cultivate sets of knowledge, skills, and behavioral norms rooted in our cultural context. He referred to this as *habitus*, later extending the concept to *disposition* and *cultural capital*.

Through repeated interaction with parents, family members, teachers, community leaders, and other social influences, we learn which patterns of speaking, thinking, and behaving, and which life goals and which activities are acceptable— and which are not. The resulting collection of competencies and behaviors become assets for maneuvering within that society because they enable us to acquire the qualifications and artifacts that reflect status. These symbols include abilities such as language and talents (embodied cultural capital), possessions and tastes in music and food (objectified cultural capital), and educational and professional attainment as well as social memberships (institutionalized cultural capital). These attributes produce a social brand and validation that gives us access to certain sets of resources, networks, and opportunities within our society.

Bourdieu focused on how cultural capital works to preserve and even exacerbate social inequality. He explained that those with "more" cultural capital have more advantages and opportunities for success because the resulting resources have equipped them with the know-how to navigate social structures, gain access to prestigious networks and institutions, and achieve social recognition and status. In turn, those with "less" cultural capital face barriers to advancement and encounter difficulties in accessing educational, economic, and social opportunities. Bourdieu's view of cultural capital is reflected in the volumes of popular books and movies as well as research and initiatives aimed at leveling the playing field. (One take on this concept can be found in the 2005 book entitled *Limbo: Blue-Collar Roots, White-Collar Dreams,* by journalist Alfred Lubrano.) The efforts to make society and institutions more equitable are important and needed. And Bourdieu's logic makes sense—in homogeneous societies.

But the shifts I have seen in the boardroom suggest that we have entered a new era. As society becomes ever more diverse and our organizations need to understand and serve an increasingly heterogeneous group of stakeholders, cultural capital ceases to be measured along a single dimension where some have more and some have less. Instead, the imperative in organizational leadership and governance becomes ensuring that we have not only density but also *diversity* of cultural capital. Without that, we will be unable to speak the language, understand the unwritten rules, and navigate the structures embedded within the multiple and diverse social groups we serve. Those organizations and boards who fail to recognize that place themselves at significant risk for missteps and strategic errors—such as H&M's 2018 ad campaign featuring a Black child wearing a hoodie stating, "Coolest Monkey in the Jungle."

The growing understanding that we need a diversity of cultural capital in the boardroom means that understanding and articulating your own cultural capital is more important than ever. That is why I seek to understand the backgrounds of potential board members. In our increasingly diverse social and business landscape, cultural capital is your signature brand of strength and drive forged through your formative years and subsequent experiences. In the remainder of this chapter, we explore how cultural capital forms, what it creates, how it affects your board search, and how to leverage your own unique capital.

THE ORIGINS OF CULTURAL CAPITAL

Cultural capital is produced through the cumulative influences of your personal, academic, and professional experiences, the socialization that occurred within these spheres, and the conscious and subconscious sensemaking you engaged in while all of this was happening.

Our family history provides the earliest and potentially most profound formative influence. Through our caregivers' explicit guidance, tacit role modeling, and storytelling, we learned and inferred what the world is, who we are, and what is possible for us, and we developed a corresponding set of beliefs, values, and ways of operating. Sheila explained that her grandparents had raised her to understand the inequity of opportunities presented to people of color. As a result, she persisted through barriers because, as she put it, "I had no choice. Like other women of my generation, we were told by our parents and grandparents to just get out there and do it. Make it happen. If you're given an opportunity, demonstrate to them that you deserve the opportunity."

Those early beginnings set us on a path for how we navigate and make sense of the circumstances, obstacles, peaks, valleys, and other events we travel. Through the resulting combination of adversity and success, we gain in-depth understanding of our own sliver of the world and the unique personal, academic, and professional circles in which we operate. For example, Sheila—along with many of the women of color board members I have interviewed—explained that they learned to ignore, go under, go over, go around, or go through any obstacles put in front of them. One of these board members explained, "You always see the walls. But you just go around them and do something different. And just keep moving forward. Sometimes you can only move a little bit. Sometimes it feels like you're standing still. But you just keep going."

As we move beyond our family and encounter knowledge and influence within academic, professional, community, and social spheres, we continue to experience socialization through role modeling, imitation, observation, and social interactions with peers, mentors, and role models. This socialization transfers to us the social expectations, cultural norms, and traditions of that sphere, which in turn shape our attitudes, values, and beliefs. Jaleh, a private company director, explained how her experience at a Fortune 50 firm shaped her career trajectory:

> It was there that I felt the frustration of not being promoted. It was not about the money, it was about, "Why am I not being recognized?" That led me to take executive roles in smaller companies. When I was put in charge of a marketing department, I learned I had powers I didn't realize I had. And this produced in me an incredible sense of resourcefulness.

The knowledge we gain through informal learning and formal education provides further socialization as well as philosophical and theoretical lenses for understanding our world. Whether that learning occurs on the job through personal reading and exploration, mentoring and apprenticeship, or via professional training programs, or through formal education (and where that education was earned) it further influences who we encounter on the path, what we come to see in the world, and what we understand and experience within it. For example, several of the board members chose their first careers based on where they went to school, such as Ariana, who shared, "because I graduated from Stanford, I went into venture capital for a couple of years completely by happenstance."

Our cultural capital is made even more complex and differentiated by the fact that we use the formative experiences to learn, change, and grow—often in diverse ways. We then revisit the lessons passed to us by our family, early upbringing, professional experiences, and personal interactions. By evaluating and integrating new information, we gain the opportunity to gauge the accuracy of our perceptions of the world, who we are, and what is possible for us. This evaluation may shift our values and our behaviors.

As a result, each of us is a dynamically and finely sculpted unique creation resulting from innumerable influences over time and how we used these to make sense of the world and our place in it. Thinking about this, it seems ludicrous to distill each other down to simple classifications of gender, ethnicity, and (sometimes) age.

Knowing more about a person, such as their industry and positions held, professional experiences and achievements, alma maters, behaviors and traits, personal achievements, family culture and experiences, formative community culture and experiences, and hardships, difficulties, and other formative experiences provides only slightly more information about that person. The reason is that the most important effects of cultural capital—which is how they made sense of these experiences and how these interpretations affected their behaviors, values, and assumptions—remain relatively unobservable.

That's why it is critical for you to understand both what your cultural capital is, how it has shaped your path, and how it continues to influence you today. As Jaleh reflected, "Looking back on my career, I always say to my daughters, I didn't run toward leadership positions, I ran away from the Fortune 50 company. I did it out of frustration. And that's a good thing to be aware of. You have to understand the lens you're putting on things because it helps you realize where you are and why."

THE IMPACT OF CULTURAL CAPITAL

Cultural capital produces personal and leadership attributes that can be used as assets—if you understand and use them. One such attribute is developing an ability and habit of self-reflection and growth. Reflecting on your cultural heritage and background gives you the opportunity to understand your roots and engage with the traditions, values, and rituals that have influenced your family and community. Akiko shared the following regarding her parents' influence:

> My parents modeled a sense of optimism where they always saw the positive in things. I didn't even realize that my mom had been in an internment camp until I went to college and read about the Japanese American experience during World War II. All she talked about when we were growing up is, "Oh, I met so-and-so at camp. … I met him at camp. … I met her at camp." I'm imagining Girl Scout camp or summer camp. I go away to college, come back, and ask her, "Did you go to one of these *concentration* camps?"

"Yeah. That was camp."

I countered, "Why didn't you ever tell us? We thought it was a good thing!"

She answered, "In a way, it was, because it took us to other parts of the country."

Combined with the mantra of *gumbaro* they taught us at home (never, *ever* give up), I now describe myself as an eternal optimist. That comes from not taking things for granted, knowing it's not going to be easy, but also knowing I just have to keep at it.

This process of discovering your cultural capital typically requires self-discovery and personal growth as you explore your values, beliefs, identity, and sense of belonging within your business, social, and global contexts. Importantly, both supportive and adverse experiences can yield personal strengths. Board member and angel investor Jessenia summarized that her experiences of childhood hardship "created a lot of strength, drive, and perseverance to just keep going forward. And you need that in corporate America because, man, the door gets slammed on you all the time—if you even get to *see* the door. Looking back, all those experiences from my early years created the resilience I needed."

Gaining this awareness, in turn, enables you to become more authentic in your leadership and helps you better understand your differences from other cultures, potentially leading to improved understanding, empathy, communication, and connection with your various stakeholders. Miranda, a woman of color board member I interviewed for my research, emphasized why socioeconomic diversity is so important in leadership and on boards. She explained, "Many of these leaders and board members come from very affluent upbringings and don't really understand the kind of decision-making that people who don't have money must make. And those people are their customers."

Cultural capital also influences the mental models we use to navigate our world. Philip Johnson-Laird, philosopher and former professor of psychology at Princeton University, explained that mental models represent our internalized ideas about reality that give rise to habitual ways of thinking and responding. By definition, our mental model is unique to us and offers a simplification of reality so that we can efficiently navigate our world. Mental models work by filtering the information available to us, providing rapid interpretations of that data, and guiding our subsequent emotional and behavioral responses. This explains why two people observing the same conditions can walk away with very different conclusions—such as one perceiving a growth opportunity and another perceiving an unwise risk. This further begins to reveal why diversity and complementarity of mental models across a board of directors is so critical for effective functioning.

CULTURAL CAPITAL AND BOARD DIVERSITY

The importance of cultural capital may be receiving increased and needed attention as the issue of board diversity falls under intense scrutiny. Historical and formal definitions and efforts related to diversity to date have centered on gender and race. Therefore, when executive teams or corporate boards initially faced internal or external pressure for more diversity, the search began for a female director and fewer boards looking for directors from other underrepresented groups. Age diversity then gained more attention due to mounting pressures for social and digital transformation across industries. This tendency for boards to lack ethnic, gender, and age diversity has been referred to as problems of being "pale, male, and stale."[2]

However, an equally valid backlash has emerged, with critics expressing concern about boards focusing too heavily on observable diversity. Lisa M. Fairfax, American legal scholar and Presidential Professor at the University of Pennsylvania Law School, argued in her critique of dominant rationales for diversity[3] that making the argument for demographic diversity via any rationale beyond a moral one is just another means for commodifying underrepresented individuals. She further warned that these rationales can create unrealistic expectations regarding how and how much diverse individuals may affect the corporate bottom line, potentially creating a backlash effect.

Optimal Diversity builds on demographic diversity by additionally assuring that diversity *of thought* is present. That is where your cultural capital comes in, because this capital powerfully and personally differentiates you from other candidates. However, gaining the full benefit of your cultural capital requires deliberate planning.

YOUR CULTURAL CAPITAL DEVELOPMENT PLAN

Creating your cultural capital development plan requires three steps:

1. **Discovering your cultural capital.** Discovering your cultural capital begins with taking stock of your personal history. A helpful exercise for doing that is creating a life map, where you reflect on important life events, pivotal moments, key relationships, professional choices, personal growth, significant challenges, and the contexts within which these occurred.

   Creating a visual representation of these events—whether digitally or in hard copy—is essential for supporting subsequent reflection. Additionally, you may choose to create your map chronologically (e.g., from birth to the present day) or thematically (e.g., organized by life lessons or challenges).

   With the map created visually, consider the significance of each major event or milestone. Identify how each shaped your identity, values, beliefs, strengths, limitations, and goals. Next, identify the patterns that appear related to key events and their influences.

   The themes you identify capture the elements and influences of your cultural capital. For additional insights, share your map and reflections with a few trusted others. These individuals may offer additional observations and questions that further deepen your self-awareness and understanding of your cultural capital.

2. **Developing your cultural capital.** Developing your cultural capital involves discerning the ways in which your culturally based identity, values, beliefs, strengths, and goals are serving your career and board journey and the ways in which these may be limiting your achievements.

   Engage in experiential learning[4] to deepen your self-awareness and to expand your mental models related to the attributes you consider limiting.

Experiential learning is a methodical, hands-on process of learning through experience, reflection, and action involving the following:

> *Concrete experience,* meaning you actively tackle a project, simulation, or real-life problem
>
> *Reflective observation,* when you deliberately reflect on what happened, what you observed, and how you felt during the experience
>
> *Abstract conceptualization,* when you turn your observations and learnings into general principles for understanding and responding to future situations
>
> *Active experimentation,* when you deliberately try out the newly formed principles in a new situation

In this way, the experiential learning process repeats in cycles of ever-deepening awareness and refinement of your knowledge, skill, and approaches. The benefits of this process can be enhanced if you also incorporate feedback on your actions and reflections from trusted mentors and advisors.

3. **Communicating your cultural capital.** Having discovered your cultural capital and fine-tuned its effects, it is critical to powerfully communicate that in your board readiness story. Chapter 11 dives deeply into how you will leverage your capital portfolio to improve your search, but you can prepare for that chapter by completing the exercises in this chapter.

TWO CASES OF CULTURAL CAPITAL

In Denise's life map, she noted how difficult some of her college courses were. She explained, "I had to take statistics, data science, advanced natural sciences, and logical reasoning, but without the years of preparatory courses my prelaw classmates had. I had so many questions that no one else seemed to have. Every day I came to class, it was under the weight of judgment from my classmates, teachers, and even my academic advisor. No one believed I belonged there. They refused to help me when I was at such a rudimentary level. And because I was a first-generation college student, my family couldn't help either. The few times I shared my frustration and worry, they only listed all the ways I could start making money now instead of wasting time on a degree." Despite the adversity all around her, Denise overcame her challenges by staying up late, reading more than the assigned work, reviewing notes from class multiple times, and assigning herself extra homework. Over time, she caught up and then surpassed many of her classmates. Denise realized that, although she hadn't thought about this time in her life for many, many years, she realized that being the first of her family and persevering despite all the odds instilled in her a profound self-confidence and ability to self-advocate. She also realized that this experience gave her a taste for seemingly impossible challenges and a hefty dose of work ethic, self-discipline, and ability to engage in self-guided learning. Denise was surprised by the renewed sense of self and deeper cultural awareness she gained through the life map exercise.

Her results also revealed that she was quick to detect judgment and exclusion from others—perhaps when it didn't exist. She wondered about the role this played in some contentious career battles she had had and in her refraining from seeking a corporate board seat. To explore this, she created some social experiments for herself where she would once again be the least experienced in the group. She enrolled in an improv comedy class. At the first session, she immediately regretted her decision. Her extreme discomfort was a marked contrast to the ease and confidence she felt at work. She noticed side-eye glances and chuckles that seemed pointed at her. When it was her turn, her mind went blank more times than she wanted to admit. She valiantly fought against her urge to quit but was relieved when the session was finally over. She carefully recorded her observations of herself and others. She debriefed these with a close friend, leading to some new realizations about herself and her group members. She made decisions about what to do differently the next time. Over time, this exercise enabled her to perceive others without the automatic filters from her college days, enabling her to make new, more authentic choices.

Sharon had an equally illuminating experience when she completed the exercise. What appeared prominently on her life map was that both her parents were very busy with the family business throughout her childhood. As a result, she was left to provide a lot of the care for her brother who was 12 years her junior. She was surprised to discover that her background produced some strengths but also some liabilities she needed to negotiate. For example, her early experiences instilled in her a sense of duty, responsibility, and pride in her ability to care for her brother. It was this fortitude that she dug into as a single mom returning to the workforce and quickly learning the ropes of the family business after a 10-year absence. On the flipside, she realized that her early appointment to being her brother's caretaker planted within her a tendency to take on too much and to neglect cultivating her own authentic identity or advocate for her own wants and needs. One noteworthy example that showed up in her life map was the time she failed her American History final exam in 11th grade (right before having to fill out college applications) because she felt obligated to clean the house and care for her brother rather than study for her own test. Remembering this event helped her recall other similar instances of neglecting her own needs, wants, and goals. She hired a coach to support her work in shifting this pattern.

ACTION ITEMS

The process of discovering your cultural capital is a journey of self-discovery that will help you put words to the unique experiences and assets you used to get you to where you are today. This process will also help you uncover the experiences you will bring to the boardroom and reveal areas you may need to work on to complete the board search journey successfully. Try the following steps to discover and enhance your own cultural capital:

1. **Become a student of your cultural, familial, and personal history.** Regardless of your racial, ethnic, or cultural background, your ancestral history reflects a story of unique challenges and successes. Learn as much as you can about your cultural history. Gather the family stories that convey the patterns of experiences and competencies characteristic of your immediate and extended family. Create a life map of your important life events, pivotal moments, key relationships, professional choices, personal

growth, significant challenges, and the contexts within which these occurred.

2. **Consider the impact.** Identify how your cultural, family, and personal history have shaped your identity, values, beliefs, strengths, limitations, and goals. Note the common themes that emerge across your cultural, family, and personal histories. These themes become the elements of your cultural capital and their influence. For additional insights, share your reflections with a few trusted others. These individuals may offer additional observations and questions that further deepen your self-awareness and understanding of your cultural capital.

3. **Fine-tune your cultural capital.** Through this exploration, you will discover assets that explain your success as well as liabilities that have limited your options and achievements. For attributes you find limiting, plan experiments that enable you to cultivate and adopt alternate approaches. Engage the help of friends, family members, coaches, and supportive others to help you.

SUMMARY

Cultural capital refers to knowledge, skills, and behavioral norms we possess, rooted in our cultural context as well as formative and subsequent experiences. Discovering our cultural capital takes work, and fine-tuning your cultural capital requires even more work; however, the results are worthwhile. When we understand and can articulate our specific attributes, we become able to differentiate ourselves based on what we will add to the boardroom. This helps boards satisfy a critical imperative to ensure they have the diversity of thought they need to navigate the competitive challenges ahead. Given our increasingly diverse business landscape, diversity of thought is no longer a nice idea; it is a governance requirement for survival.

CHAPTER SEVEN

DIRECTOR CAPITAL

If you're interested, you will do what is convenient; if you're committed, you'll do whatever it takes.

—John Assaraf

irector capital relates to the knowledge, skills, and attributes you need to function well as a board member. Although these competencies overlap to some degree with those required for executive roles, the unique nature and purpose of an independent director means that you will need certain additional experiences, training, knowledge, and traits. In this chapter, we review the elements of director capital, how your amount of this type of capital affects your board search journey, and how to develop it. We find out how two of our aspiring directors reviewed and enhanced their director capital. The chapter closes with practical action steps you can take to assess and improve your board readiness.

WHAT IS DIRECTOR CAPITAL?

Director capital refers to the personality traits and working style, training, experience, and knowledge specific to filling the role of a director on the board. Possessing specialized knowledge that enables you to offer acute insights and know-how related to emergent organizational challenges comprises a second source of capital critical for aspiring and existing independent directors.

Board-related personality traits and working style. Boards need competent thinkers who improve the quality of decisions and are collegial and pleasant to work with on the team. Fulfilling this need begins before the board meeting with your preparation, including reviewing any relevant documents and recognizing and taking any action needed to upskill or increase your knowledge. These attributes support your ability to engage in strategic thinking, demonstrated by being able to anticipate what may be around the corner and factoring that into present-day activities and decisions. For example, you may recognize blue oceans, industry trends and disruptions, and emergent threats or opportunities that indicate the need for risk mitigation or the timely exploitation of opportunity. For example, Najma's ability to provide value to boards was evidenced in her track record of transforming her own company through digital and technology platforms in order to innovate and stay competitive. She explained:

> I built the company and gutted it in a good way, meaning I left no stones unturned to build. And my idea was that we could build a platform of synergistically operating brands that can work together. And we did. We created new technology platforms from the ground up. We created new digital marketing platforms from the ground up, with the idea that many brands could all utilize the same platform. The result was that the company we had already grown for 20-some years more than doubled its value in four short years due to these enhancements.

Once in the board meeting, you need to exercise a collegial and collaborative style, facilitating the board's work together. Specifically, these traits encourage productive and open team communication, sharing of resources and expertise to achieve the board's aims, increased morale, motivation, and engagement, improved problem-solving, and smoother negotiation of conflicting views. Cherise, a CFO and experienced board member, emphasized the importance of building trust, maintaining a cooperative attitude, and fostering strong relationships with other board members. She explained:

> You have to build trust with your fellow board members. That means being prepared, being respectful of others' opinions, and always acting with integrity. When everyone is on the same page and working towards the same goals, the board can achieve great things.

Additionally, it is important to add value to the board discussion by demonstrating intellectual curiosity, listening to other board members and asking thought-provoking questions, and challenging suggestions, decisions, and assumptions when appropriate. Moreover, you need to effectively balance a tolerance for risk with prudent decision-making to fulfill your duties of care, loyalty, and obedience. Dara, who has served on an impressive portfolio of seats across nonprofit, private, and public boards, emphasized the importance of curiosity and questioning in the context of technology adoption. She shared, "I always make it a point to ask detailed questions about how new technology will be integrated and its potential impact. It's through these questions that we can foresee challenges and address them proactively." Imani added, "Asking the right questions is crucial. Sometimes it's not about having the answers, but about challenging assumptions and digging deeper. It's those thought-provoking questions that can lead to breakthroughs and better strategies." In this way, your insightful questions as a director can uncover important details that help the board make more informed decisions.

Board training. The role of an executive and the role of a board member are not equal. Therefore, I advise aspiring directors seeking their first seat or a subsequent seat at the table to adequately equip themselves for the role of director through general board education, completion of certificate programs, and maintaining active memberships in board-related organizations. In other words, joining a board of directors is far more than the club experience it initially appeared to be to Denise. Instead, fulfilling the role of director comes with substantial responsibility. As such, it is appropriate to become a student of this profession if you desire to start the journey. Several directors I interviewed as part of the research for this book described training they intentionally sought to enhance their competence as board members. Jayla underscored the importance of continuous learning and adapting to new challenges, identifying several training opportunities and resources she sought out to stay updated on best practices and governance standards to enhance her effectiveness as a board member. She urged, "You have to stay curious and never stop learning. I've attended numerous workshops and training sessions on corporate governance, risk management, and financial oversight. It's essential to keep improving and staying current with the latest developments to be an effective board member." Similarly, Carmen shared, "I made it my mission to enroll in several director training programs. These courses were invaluable for giving me a comprehensive understanding of board governance, fiduciary duties, and strategic oversight. They equipped me with the knowledge and confidence to make meaningful contributions to the boards I now serve."

Board experience. As with many professions, the paradox of obtaining a board seat is that you need experience on a board to get a board seat, and you need a board seat to get experience. Fortunately, you may have more board experience than you realize if you have presented to or frequently observed your own company's board, or if you have served on the board of a nonprofit or civic organization. The more extensive your board service history, the better. Service on nonprofit fiduciary boards are ideal, with additional credit given to those with experience serving on committees within the board or holding board leadership positions. For example, Daiyu gained extensive involvement in different boards and took care to extract valuable lessons from these experiences. She emphasized the importance of continuous learning and staying engaged with various aspects of board service. She explained, "Serving on several nonprofit and corporate boards provided me with diverse perspectives and a deeper understanding of governance. Staying engaged and continuously learning from each board experience was crucial for my development as a competent board member."

General and specialized knowledge. Serving on the board of directors involves advising and guiding the organization through challenging regulatory, competitive, and social waters. As a result, board members need strong business acumen and a broad understanding of the entire business ecosystem; financial acumen, with the ability to understand the company balance sheet, income statement, cash flow statement, and other financial documents; and specialized knowledge related to current board trends, such as artificial intelligence; environmental, social, and governance (ESG), cybersecurity, talent management, risk management, board composition, and more. Bethany, a law school dean who currently serves on multiple boards, shared her realization that to be taken seriously for leadership and governance positions, she was going to need to strengthen her financial knowledge. Despite already having a JD and significant experience, she decided to pursue an MBA to ensure she was well-positioned for the path ahead. She recalled:

> I could see that I was probably heading down the road to get the dean position. But I had sat in on so many search procedures for leadership positions that I knew that women and people of color are presumed to be incompetent on financial questions—whether that's true or not. In fact, many times, the other people around those rooms know less about what they're looking at than the candidate does. But I realized that that was going to be an impediment to me

being able to take that next step. So I went back and got my MBA, even though I already had my JD and 15 years of experience. That put that conversation about my financial competence to bed.

IMPACT OF DIRECTOR CAPITAL ON YOUR BOARD SEARCH

The amount of your director capital substantially affects your board search journey. Naturally, the more director capital competencies you have and the more you showcase these capabilities, the more competitive you are compared to other candidates and the more likely you are to be strongly considered for an open seat. Additionally, assessing your director capital gives you stronger self-awareness of your capabilities, and that awareness increases your ability to navigate toward a suitable board and away from those boards that represent a poorer fit with the value that you bring. Once you secure a seat, continually assessing and upgrading your director capital prepares you for assuming leadership roles on the board. Demonstrating strong director capital also can help you expand your network of other aspiring and existing board members. That is, by seeking to continually strengthen your board readiness, you are more likely to connect with other executives and directors who can provide valuable insights, mentorship, and refer you for potential board opportunities. The directors I spoke with in preparation for this book offered many examples of how their efforts to grow their skills and provide value rooted in their competence attracted board service opportunities. Lucia, whose reputation is rooted in her experience founding a successful business, shared "private company boards found me. I was just shy of 40 when the first opportunity came to me. Someone said, 'Hey, somebody's looking for a director for a hedge fund. Can I give them your name?'" Similarly, Holly stated she was sought out by the CEO of a health care organization for an independent director position due to her active involvement in the community and her professional reputation.

ASSESSING AND DEVELOPING DIRECTOR CAPITAL

Assessing and developing your director capital requires attention to your personality traits and working style, board training, board experience, and general and specialized knowledge. Zuri, an experienced director with experience across several types of boards, emphasized the importance of dedication and leadership qualities. Her commitment to governance and her ability to lead effectively have been recognized and valued in her roles. She explained, "You have to be dedicated and lead by example. Being on a board is not just about attending meetings; it's about being actively involved and contributing to the organization's success." Others, such as Martina, actively seek opportunities to enhance their skills and knowledge through training programs and educational courses. Martina explained, "I am committed to continuous learning and development. I regularly participate in training programs and educational courses to enhance my skills and knowledge as a board director."

Assessment

Developing your director capital begins with honest assessment. Gauge your current attributes using the questionnaire that follows. Circle your answer for each question. For additional insights, ask one or more trusted mentors or colleagues to rate you as well.

Personality Traits and Working Style

1. As it pertains to board-related documents sent to me in advance of a board meeting …

   A. I would not review them because I already have a good grasp of what's going on. (1 pt)

   B. I would glance through them, but I don't have the time to carefully read everything. (3 pts)

    C. I would make the time to carefully read and review everything in advance to make sure I'm up to speed and able to contribute productively to the board's discussion and decisions. (5 pts)

2. When it comes to my board-related skill and knowledge …

    A. If I had any competency gaps, I would know it or I would hear about it in my performance review at work. (1 pt)

    B. I would evaluate my board-related competencies once when I'm first seeking a board seat. I wouldn't need to do ongoing evaluation after that. (3 pts)

    C. I would deliberately evaluate myself and gather feedback from trusted peers and mentors at least annually and then implement a development plan to close any gaps. (5 pts)

3. To actively identify and anticipate upcoming threats and opportunities that could affect the board …

    A. I rely on strategic thinking and forecasting I've already done as part of my work. (1 pt)

    B. I would chat with my fellow directors at board meetings about developments in the industry and competitive landscape. (3 pts)

    C. I regularly review industry-specific reports and deliberately apply strategic thinking and forecasting tools to anticipate trends that relate to my board service. (5 pts)

4. In team settings, regarding sharing responsibility and authority for making decisions …

    A. Some people will drive the discussion and decision and others will sit back. Depending on the discussion, I usually fall into one of those two camps. (1 pt)

    B. If at least a couple of people are participating, a sufficient level of shared responsibility and authority is present. (3 pts)

    C. the best decisions are reached when every member is heard and engaged and no one person is bent on having their way. (5 pts)

5. When I disagree with the direction a discussion or decision is headed …

   A. I point out how the others' viewpoints are wrong, and I do everything I can to get the group on the right track. (1 pt)

   B. I don't get involved because I don't want to hold up the group discussion. (3 pts)

   C. I ask questions that test the underlying assumptions others are operating on and propose alternate interpretations and solutions for us to consider. (5 pts)

6. If I am unclear or confused during a team discussion or decision-making process …

   A. I don't get involved because it might eventually make sense or it doesn't involve me. (1 pt)

   B. I don't get involved because I don't want to hold up the group discussion. (3 pts)

   C. I ask probing and clarifying questions to gather more information that clear things up because if it's not making sense to me, some of the logic may still need to be worked out. (5 pts)

7. When I need to make decisions …

   A. I almost always default to the high-risk or the low-risk choice. That's how I operate, and it has worked for me so far. (1 pt)

   B. I default to the high-risk or the low-risk choice, unless someone else with a different point of view is driving the decision toward a different outcome. (3 pts)

   C. I carefully evaluate the details of the situation. Based on that, I may choose a higher risk option, a lower risk option, or something in between. (5 pts)

Board Training

8. Regarding membership in a board-related professional association …

   A. I don't have the time or need for membership in a board-related professional association. (1 pt)

   B. I am considering membership in a board-related professional association but have no immediate plans to join. (3 pts)

   C. I am an active member of at least one board-related professional association. (5 pts)

9. As it pertains to completing board general certification programs offered by board-related professional association (e.g., NACD, ELC) …

   A. I have what it takes to be an effective board member and cannot justify the time and expense of seeking a certification. (1 pt)

   B. I am considering or would consider seeking certification but have no immediate plans to obtain one. (3 pts)

   C. I have enrolled in, am actively progressing through, or have earned a board member certification through a recognized board-related professional association (e.g., NACD, ELC) (5 pts)

10. As it pertains to completing specialized certificates (e.g., AI, ESG, cybersecurity, risk management) …

    A. I am not interested because any specialized expertise can be accessed through board consultants or other directors. (1 pt)

    B. I am considering or would consider seeking a specialized certificate but have no immediate plans to obtain one. (3 pts)

    C. I have enrolled in, am actively progressing through, or have earned a specialized certificate. (5 pts)

Board Experience

11. How much experience do you currently have serving on boards?

    A. No experience or experience only with nonprofit fundraising boards (0 pts)

    B. Presentation to or nonvoting member of any corporate board (1 pt)

    C. Voting member of nonprofit fiduciary board (2 pts)

    D. At least one committee member or leadership role on a nonprofit fiduciary board (3 pts)

    E. At least one voting member role on any corporate board (4 pts)

    F. At least one committee member or leadership role on any corporate board (5 pts)

General and Specialized Knowledge

12. Given a real or hypothetical business scenario, I can swiftly identify the key issues and propose solutions.

    A. Strongly disagree (1 pt)

    B. Disagree (2 pts)

    C. Neither agree nor disagree (3 pts)

    D. Agree (4 pts)

    E. Strongly agree (5 pts)

13. I easily understand financial statements such as the company 10k, balance sheet, income statement, and the cash flow statement.

    A. Strongly disagree (1 pt)

    B. Disagree (2 pts)

    C. Neither agree nor disagree (3 pts)

    D. Agree (4 pts)

    E. Strongly agree (5 pts)

14. I understand the key financial metrics relevant to business success and can interpret financial data to make informed business decisions.

    A. Strongly disagree (1 pt)

    B. Disagree (2 pts)

    C. Neither agree nor disagree (3 pts)

    D. Agree (4 pts)

    E. Strongly agree (5 pts)

15. I understand the market trends, competitors, regulatory environment, and potential challenges and opportunities in the industry in which I would like to serve as a board member.

    A. Strongly disagree (1 pt)

    B. Disagree (2 pts)

    C. Neither agree nor disagree (3 pts)

    D. Agree (4 pts)

    E. Strongly agree (5 pts)

16. I effectively communicate my ideas, plans, and strategies verbally and in writing.

    A. Very rarely true of me (1 pt)

    B. Occasionally true of me (2 pts)

    C. Sometimes true of me (3 pts)

    D. Frequently true of me (4 pts)

    E. Almost always true of me (5 pts)

17. I have at least some experience navigating the market trends, regulatory environment, and issues and opportunities related to _____ of the following board challenges: ESG, cybersecurity, talent management, risk management, and board composition.

    A. None (1 pt)

    B. One (2 pts)

    C. Two (3 pts)

    D. Three (4 pts)

    E. Four or Five (5 pts)

Scoring

Calculate your director capital score by computing the total for each area and then adding the area totals for an overall total:

Area of Director Capital	Questions	Score Range	Your Score
Personality Traits and Working Style	1–7	7–35	
Board Training	8–10	3–15	
Board Experience	11	1–5	
General and Specialized Knowledge	12–17	6–30	
Overall	1–17	17–85	

Compare your scores to those in the next table to determine whether each area of your director capital constitutes a strength to sustain, a competency to develop, or a significant development need. If an area falls into the "revisit" range, it may be helpful to revisit the strength of your desire to pursue board service (see Chapter 3) or your Commitment Capital for this effort (see Chapter 10). Circle where your score fell in the following table.

Area of Director Capital	Strength Range	Development Need Range	Significant Development Need Range	Revisit Motivation and Commitment Range
Personality Traits and Working Style	30–35	25–29	14–24	10–13
Board Training	13–15	11–12	6–10	4–5
Board Experience	4–5	3	2	1
General and Specialized Knowledge	26–30	21–25	12–20	9–11
Overall	73–85	60–72	34–59	25–33

DEVELOPMENT

With the results of your director capital assessment in hand, you now have the ingredients to design a customized development plan. If one or more of your scores fell into the revisit range, I suggest beginning with working through Chapters 3 and 10 to ensure that you have the willingness, motivation, and availability to pursue your journey to the boardroom at this time.

Next, turn to those areas that fell into the significant development need range. Examine your answers to find the specific elements that brought down your score and plan specific activities and goals to boost these scores. Repeat this process for those scores that fell into the development need range. Last, ensure that your activities will continue to sustain and build your strengths.

After planning your development activities, review your list to consider whether you could achieve several development goals with a single activity. For example, securing a seat on a nonprofit fiduciary board could strengthen your financial acumen as well as your board experience scores. As a final step, select three activities that will most affect your director capital based on your analysis.

As with many of the activities outlined in this book, seek the advice, insights, and recommendations of trusted mentors in designing your development plan—especially those who are serving on boards.

CASE STUDIES

After completing the director capital assessment, Lauren identified several areas in which she needed development. Of these, she selected the two areas to focus on first: getting board training and building her general and specialized knowledge. In particular, she decided to enroll in NACD's Directorship Certification Program. Additionally, she began reading articles about the challenges boards face related to ESG and talent management and deliberately reflected on how these issues were affecting her current employer. These exercises helped her develop her skills in detecting trends as well as strategic threats and opportunities. She also explored opportunities for obtaining ESG specialization certificate, with plans to enroll in a program after she completes her general director certification. Since beginning her board journey, she had gained a seat on a nonprofit fiduciary board. In this role, she sought opportunities to review the organization's financial statements; identify potential key issues and possible solutions based on industry and market trends, competitors, its regulatory environment; and strengthen her abilities to communicate her ideas by initiating discussions about these with her board colleagues.

The results of Michele's assessment reflected her additional years of professional and board experience, given her role as an executive vice president of technology at a Fortune 500 technology company and having already secured a board seat at one large cap public organization and one private organization. Additionally, she had served on the audit, compensation, and nom-gov committees. Her main development needs are to secure a board leadership role and, especially given her professional role, to obtain a specialization certificate in cybersecurity from a board-related professional organization. Her general and specialized knowledge score fell into the development need range, suggesting that her competency in this area was sufficient for board service but that she could continue to improve. She examined her answers within this area and decided to focus on strengthening her financial acumen. Similarly, her personality traits and working style also fell into the development need range, with her lowest scores for document review and monitoring and upgrading her competencies. These results revealed why she did not enjoy serving on a large cap public board. She also recognized the need to be in board environments that practice strong refreshment and development practices that would support her development rather than having to take the initiative to complete these activities on her own.

ACTION ITEMS

You cannot use your director capital to attract a seat at the table unless you understand what your current amount of capital is and what it will take to grow it into what it needs to be. Take action growing your capital using the following steps:

1. The table below lists five types of board roles directors hold and five types of boards that directors serve. List the board experiences you have to date. For example, if you served as a voting member and audit committee chair of Walmart, you would list "Walmart" in the bottom row in the "voting member" and "leadership role" columns. Additionally when possible, list the specific nonvoting member roles, committees, and leadership roles you held.

Board Type	Role on the Board				
	Presentation (no director seat)	Nonvoting member	Voting member	Committee member	Leadership role
Nonprofit fundraising	———	———	———	———	———
Nonprofit fiduciary	———	———	———	———	———
My employer's board	———	———	———	———	———
Private company	———	———	———	———	———
Public company	———	———	———	———	———

2. Complete the steps in the Assessing and Developing Director Capital section earlier in this chapter.
3. Ask one or more trusted colleagues and mentors to review your assessment results and development plan with you. Seek their advice, insights, and recommendations to help you fine-tune your development plan.
4. Reflect on your experience of assessing your director capital:
   - Do the results seem accurate?
   - What surprised you?
   - Does the development plan seem realistic?
   - What would support you in helping complete your plan?

SUMMARY

Understanding and developing your director capital helps give you a competitive edge as an aspiring board member. Relying on your executive success and competencies will not be sufficient to demonstrate the value you can provide to a board, as the directors require a different perspective, working style, and collection of knowledge, skills, and abilities than you rely on in your daily role. Successfully securing a seat will require the development of certain additional experiences, training, knowledge, and traits. This chapter reviewed the elements of director capital and how your amount of this type of capital affects your board search journey. You also completed an assessment of your own director capital and designed a custom plan for developing it. Implementing your plan will help you take a large step forward in distinguishing yourself as a competent candidate. Finally, keep in mind that developing your director capital is a long-term effort. Reassess yourself every six months until all areas fall into the development need range at a minimum. After that, continue assessing yourself annually.

CHAPTER EIGHT

HUMAN CAPITAL

Build your skills, not your résumé.

—Sheryl Sandberg

Your human capital profile indicates your strengths, development areas, and blind spots as a prospective board member. Having this understanding is crucial to shaping and expediting your path to the boardroom. This chapter introduces what the core elements are in your board member human capital area and describes how directors' human capital affects governance quality. This chapter also provides tools for assessing and developing your human capital, followed by a presentation of what happened when two of our board seekers evaluated their own human capital. By implementing the assessment, planning tool, and action items offered in this chapter, you can ensure that you are aware of your own human capital strengths and development needs.

THE MAKEUP OF HUMAN CAPITAL

Human capital encompasses the combined expertise, know-how, talents, background, and qualities that individuals bring to an organization or society. It exemplifies the immense worth that individuals bring to an organization with their intellectual and personal qualities, which greatly contribute to productivity, innovation, and overall success. Human capital encompasses a broad spectrum of factors:

Education and training. Investing in education, vocational training, and ongoing learning opportunities can greatly enhance your skills and knowledge, enabling you to become more a valuable contributor to the workforce. Vivian, an experienced director I spoke with, discussed her efforts to enhance her strategic planning skills through specialized training programs. She explained, "Strategic development training has been a game changer for me. It's important to understand not just the current market landscape but also anticipate future trends and disruptions. This kind of training helps me provide better strategic guidance to my boards."

Skills and expertise. Having a strong set of skills and expertise is crucial for individuals to excel in their roles. This includes technical proficiency, effective communication, problem-solving capabilities, strong leadership qualities, and in-depth knowledge of the industry. Rosalyn, who has a long history of board service and board leadership, highlighted how her leadership qualities were essential to her role chairing the corporate social responsibility and sustainability committee. She relied on her leadership skills and expertise to help guide the company through the COVID-19 pandemic and ensure it remained committed to social responsibility and sustainability.

Professional experience. Practical experience gained through previous work, projects, and challenges enables individuals to apply their knowledge and skills effectively, make informed decisions, and handle complex situations with confidence. Simone shared her journey to becoming a board member and highlighted how her extensive experience in finance and her role as a CFO prepared her for board service. She emphasized the importance of continuously developing industry knowledge and how it opened doors for her to join various boards. She shared, "Over my financial career, I checked all the boxes to become CFO. I built my expertise in M&As [mergers and acquisitions], strategic planning, banking relationship management, capital markets, and foreign currency management. I served as CFO at an international location, so I ticked that box. And I served in three CFO roles—two of which were at Fortune 300 companies. That opened the door to the boardroom."

Creativity and innovation. The capacity for creativity, innovation, critical thinking, and adaptability is crucial for driving progress, problem-solving, and exploring new opportunities. These qualities are essential for success in any leadership role. Sheryl, currently a director serving on three boards, described how she carried forward a mentality and habit of creativity exercised in collaboration during her early career that continues to influence her approach to board service. She shared:

> We would have these sessions where if one of us young engineers had a problem to solve, we would all camp at the engineering supervisor's house. He would say, "Okay, everybody at my house at 6 o'clock." We'd get pizza. We'd get out the flip charts, and we would work out the problem. It was this world of ideation and creativity and knowing that if we had the strength of the collective that we could attack anything.

Working style and motivation. Aspects like working style, ethics, motivation, passion, resilience, and commitment play a crucial role in determining individuals' productivity, engagement, and overall contribution to organizational goals. Several directors I spoke with had a deeply rooted passion for their board work, such as Monica, whose service on the board of a lithium mining company aligned with her commitment to clean energy, or Sophia, whose service on the board of a children's hospital aligned with a steadfast passion she has for children's health and well-being. Arlene additionally noted that her approach to work and board service reflects having a learner's mind, becoming a student of governance, and her particular areas of expertise. This dedication and working style has served her well and led to high performance in her professional roles as well as those on her boards.

Organizations and societies prioritize the development of human capital by investing in training programs, career development initiatives, mentorship opportunities, and creating a work environment that encourages continuous learning, collaboration, and growth. Understanding and harnessing the power of human capital is crucial for attaining long-term growth, staying competitive, and achieving success in the fast-paced and knowledge-based environment of today.

IMPACT OF DIRECTOR HUMAN CAPITAL ON GOVERNANCE

Directors accept substantial legal and ethical responsibilities when they accept a position on a board, and these responsibilities are assumed collectively. This means that knowing, trusting, and working well with one's fellow directors is of prime importance—and the search for a new director rarely, if ever, extends beyond the existing directors' networks. Nearly all the directors I interviewed in preparation for this book, in fact, were identified for their board seats through their existing networks in board-related professional organizations or their working relationships. Those who serve on nom-gov committees additionally shared that it was through their own networks that they sourced their open board seats. For example, Janae shared, "The majority of directors I've interviewed come through my relationships at the Executive Leadership Council, at the National Association of Corporate Directors, or at the Black Corporate Board Readiness program." Several other directors shared that boards found them through their networks.

Although this sourcing strategy provides the board with a sense of safety, that safety may be an illusion. The risk of searching only within the board's existing circles is cementing a homogeneity of thought, experience, and competencies that can create real difficulties when boards need to anticipate and help companies navigate the volatile environments and competitive challenges they face. I suspect that if we examined the boards of failed companies such as Blockbuster, Polaroid, Circuit City, and more before and during their inflection point toward decline, we would discover several gaps and redundancies in its human capital that ultimately explained the puzzling decisions that ensured their disaster.

This reveals that the issue of board diversity—which itself has fallen under intense scrutiny—centers on a question we can all agree on: are we, as the board, collectively and sufficiently equipped to fulfill our duty of care to the organization? Duty of care involves such things as being knowledgeable about the organization's operations, exercising long- and short-term thinking, posing incisive questions, comprehending hazards, and deliberately gauging which risks are acceptable. Confirming we are adequately fulfilling our duties requires sober self-examination that identifies human capital redundancies, gaps, and misalignments between the board and organizational stakeholders. For example, one director serving on the board of a scientific research and development company found itself undergoing significant changes and expanding its strategic focus in various sectors. The board recognized the need to align its skills and expertise with the company's evolving strategic outlook and stakeholder needs. The board underwent a refreshment process wherein it carefully assessed whether its composition matched the strategic direction of the organization. This process highlighted the need for expertise in areas such as scientific research, energy, and global operations, given the company's mission and areas of impact. Identifying these skill gaps and aligning the board's expertise with the company's strategic needs enabled leadership to ensure the board was well-equipped to support the company's mission and strategic objectives. This proactive approach helped the company navigate complex challenges and seize opportunities in its areas of focus.

This kind of board self-examination is critical because failure to fulfill our responsibilities results in disastrous missteps—such as BP's failure to swiftly and transparently handle the Deepwater Horizon oil spill in 2010—and blind spots that can lead all the way to organizational death, as in the case of Blockbuster. The longer board homogeneity is allowed to persist, the more vulnerable the board is to overlooking risks, signposts, and critical moments when executives' decisions need to be challenged rather than simply approved.

Board directors' human capital significantly affects the effective operation of the board. When board members collectively have human capital redundancies, gaps, or misalignments, the board can fail to identify emergent opportunities and markets. One symptom is when the organization's leadership, particularly the board, is unable to recognize and capitalize on new and evolving trends, needs, or potential areas for growth within the business environment. This failure can result in missed chances for innovation, growth, and competitive advantage, increasing the risks of stagnation, competitive vulnerabilities, and even financial setbacks. Organizations with these board vulnerabilities also find it challenging to stay relevant and navigate changing industry dynamics. For example, by the time Blockbuster finally attempted to become a contender in online rentals, it was hopelessly behind its competitors and never recovered. Identifying and addressing human capital gaps can help mitigate these risks by improving the board's ability to create effective strategic plans, understand their market, and architect innovation.

Problems with board members' human capital also may be the culprit when the same problems keep recurring, which suggests that the root causes have not been adequately identified, understood, and addressed, or that innovation and needed perspectives are lacking. A glaring example of this is the persistence of glass ceilings, despite Marilyn Loden first pointing out the phenomenon during a 1978 panel discussion on women's goals and dreams. The fact that women remain underrepresented at the highest levels of organizations more than 40 years later, despite the proliferation of legislation, nonprofit organizations, diversity roles, and organizational programs designed to close the gap, suggests we have not yet uncovered and solved the root problem. The lack of effective solutions reveal potential gaps in knowledge, skill, and other competencies. If these gaps are not identified and filled, recurring problems can evolve into stagnation, missed opportunities, competitive disadvantages, employee disengagement, resistance to change, poor decision-making, ineffective problem resolution, and ultimately erosion of stakeholder trust in the organization and the board.

Take the case of Blockbuster. The opening of its flagship store in the 1980s was quickly followed by the company becoming a staple of American culture. From a single storefront in its opening year, it was operating out of 800 by year three, thanks to significant contributions by investors. Eleven years later, the company went public and swiftly reached its pinnacle, with a worldwide presence of 60,000 employees across 9,000 stores, a market value of $5 billion and revenues of $5.9 billion. The company's stunning success made its demise 10 short years later all the more shocking.

Although no one denies that Blockbuster's infamous refusal to acquire Netflix in 2000 was the beginning of the end, there is more to the story—especially for those of us concerned about sound governance. In reviewing the history of Blockbuster's missteps, many more errors become apparent, such as late fees making up a whopping 16% of its revenues in 2000 (Blockbuster's late fees played a central role in Netflix's origin story), frequent CEO and strategic changes, and the bewildering decision to abandon online access and streaming in favor of storefront rentals from 2005 to 2007. To a governance researcher and practitioner, Blockbuster's story points to a core problem of human capital redundancies and gaps within the board.

Addressing these human capital redundancies and gaps in a lasting way requires a comprehensive framework of periodic board evaluations and board refreshment practices, which include director self-assessments and peer-to-peer assessments. As an aspiring board member, you can develop your ability to understand and participate in these practices by assessing your own human capital.

ASSESSING YOUR HUMAN CAPITAL

Every member on a board bears the responsibility to ensure that, as a group, it has the knowledge, experience and viewpoints needed to effectively monitor company performance and constructively challenge new ideas and strategy. As an aspiring director, it is your responsibility to evaluate your own human capital, including your skills, knowledge, experience, and other attributes. This kind of self-examination featured prominently in the stories of successful directors I spoke with. For example, Adeline spent her career in finance, culminating in the CFO role, which made her an attractive candidate for corporate boards. Her account of her path from her college years to the current day demonstrates her dedication to continual self-improvement, culminating in gaining the necessary skills for effective board service. She explained:

> I am a lifelong finance person. I have an undergraduate degree in accounting and information systems. I have a CPA. I spent years in public accounting and then went into corporate finance. I meandered my way through every aspect of finance, whether it was controllership, reporting, internal controls, or internal audit. Then I also did the more strategic side.

Assessing your human capital involves several steps, which this section will guide you through. You will begin by evaluating your job history and key accomplishments to identify your industry expertise, education, core skill sets, and personal traits. Next, you will rate your expertise on a range of board director competencies. This quantitative evaluation will help you pinpoint your key strengths and chief areas needing improvement, providing you with clear guidance for goal setting and development. By periodically repeating this process, you can stay ahead of emerging trends and remain competitive and relevant both in your field and in your board search. This targeted approach ensures that you not only pursue board opportunities that align with your skills and interests, but also differentiate yourself as a director.

To begin your assessment, take note of your:

- Job history and key accomplishments
- Industry and knowledge expertise
- Education, including formal degrees, certifications, and professional training
- Core skill sets
- Personal traits and approaches that reveal *how* you carry out your professional roles

Next, rate yourself according to standardized board director competencies (see Table 8.1), taking care to add any specific competencies needed within the target board type you identified in Chapter 4. Such competencies might include deep knowledge of the operational or market dynamics of specific regions critical to the company or skills in managing relationships with investors, regulators, or key business partners. Rate yourself according to your degree of mastery in that competency using this four-point scale:

0—I do not have this competency.

1—I have minimal expertise or knowledge in this competency.

2—I have sufficient expertise or knowledge in this competency.

3—I have strong expertise or knowledge in this competency.

Table 8.1   Human Capital Self-Assessment.

Competency	Rating
Management and Leadership Expertise	
CEO experience	
CFO experience	
CTO experience	
Profit-and-loss experience	
Management and Leadership Expertise Subtotal	
Functional expertise	
Accounting	
Finance	
Human resources	
Legal/regulatory	
Marketing/sales	
Technology	
Functional Expertise Subtotal	

(Continued)

Table 8.1 (Continued)

Competency	Rating
Governance-related expertise	
Corporate leadership and governance	
Board expertise	
Governance Expertise Subtotal	
Specialized expertise	
Compensation	
Environment	
Government affairs and public policy	
Mergers and acquisitions	
Operations	
Strategy development	
Talent development	
International business experience	
Specialized Expertise Subtotal	
Emergent Challenges Expertise	
Artificial intelligence	
Cybersecurity	
Risk management	
Supply chain	
Emergent Challenges Expertise Subtotal	
Leadership Qualities and Behaviors	
Dedication to social issues	
Emotional intelligence	
Genuine concern for the company	
Intellectual curiosity	
Professional and personal ethics and integrity	
Time to devote to board work	
Working style that reflects collaboration, collegiality, and a consultative approach	
Leadership Qualities and Behaviors Subtotal	

Competency	Rating
Target-Specific Expertise	
Target Specific Expertise Subtotal	
Total	

The next step is to carry forward your subtotals into Table 8.2 in the rating column (Column 1). For your target-specific expertise subtotal, calculate the max possible score by multiplying the number of competencies you listed by 3 and enter this number into Column 2. Then, calculate your percent score for each competency type by dividing your rating by the max possible score for each. Record your percent score for each area of expertise in Column 3.

Table 8.2   Human Capital Competency Percent Scores.

Competency Subtotals	Rating	Max Possible Score	Percent (Rating/Max)
Management and leadership expertise		12	
Functional expertise		18	
Governance expertise		6	
Specialized expertise		24	
Emergent challenges expertise		12	
Leadership qualities and behaviors		21	
Target specific expertise			

Table 8.3 Human Capital Top Strengths and Development Areas.

Top Three Competency Strengths	Top Three Development Areas
1.	1.
2.	2.
3.	3.

Finally, in Table 8.3, list your top three competency strengths based on the three highest percent scores from Table 8.2. List your top three development areas based on the three lowest scores from Table 8.2.

YOUR HUMAN CAPITAL DEVELOPMENT PLAN

Your human capital assessment provides in-depth insights into your strengths and weaknesses as a potential board member. These results should be empowering rather than discouraging. Growth and change are inevitable. Do not be alarmed or dismayed if you discover you need to grow to make your goals of board service a reality. Many successful directors can tell stories of the times they realized they too had competency gaps. For example, Jessica realized she needed to improve her audit skills to be more effective in her board roles. She explained, "My goal when I first joined the board was figuring out what I had to do to obtain leadership positions on the board. I noticed who was chairing each committee and what their credentials were. Then I asked myself, 'What do I need to do to get there?' I refused to let a title like a CEO get in my way."

Where gaps exist, seek developmental experiences and activities to cultivate what you need. The directors I interviewed shared that they regularly develop their competencies and capabilities through activities such as acquiring profit and loss experience, improving their internal and external networks, building more trusted relationships, repairing broken professional relationships, creating more mentor relationships for specific skill sets, positioning themselves for different executive roles internally or externally, seeking opportunities to have interactions with their firms' internal boards, joining external board-related groups, becoming students of corporate governance, and ensuring they are seen and known. For example, in addition to carefully constructing her competencies over her career, Fatima worked to strategically position herself through relationships, performance, and continuous learning to ensure that others would recognize her skills and consider her for board positions. Her proactive approach in seeking out sponsorship, leveraging her network, and demonstrating her capabilities made her a sought-after board member. This is why she often received unsolicited calls inviting her to serve on boards. She shared:

> The CEO of a prominent energy company called me and said, "Fatima, you're going to get a call for a board position." I responded, "With all due respect, I am serving on many, many boards right now." At the time, I was serving on 10 or 12 when you include the local community and chambers and things like that. He said, "This is one you cannot say no to."

Fatima's reputation, combined with the sponsorship she had cultivated, helped her assemble an impressive portfolio of board service. Fatima's experience also demonstrates that these efforts of evaluating and developing your human capital does not end once you secure a seat. Boards are becoming more transparent in response to shareholder engagement and activism, and a critical consideration is whether the directors' collection of expertise and skills align with company strategy and investor value creation. For this reason, more and more company boards are disclosing their composition in the form of board skills matrices. Implementing your own rigorous and repeated self-assessment practices will help ensure you are keeping pace with the needs of boards and their organizations.

Your action plan should focus on closing competency gaps through specific development activities and experiences such as:

- Job moves and positions you need to hold
- Experiences you need to gain (e.g., M&A, turnaround, industry disruption)
- Industry expertise to acquire

- Formal education, certifications, or professional training to obtain
- Skill sets to develop
- Personal traits to cultivate

Once you create your action plan, be sure to track and report on your progress. Coaches, mentors, peers, and support groups can be invaluable for providing accountability as you implement your action plan.

CASE STUDIES

Lauren had come a long way since the start of her board journey. She had almost finished NACD's Directorship Certification Program and had already enrolled in the ESG specialization certificate, which she would begin when the general certification was complete. She also had joined a local nonprofit fiduciary board focused on leadership in girls. Through this exposure, she gained experience reading financial statements and created a weekly habit of reviewing industry and market trends and then deducing how these may affect the board. She also reached out to a different board colleague each month to discuss her thoughts, which helped further sharpen her critical thinking skills. She was excited to notice that insights were more easily and rapidly coming to her over time. When she assessed her human capital, she decided her leadership qualities and behaviors comprised her strongest area. She was glad that her genuine concern for the company; intellectual curiosity time she devoted to board work; and collaboration, collegiality, and consultative approach were valuable. Lauren shared her self-assessment with her uncle, who gave her some concrete suggestions for how to start gaining the leadership experience she needed to continue developing. He began by painting the vision of landing her first corporate board role by age 45. To get there, he explained she would need to both advance and expand in her expertise. Specifically, he advised getting promoted from district to regional manager or area vice president in sales and then making a lateral move to operations management to gain the profit-and-loss (P&L) experience she needed. "It is not enough to be conversant about other areas," he explained. "You need actual experience if you really want to make it to the boardroom." He further explained to her that although her career path may not be as straightforward as he suggested, the point is to acquire the skill sets she needs, and she must evaluate every career move in light of its alignment with her long-term knowledge and skill development goals.

Sharon began her journey from a very different starting point than Lauren. Sharon had 12 years of CEO experience and was an executive board director for her father's $45 million original equipment manufacturer family-owned business. Given her experiences, she had set the goal of securing a seat on another family-owned company's board. Based on her self-assessment, her top three strengths were her management and leadership experience (specifically CEO and P&L experience), and her leadership qualities of genuine concern for the company and professional and personal ethics and integrity. She identified her top three development needs as lacking expertise in boards' emergent challenges, lacking the other specialized expertise desired by boards, and tending to take on too much rather than adopting a working style that reflects collaboration, collegiality, and a consultative approach. She shared her reflections with an independent director who had served with her in the past. Together, they outlined a pathway forward, which included attending the Director Development Initiative's Board Boot Camp, and completing specialized certificates in artificial intelligence and M&A. Additionally, she decided to join a doubles pickleball league to gain more practice with doing unfamiliar things, letting go of the outcome, and having no choice but to listen to and collaborate with others.

ACTION ITEMS

Building your human capital in preparation for board service requires careful assessment and development. Take the following steps to sharpen your knowledge, skills, experience, and abilities:

1. Review the general destination you selected in Chapter 4 and the insights you gained from evaluating your board fitness in Chapter 5.
2. Using the results of Step 1 as a lens, reflect on your professional, academic, and personal background and make an inventory of your job history and

key accomplishments; industry and knowledge expertise; education, including formal degrees, certifications, and professional training; core skill sets; and personal traits and approaches.

3. Rate yourself against the standard board director competencies provided earlier in this chapter. Identify your top three strengths and top three development areas. Design a development plan for yourself based on the results of Steps 2 and 3.

4. Ask one or more trusted colleagues and mentors to review your assessment results and development plan with you. Seek their advice, insights, and recommendations to help you fine-tune your human capital development plan.

5. Reflect on your experience of assessing your human capital and journal your responses to the following: Do the results seem accurate? What surprised you? Does the development plan seem realistic? What would support you in helping complete your plan?

SUMMARY

When it comes to securing a seat at the table, taking the initiative to deliberately and regularly evaluate your human capital is vital to the personal and professional growth you need to get there. Developing these practices gives you the ability to take charge of your professional life, make the most of your potential, and succeed in a dynamic and competitive landscape—both in your industry and on your path to the boardroom. At the same time, as you become an increasingly careful curator of your own expertise, you will attract attention. You will be tapped for an increasing number of roles. It is critical to neither automatically accept nor decline these. Instead, you must carefully evaluate each by gauging how it fits your goals and development needs. This does not mean your career path will progress along a straight line, as few (if any) do. However, it is important to remain mindful to evaluate each twist and turn and then select those that complement and refine your path.

CHAPTER NINE

SOCIAL CAPITAL

There's no fall greater than one from a burnt bridge.

—Carlos Wallace

We have all heard, "It's not what you know, it's who you know." Very few recognize that even knowing the right people is not enough. Instead, *who knows you* actually drives the opportunities we find ourselves presented with. Usually, when opportunities emerge, we are identified, vetted, and selected (or weeded out) completely outside our awareness based on the network of our past relationships—all made visible by social media. This leads to the critical imperative that we must build, continually examine, and then nurture and repair our relationships throughout our careers, especially if we want to architect a fulfilling and impactful post-career. In this chapter, we discuss what social capital is, why it is important, how it affects your board search, and how to evaluate and strengthen your social capital.[a]

---

[a] Portions of this chapter first appeared in Dorsey, Keith D. (2022). 4 strategies to secure a corporate board seat. *Harvard Business Review* (December 14). https://hbr.org/2022/12/4-strategies-to-secure-a-corporate-board-seat

WHY SOCIAL CAPITAL IS SO POWERFUL

The social media age has allowed covert recruiting to flourish so that, whether you like it or not, your past relationships become your character references. People's impressions of and experiences with you, as well as their knowledge of your goals, interests, and abilities, can make the difference between being offered an opportunity and being excluded from the running.

The importance of making a good first impression, networking, and relationship building have long been the focus of books, articles, and corporate training. Efforts to increase diversity, equity, and inclusion have focused on leveling the playing field, bringing diverse voices to the table, and identifying and eradicating systemic and institutional racism—often through top-down and system-wide actions. Although these efforts have merit, individuals seeking board seats do not need to wait for such changes to occur to secure the opportunities they want. What I realized through my research on women's pathways to the corporate boardroom is that much traction can be gained when we carefully examine and nurture our network of relationships—both past and present—so that our contacts know us, know what we want, and maintain a positive impression of us and our contributions.

Two theories from social psychology help us understand why it is so important for others to know us and to know what we want. First is social capital theory, where social capital refers to a kind of interpersonal "currency" that enables you to access structural, cognitive, relational, and other resources through your connections to others and through your membership in social networks. When you have social capital in your workplace, for example, you tend to have better access to information, resources, and sponsorship. Social capital builds as you increase your number of relationships and deepen the relationships you have through reciprocity and shared norms, values, and trust.

The second theory relevant to this discussion is uncertainty reduction theory, which begins by acknowledging that the unknown makes us uneasy—and when it comes to interpersonal workplace situations, not knowing someone or how they are likely to react makes us especially uneasy. To avoid this discomfort, we collect as much information as possible about the other person to reduce our sense of uncertainty and help us predict the other's behavior and resulting actions. That greater sense of predictability helps us interact better, build a better relationship, and create better outcomes.

Applying these theories to the task of finding directors for a corporate board, it follows that the people tasked with filling open board seats are far more likely to select someone they know (or someone whom they trust knows) than they are to choose unknown candidates—even if those candidates look great on paper. This means you will have an easier time securing a seat at the board table when you have a broad and deep network of healthy relationships and when you make known (1) that you want to serve on boards, (2) why you want to serve on boards, and (3) what types of boards you are best equipped to serve.

The bottom line of covert recruiting is that you must carefully maintain your past and present relationships—and this can be even more important than expanding your current network. Jocilynn emphasized, "Your social networks are key to securing board positions, but what is even more important is maintaining positive relationships with those in your past because recruiters and boards do reach back into your background." She added, "I am so thrilled that I never carelessly left a company, that I always had a good transition plan, and that I stayed connected to former executives."

HOW RELATIONSHIPS AFFECT YOUR BOARD SEARCH

The impact of social capital on aspiring directors' efforts to secure a board seat was evident in my research on women's pathways to corporate board room. The female directors I interviewed emphasized the importance of improving their internal and external networks, building more trusted relationships, repairing broken professional relationships, and ensuring they are seen and known. They also stressed the importance of sustaining not only their current relationships but also those from the past and, specifically, taking care to nurture their entire constellation of relationships in order to be noticed by recruiters and boards.

April, an attorney with nearly 10 years of board experience across two boards, succinctly noted, "It's about who they know, who knows you, *and what that person has to say about you* that makes the difference." The directors I interviewed for my study echoed April's sentiments through numerous stories about why it comes down to the people they knew and, more important, who knew them. Elaine, a Fortune 500 executive with two years of experience across three boards, emphasized, "You probably know people on boards. You need to reach out to them and meet with them and say, 'I'm interested in serving on a board, and here's what I'm interested in,' because those of us who are on boards are often called and asked if we know anybody." After all, if you are interested in securing a board seat, you want to be the first person that comes to mind. But you won't come to mind if your relationships need work or if people don't know you want a seat.

Other research has similarly underscored the importance of relationships. For example, the NACD reports that more than 60% of independent directors find their board seats through networking (with recruiters filling the gap for remaining board seats).[1]

Recruiters and boards typically use three specific approaches to sourcing candidates that reveal how strongly your social capital affects your chances.

The C-suite Connection

Corporate boards historically have consisted of current and former CEOs and CFOs. Therefore, when they need to recruit new board members, they generally reach out to their networks of other CEOs and CFOs, refilling the stock of C-suite directors. Victoria, a CEO with 22 years of experience across five boards, reflected,

"I just think that companies are looking for the C-suite individual and are recruiting CEOs, CFOs, and CIOs." It is no surprise, then, that all the directors I interviewed served in the C-suite during their executive careers, with half holding the CEO title, and one-quarter having a CFO title. Martina, a public company CFO with 17 years of board experience across seven boards, explained that these individuals are needed because "they can see the business in its broadest, holistic form, not just their functional form." In a similar vein, profit-and-loss (P&L) operating experience has long been a prerequisite to serving on boards, and two-thirds of the women I interviewed had such experience. Describing it as "the first competency boards seek," Yvonne, who had served on five boards over the previous three years, emphasized, "the real one that I think gets you in the door is that operating experience."

This approach of sourcing new directors with C-suite executives means that boards run the risk of lacking the deep functional insights they need to navigate emergent opportunities and challenges. Although this could open up opportunities for you to differentiate your value to a prospective board through your unique expertise, the power of having C-suite experience cannot be underestimated, this doesn't help you, as an emerging candidate to attract a seat.

The Search for the Familiar

Catalyst, a global nonprofit organization dedicated to accelerating progress for women through workplace inclusion, reports that boards seek new members who resemble the board member who vacated the position, and the women I spoke with confirmed this.[2] Scarlet, an executive who has served on six boards over the past three years, shared that she was all too familiar with these responses from executive recruiting firms: "Your background is fantastic. You would be great on this board, but you are an out-of-the-box candidate" or "You are an off-spec candidate," followed by concerns about how hard it will be for them to place her.

The problem with looking for the doppelgangers of past board members is that a déjà vu effect forms where the more things (i.e., directors) change, the more things (i.e., boards) stay the same. Ebony, a 23-year veteran of six corporate boards, explained that this déjà vu dynamic happens because "board members and recruiters get nervous when they're looking at people they don't know, and most minority candidates fall into this category." Instead of facing that nervousness, boards instead keep selecting the same kind of director over and over again. First, that makes recruiting a new director easy: they expediently fill open seats because they just tap into their usual networks. Second, sourcing directors this way feels good because they get to avoid the uncertainty and discomfort of having to figure out how to collaborate with a new type of person in the director seat.

The easy pick comes at a significant cost: when boards choose déjà vu over diversity, they risk homogeneity of thought, experience, and competency. This homogeneity, in turn, can pose real risks for board effectiveness given the volatile environments and competitive challenges companies face today. Understanding boards' tendency toward familiarity and the risks they place themselves in as a result can help you differentiate your value during your own search.

The Hidden References in Your Network

To reduce uncertainty and improve the success of a director sourcing effort, recruiters and boards tend to rigorously vet director candidates—often well before the candidate even learns of the open board seat. Before social media, vetting was far more controlled, largely with the candidate identifying references who would speak positively about them. Now, nearly your entire network is on display for the world to see—even those who might not remember you so fondly. The transparency of our social networks, connections, and past work experiences enables unprecedented opportunities for boards to get the *complete* story on you.

The directors I interviewed shared that they had been pre-vetted by the recruiters and other board members and that they were contacted only when the information gathered was favorable. Nicole, an executive who had accumulated 19 years of experience across four boards explained, "Boards are looking for the skills, the background, but honestly, you've been pre-vetted before they even talk to you." The other executives I talked with added that the recruitment process becomes significantly abbreviated as a result, because the board contacts only the candidate they want. Jocilynn, an executive who had served on four boards, all within the previous two years, shared her story: "We hadn't even spoken on the phone, but the board chair sent me an email saying, 'I've heard so much about you. Everyone that I've interacted with knows you're fantastic. Would you be willing to consider this particular company?'"

EVALUATING YOUR SOCIAL CAPITAL

Before you can optimize your social capital, you need to know where you currently stand. Four steps help you do this:

1. Identify your past and present professional relationships—names, contact info, date of last contact, status (active [in touch within last 12 months], inactive), quality (healthy, strained but reparable, broken and irreparable, unknown). Think about every job you've had and every club you've been in. Although this takes effort, the pre-vetting that has become a normal part of any board search effort means you *must* do this work.

2. Identify your past and present group affiliations—names, contact info, date of last involvement, involvement status (active [participated within last 12 months], inactive), degree of involvement (positions held, events/ activities attended), depth of in-group network (what percent of group do you know/knows you—small, medium, large]). Also think about every association you've been a member of.

3. Identify your past and present relationships with executive recruiters— names, contact info, date of last contact, status (active [in touch within last 12 months], inactive), quality (healthy, strained, broken, unknown).

4. Identify your past and present relationships with active and inactive board members—names, contact info, date of last contact, status (active [in touch within last 12 months], inactive), quality (healthy, strained, broken, unknown).

The outcome of this effort is having an inventory of who you need to let know of your interest, which affiliations you need to strengthen to enhance your pre-vetting outcomes, and which you can offer as capital to boards you serve on. The next section presents a detailed approach to accomplishing this effort.

YOUR SOCIAL CAPITAL DEVELOPMENT PLAN

Now that you have evaluated your current social capital, it is time to develop a specific plan for your relationships, group affiliations, executive recruiter connections, and board member connections.

Relationship Action Planning

The primary criterion for continuing any relationship and planning how to strengthen it is that the relationship is aligned with your career and board service goals. If it is not, it is best to honor and celebrate the mutual enjoyment and benefits gained from the relationship for the time it was active and to part ways amicably.

For the remaining relationships that are aligned with your goals, I recommend five possible relationship actions to take, depending on the status and health of the relationship: prune, follow, reconnect, broadcast, and reconcile. These actions vary in the degree of self-advocacy and level of engagement involved (see Figure 9.1).

Figure 9.1 Possible Relationship Actions.

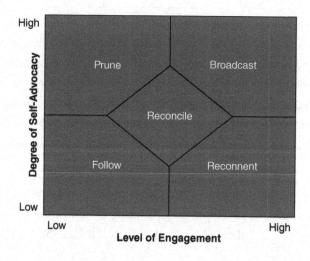

Prune

Pruning involves a conscious decision to discontinue relationships that are broken beyond the point of repair and reconciliation. In this way, this relationship action reflects high self-advocacy. In situations in which there is no need to deliberately cease a formal legal contract or business relationship, it also is a low-engagement strategy. Pruning relationships is crucial because it enables you to prioritize meaningful key connections instead of stretching yourself too thin across multiple superficial relationships.

For example, Melissa began her career on the leadership track at a prominent consulting firm. Her early days of onboarding, training, and early team projects were stimulating and great fun. In particular, she formed fast friendships with Sarah and Mary, two other college hires. She recalled many days and happy hours expressing mutual respect and discussing shared goals with her friends. But over time, cracks began to appear as their respective careers unfolded. Their communication styles and values clashed. Distrust and dissatisfaction grew as Melissa's and Mary's careers advanced faster than Sarah's. When they did find themselves together on a team project again, Melissa discovered that her communication style clashed with those of her two friends, leading to tension, inefficiency, and frustration. Mary missed key deadlines and all of them failed to meet commitments made to each other. Her early friendships had officially soured, and they no longer had the same aspirations, much to talk about, or even enough good will or shared experience to support each other's success. Melissa ultimately made the difficult decision to end these friendships by acknowledging all she and her friends had once enjoyed together but ceasing any further attempts to maintain or rekindle the friendships.

When we end relationships that no longer are mutually beneficial, we conserve our emotional and mental energy so we may prioritize and invest in the relationships that align with our values, goals, and overall well-being. Our emotional well-being also is enhanced because the stress, conflict, and negativity we may otherwise experience from unhealthy or draining relationships is avoided. We also gain bandwidth and energy for those connections that foster our personal growth and development. In general, trimming down our relationships enables us to foster and develop a network that brings value to our lives, while reducing the distractions and negativity that can arise from maintaining an excessive number of connections or unsuitable ones.

Follow

Following is a low-self-advocacy, low-engagement action designed to rekindle and nurture a relationship in a nonintrusive way. For this reason, it is a helpful strategy for strained but inactive relationships and for those relationships for which you are unsure of its status. Following includes activities such as liking, commenting, and sharing their social media posts that resonate with you. You also may engage in conversations with individuals you follow, using methods such as direct messages or actively participating in discussions on pertinent subjects. Share valuable content on your own profile to establish credibility and demonstrate your alignment with this individual. Miranda, a tech executive and aspiring director, shared an example of one particular social media group she belonged to. Although the group as a whole was active in sharing their insights, ideas, and expertise, one contributor in particular consistently caught her attention with his thought-provoking content and engaging perspective. Intrigued by his insights, she followed and began regularly engaging with his posts, offering comments, sharing her own thoughts, and sparking discussions. As her interactions continued, a sense of camaraderie and mutual respect developed between them. They discovered shared interests, complementary skills, and overlapping goals in advancing their respective industries through technology. Over time, their online exchanges evolved from casual interactions to meaningful conversations about potential collaborations and business opportunities. They also were able to meet in person at a recent professional conference. After that, they formed a rewarding peer mentorship and met regularly as they both sought to advance in their careers and in board service.

When you use this strategy, take care to prioritize authenticity in online interactions by embodying genuineness, transparency, and approachability. Express gratitude toward them if they engage with your posts by sending thank-you messages, giving shoutouts, or showcasing their content. Begin reaching out from time to time to acknowledge their accomplishments or send personalized messages for special events. Ensure prompt and courteous responses to comments, messages, and feedback, showcasing attentiveness and fostering positive connections. Monitor and analyze your social media interactions to gain valuable insights into what connects with them and enhance your strategy for building strong relationships. Your aim through these activities is to gauge the health of this relationship, ultimately gaining clarity about whether it is strained and in need of reconciliation, a broken relationship that needs to be pruned, or a healthy relationship that could be ready for reconnection.

Reconnect

Reconnecting with past relationships is a high-engagement strategy involving low to moderate self-advocacy. This involves making genuine connections and providing value in exchange. For example, you can reconnect by arranging a virtual coffee chat or a lunch meeting to discuss a potential collaboration or simply shared interests. When you do reconnect, be authentic and practice active listening, displaying a sincere curiosity about how your contact's professional journey has unfolded since you last connected. Moving forward, take care to stay connected and maintain active involvement by sending follow-up messages expressing gratitude and delivering promised resources.

The directors I spoke with emphasized the importance of their informal networks and serendipitous connections. Jada recalled, "Once, I interviewed with a board member and as soon as he got off the phone with me, he sent a note asking if I know Mike. I said "Yeah, very well. I worked with Mike many years ago, and now we have dinner once a quarter." The board member responded, "Mike lives on my street." What the board member didn't know is that Jada had reconnected with Mike only nine months earlier when she began her board service journey and learned about the importance of rekindling her relationships. This informal conversation and mutual acquaintance helped pave the way to Jada's next board opportunity. Approach rekindling relationships with patience and respect, and take care to avoid unrealistic expectations. These steps will help you reignite previous professional connections and use them to propel your board service aspirations because these connections can endorse you for seats and offer testimonials that enhance your candidacy. This also helps ensure you remain in their thoughts when encountering relevant opportunities.

Broadcast

Broadcasting is a high-self-advocacy, high-engagement strategy in which you share your board service goals with others. Broadcasting is an essential part of any board search because of the enhanced connections, visibility, and advice you gain. Ava, a director who has accumulated a range of nonprofit, public, and private board seats over years, emphasized, "You do have to be intentional. You have to promote yourself as a director," acknowledging that "this really feels uncomfortable for a lot of people." Nonetheless, proactive engagement and strategic networking is critical for successfully navigating the path to board membership. Sharing your goals also enhances your reputation within your professional community, as it demonstrates your expertise, interests, and ambitions. It also serves as a support system, as individuals who understand your professional aspirations can offer emotional support during difficult times. Sharing your board service goals with others also helps you stay on track, build your professional connections, learn from others' perspectives, increase your visibility, and create a supportive community to help you reach your goals. By fostering a supportive environment, individuals can stay focused on their goals and achieve their professional aspirations.

Reconcile

Reconciling is the most complex activity of all the relationship actions and can vary greatly in the degree of self-advocacy and engagement needed, depending on the specific circumstances surrounding the events that strained or damaged the relationship. Relationships that are strained but not unknown or broken may be appropriate for reconciliation. To proceed with a reconciliation strategy, you will need to be willing to admit your own mistakes and take proactive measures to restore the relationship. Specific activities include reflecting on the circumstances that led to the relationship becoming strained or broken, taking responsibility for one's actions, initiating contact, scheduling a meeting, expressing regret, setting clear expectations, proposing solutions, following through on commitments, requesting feedback, and maintaining open communication channels. For example, in my interview with Joann, she described a challenging situation where she felt her voice wasn't being heard on the board. She decided to address the issue directly but tactfully. She explained, "When I first joined the board, I felt that no one was hearing me. I had to fix that." She decided to engage with another board member privately. "I literally just reached out to one of the other board members outside of the board meeting and said, 'Joe, I think I'm having trouble being heard.

I read the pre-materials, and here are a couple of points I want to make. Do you think those points are reasonable?' He said, 'Yes.' So I asked, 'When I make them at the meeting, would you mind just echoing them for me?'" By doing this, Joann reconciled her relationship with Joe, which was starting to feel strained, and she leveraged this relationship to ensure her points were reinforced, helping her regain credibility and influence on the board.

The ultimate aim of these five activities is to create clarity about your relationships, focus your energy on those relationships aligned with your board service goals, and increase your opportunities for support. Taking these steps should enable you to classify unknown relationships as healthy, strained, or broken and strained relationships as healthy or broken. Through this process, you also gain clarity about which relationships to prune, which to reconcile, and which to strengthen. Table 9.1 presents guidelines for relational end goals and actions based on relationship status and quality.

Table 9.1 Relationship Action by Relationship Planning for Aligned Contacts.

Relationship Status and Quality	Relationship Action	Goal
Active		
Healthy	Broadcast	Maintain as active and healthy
Strained	Reconcile	Convert to any discontinue or active and healthy status
Inactive		
Healthy	Reconnect	Convert to active and healthy
Unknown or Strained	Follow	Convert to any active or discontinued status
Discontinued		
Amicably Closed or Broken	Prune	Deliberately discontinue relationship

Group Involvement Planning

For each group you identified in the previous section, decide which groups you will get more involved in and specifically what you will do as well as how you intend to remain engaged. Many directors I speak with opt to become involved in board-related professional organizations; however, other professional organizations as well as charity and other community organizations can be equally beneficial for expanding your social network in valuable ways. Groups with similar interests provide a wide range of advantages, such as a supportive atmosphere, chances to connect with others, opportunities for personal development, and the ability to foster a sense of community. These groups foster connections among individuals who share similar interests, creating a strong sense of camaraderie and mutual understanding. They also provide excellent prospects for professional development, collaborations, and career progression. Engaging with individuals who share similar interests and goals can provide valuable insights and perspectives, which can greatly contribute to personal and professional development. In addition, groups with similar interests promote a sense of belonging and community, which enhances overall well-being and social connection. Selecting groups that have members and activities aligned with advancing your board service goals will help you make significant strides toward your goals. To keep this manageable and to be able to maintain active membership, I advise clients to select one to three groups to focus on.

Having done that, decide specifically how you will engage with this group and confirm that this group and level of involvement will enable you to gain a community of like-minded individuals within a supportive atmosphere, opportunities for personal development, ample opportunities to form connections with other members, and the ability to foster a sense of community. For example, Larissa described her initial experience with one group as "initially challenging due to its clique-like nature." She added that the COVID-19 pandemic transformed the group's dynamics by making interactions more inclusive through virtual meetings. This enabled her to engage more deeply and derive more value from her membership. As a result, she soon took on a leadership role, focusing on onboarding new members and fostering regional and cross-regional interactions. Larissa's story highlights the importance of engaging deeply with social groups to build meaningful connections and drive collective advancement.

Executive Recruiter Contacts

Executive recruiters often play substantial roles in placing new board members. Based on my own research and observations, search professionals get involved in roughly one of every four board searches by either sourcing and vetting candidates or helping boards vetting their chosen candidates. Begin by conducting thorough research to find well-established firms or individuals who have a wide range of connections and a wealth of experience in board recruitment in your industry or sector. Reach out to the executive recruiter by sending a tailored email or making a professional phone call. Provide a concise introduction, expressing your keen interest in serving on boards, and convey your openness to further discussions regarding potential opportunities. For example, Amira shared that she talked with one particular recruiter about several executive roles over seven years. Once Amira clearly articulated that her interest was finding board opportunities, the recruiter immediately launched her efforts to get Amira on the board of a large insurance company. Amira's story demonstrates how clear communication about one's career aspirations can help you stay top of mind for recruiters.

You may then schedule a short meeting or call with the executive recruiter to have a conversation about your aspirations for joining a board, your career objectives, and the types of board positions that align with your goals. Be prepared to provide your board profile (see Chapter 11), an updated résumé, and any relevant documents. Ensure that your materials highlight your leadership capabilities, strategic vision, governance experience, and contributions to previous boards or organizations. During the meeting, ensure clear communication by openly discussing your expectations, preferred industries or sectors, and geographic preferences.

At the same time, it is critical to be judicious about when you schedule these meetings to make sure the recruiters first have been vetted by your mentors and sponsors. Then determine which recruiters are worth your continual investment. You have a limited amount of time, and these relationships must stay active so you are at the top of their list when boards approach them for candidates.

The benefit of working with an executive recruiter is the extensive network and industry connections they have for investigating potential board openings.

Explore opportunities to connect with board nominating committees, search firms, or organizations that are currently seeking board candidates with your qualifications. Additionally, it will be helpful to ask them for input and advice on how to strengthen your board candidacy, elevate your presence in the boardroom, and successfully navigate the board recruitment process. Integrate this feedback into your strategy to keep improving your board profile.

Board Member Contacts

Building connections with current board members is an effective tactic that can greatly increase your likelihood of obtaining board positions. Begin by identifying five board members who serve on boards similar to your target destination. Create an interview script of questions about their journey to the boardroom, what they are seeing on boards, and what tips they have for you in your board search. Throughout these discussions, showcase your ability to elevate the conversation and showcase your ability to be a board member. For example, Joan, an accomplished leader and board member, explained that in most conversations, she raises questions of "What's the root cause? What are we trying to solve for?" She often questions conventional thinking to foster deeper insights and more robust strategies.

This step of reaching out to existing board members is crucial for gaining access to these members, valuable insights into upcoming board vacancies, industry trends, and organizational priorities. This kind of valuable insider information may not be widely known. These conversations also will provide you with a valuable opportunity for mentorship, professional growth, and enhanced understanding of board governance practices as you learn from their wealth of experience, unique perspectives, and leadership approaches. Deepening your understanding of governance in this way can greatly enhance both your preparation for board roles and your ability to showcase your value.

Board members also have the ability to serve as influential advocates and recommenders because numerous board search firms and nominating committees heavily depend on referrals and recommendations from current board members when searching for candidates for board seats. Nadine explained, "Relationships become the key in how board seats are sourced. For example, when we were looking for new board members at the private equity firm, we didn't want to use a search firm. So we leaned on each board member, asking, 'Who is in your network?' And that's how it typically gets done." It follows that developing a solid relationship with existing board members greatly enhances your chances of getting referrals, introductions, and recommendations for board positions in their networks or affiliated organizations. In this way, networking with established board members can greatly enhance your credibility and reputation within the boardroom community, potentially leading to collaboration, partnerships, and future board roles.

In sum, networking with existing board members is a strategic and effective approach to accessing board opportunities, receiving referrals and recommendations, enhancing credibility, gaining valuable insights, contributing to diversity initiatives, expanding your network, and positioning yourself as a strong candidate for board seats.

All Roads Lead to Networking

As you probably have noticed, the steps involved in developing your social capital center on networking. This is key to getting on boards because of the inherently social nature of recruiting and placing new directors. If you desire a board seat, you need to make sure the right people know you and say positive things about you, that you learn from their experiences, and that you maintain positive relationships throughout your network—even if it has been years since you worked together.

One director I interviewed for my research summarized that when it comes to filling a board seat, "It's about what candidates the recruiter and remaining board members know, who knows those candidates, and what those people say about the candidates that makes a difference." Another director added, "I had to learn that being great in my business unit wasn't enough. I had to make sure people *outside* my business unit knew me. It wasn't enough for me to know them." Your network should include mentors and sponsors who can help guide and facilitate strategic career decisions as well as recruiters, search firms, and other board members who can help you find board seats. Joining external membership groups (e.g., NACD) and attending board education and networking events also can be exceptionally helpful for building your networks, learning the unwritten rules of boards, shaping your career, and securing a board seat.

Finally, although it can be enjoyable to build new relationships and expand your network, it is equally critical to nurture your existing and past network of relationships. April shared a story of being contacted for an open board seat based partly on vetting that occurred through relationships from 20 years earlier. Several directors I interviewed reflected on the importance of treating others well; leaving lasting, positive impressions; and mending any relationships that need it, because their next character reference may literally come from anywhere. By nurturing your networks, you make it far easier for others to recognize that you are the next director they need.

CASE STUDIES

Although Michele already had board experience before she started her path to additional service opportunities, in the course of the exercises, she realized she wanted to shift her focus from serving on a large cap public board to serving growth-oriented private and/or small to mid-cap public boards. She realized that making this change happen would require some adjustments to her social network. She reviewed her contacts and identified 20 tech executives within these companies to reconnect with and broadcast her interest. She also spent time reviewing and narrowing down a list of three executive recruiters who specialize in small to mid-cap public boards and two who specialize in growth-oriented private firms. She reached out to them to begin the process of vetting these recruiters for their suitability with her aims. Through these activities, she also identified several existing board members to build relationships with and gained some insights about two groups she should consider joining.

When Sharon completed the exercises, she quickly realized that she needed to repair some relationships. At one point in her career, she had seemed to work 24/7 and expected everyone in her reporting stream to be glued to their Blackberries and be available to work at all times. Even on weekends, she recalled, "If I didn't hear from them within two hours after my email, I called them. I didn't believe in work-life balance, and I didn't think that anyone who did should have a place on my team. I pushed people out the door." It wasn't until she was 47 and her dad shared some home truths with her that things started shifting. She elaborated:

> He sat me down and said, "I am planning to retire and I want the business to stay in the family. But you're making it very hard for me. I can't move you into the CEO role with the attrition you leave in your wake." I heard what Dad said, and it stuck with me. I started noticing the strain I was causing others. But even then, it wasn't until my heart attack the next year that I changed things for good. After that, work-life balance was no longer an option. I had to make time for exercise, rest, and relaxation. I had to practice mindfulness. I had to do things outside of work mentally, physically, and socially. And to my surprise, I found I was *more* efficient and effective. I thought of all the people I pushed out and knew I needed to repair those relationships and do things differently at work.

She began by looking up each one on social media and gently engaged them by commenting on and liking their posts. Then, she began to offer her own insights and value when appropriate. After some time, she sent connection requests, which led to conversations. Although some of these relationships still felt a bit prickly, some of them were restored, and all had improved thanks to her efforts.

ACTION ITEMS

Evaluate and optimize your social capital using the following four steps:

1. Review your email, social media, résumé, and any other tools you use to maintain your list of contacts and then list your past and present

relationships. Ideally, over time, you will create a complete accounting of your relationships. To keep this effort manageable for now, you might begin with identifying 20 professional and personal relationships. Next, rate the status of each relationship (i.e., healthy, unknown, strained, broken), along with contact information, date of last contact, and whether this relationship is active, meaning whether you have been in touch within the previous 12 months. Select your actions for nurturing each relationship based on the Relationship Action Planning section in this chapter.

2. Create your group affiliation résumé noting the names, dates of involvement, and degrees of your involvement. As with your relationship inventory, over time, you will accumulate a complete accounting of your group involvement. To keep this effort manageable for now, you might begin with identifying up to 10 group affiliations. Following the steps in this chapter, select the one to three groups you will actively engage with and how you will do that.

3. Inventory the executive recruiters you have worked with in the past or solicit recommendations from others. Vet this list to ensure they are involved in top-quality searches. To keep this effort manageable, I suggest aiming for a list of five. Arrange meetings with each to get acquainted and to express your board service goals. Be prepared to provide your board profile (see Chapter 11), an updated résumé, and any relevant documents.

4. Create a list of five active and previous board members you know who have served on boards similar to those you are targeting in your search. Create your interview script of questions and schedule brief calls to solicit their perspectives about their journey to the boardroom and board service.

SUMMARY

Although you likely are well aware of the importance of networking and connections, it is important to understand that having the right connections is just the beginning. Remember that your opportunities come through those who know you. Typically, when opportunities arise, they are discovered, evaluated, and chosen (or eliminated) without our knowledge, solely based on our past connections, which are easily accessible through social media. It is crucial that we prioritize building, consistently evaluating, and actively maintaining our relationships throughout our professional journeys, particularly if we aspire to create a meaningful and influential legacy after retirement. In this chapter, you learned more about the concept and impact of social capital, how it affects your board search, how it affected two of our protagonists, and how you can evaluate and improve your relationships to support your journey to the boardroom. The ultimate aim of growing your social capital is sparking productive conversations about your board aspirations and creating solid pathways to these opportunities. Let everyone and anyone know you're interested in board work. Be your own best advocate.

CHAPTER TEN

COMMITMENT CAPITAL

*Every twist and turn in life is an opportunity to learn something new
about yourself, your interests, your talents, and how to set and then
achieve goals.*

—Jameela Jamil

Serving on a board is a serious commitment: each board seat requires approximately 200–250 hours of work per year, allocated to four to six board meetings, additional committee meetings, and time spent reviewing substantial documentation in advance of board meetings. Additionally, part and parcel with any role is legal exposure, which can lead to serious consequences if things go wrong. The recent spate of shareholder activism has made this reality very apparent. Moreover, board members can face lawsuits related to their service even years after leaving a board. In short, board service is not a cake walk or easy money (if you receive compensation as a director). To persist on the journey to board service and to deliver exemplary service, you need several kinds of resources, as I have discussed in previous chapters: cultural capital, the strength and drive we acquire during our formative years as a result of our family, friends, experiences, successes, and challenges (Chapter 6); director capital, the personality traits and working style, training, experience, and knowledge specific to filling the role of a director on the board (Chapter 7); human capital, the sum of our education, knowledge, skills, personal attributes, and experience to generate a given set of outcomes (Chapter 8); and social capital, the sum of structural, cognitive, and relational resources available to us via our social networks (Chapter 9).

Another type of resource crucial to our success is Commitment Capital, the combination of human, social, and other resources we use to execute and complete a specific task. This source of capital is critical because, as with many important things in life, it will never be the right time to start your board journey, and it will *always* be the right time to start. It is up to you to make this the right timing by setting expectations with yourself and those affected by your pursuit of this and through the dedication of capital. This chapter introduces the concept of Commitment Capital and walks you through the process of diagnosing and increasing it so that you reach your board service goals.

THE MAKEUP OF COMMITMENT CAPITAL

Volumes of research have been published and continue to be published on motivation and task performance. Motivation is a powerful force that propels individuals to take action and strive for their desired goals or outcomes. When individuals are driven, they are more inclined to put in the necessary effort, concentrate their attention, and persevere in overcoming obstacles to successfully complete tasks.

Motivation is crucial for individuals to gain clarity on their goals, priorities, and expectations regarding tasks. When individuals are driven, they possess a distinct understanding of their purpose and how it aligns with the goals of the organization. This leads to concentrated and intentional task execution. In turn, driven individuals tend to be more productive and efficient in completing tasks. They excel at prioritizing tasks, managing their time efficiently, and maintaining a strong focus and commitment, leading to enhanced task performance outcomes. Having a strong sense of motivation can help cultivate resilience and persistence when confronted with obstacles or setbacks. Motivated individuals are more inclined to persist, adjust, and discover alternative solutions to challenges, keeping their drive and accomplishing desired results. For example, one director I interviewed shared, "I could just make stuff happen out of thin air. I didn't even know how I did it. ... I never took no as an answer. I had incredible tenacity and resilience."

However, what I have noticed time and again is that motivation is not always sufficient to get someone across the finish line—whether that is the physical finish line of a race or a metaphorical finish line of completing an important task. In fact, I grappled with that myself related to the research that helped inform this book.

For months, I had to face the fact every Friday evening that another week had slipped by without me moving the needle on my research project. I'd gone through all the usual tactics: setting the goal, breaking it into tasks, blocking off time. It still wasn't happening.

Then I thought about this: if it's been on my task list for several weeks (or months) and I still have made no progress, maybe this goal isn't as important to me as I thought it was. Maybe my *why* wasn't strong enough. According to Simon Sinek's golden circle, lacking a strong why could explain my stagnancy.[1]

But the project was important. The project involved interviewing women of various backgrounds about their journeys to secure a corporate board seat. This research project strongly aligned with my professional contributions, personal passions, and thought leadership. Gathering these women's stories was a vital part of continuing to gain the fresh insights that make true change possible. My driving why was to better understand why some qualified executive women were securing board seats while other equally qualified executive women were not. Finding those answers, I believe, is central to improving the parity issues surrounding corporate board diversity.

Yes, this project was really important. So what was the problem?

A colleague suggested that maybe I was trying to bite off too much. She suggested I interview a smaller set of women and proceed from there. "No," I immediately protested. "The stories are too varied, and too rich. I don't want to shrink the sample size."

Back to the drawing board again.

If you've ever set a challenging goal, you know the battle I was facing. These kinds of goals can span all areas of life: Why train for a 5K walk/run when I could train for and complete a marathon? If I'm going to get more education, why settle for a continuing education certificate when I could earn a master's or doctoral degree? Why do a bit better than last year's sales figures when I could double them?

These kinds of goals could be called big, hairy, audacious goals (BHAGs, pronounced bee-hags), a term first coined by James Collins and Jerry Porras in their 1994 bestseller *Built to Last: Successful Habits of Visionary Companies*. A BHAG reflects a clear, focused, long-term, and outrageous commitment, such as Henry Ford's goal to democratize automobiles, Kennedy's moon mission, or GE's goal to be number one or two in each of its markets. The nature and seeming impossibility of the BHAG are what makes this kind of goal grab you in the gut, as described by Collins and Porras. These goals have higher stakes, require more of you, and push you to your limits. All these characteristics make BHAGs that much more compelling and exhilarating to achieve—whether the BHAG concerns a national or organizational goal or your own personal or professional goals. And when these BHAGs are aligned with your own personal why—the guiding purpose in your life—the rest falls into place, right? Not always.

In my own experience as well as those I have led and coached, even when you have a clear and compelling goal powered by a heartfelt why, you may still find yourself stuck in place.

For decades, motivation theories have attempted to explain why we fail to progress in our work tasks. For example, Victor Vroom's expectancy theory (Figure 10.1) suggests that we tackle tasks when we believe our effort will produce satisfactory performance and that this performance will lead to an outcome we value.

Figure 10.1   Vroom's Expectancy Theory.

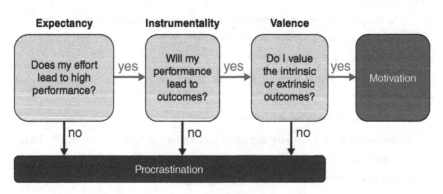

I put this theory to the test. I had blocked out two workdays per week for my research project. If I had spent that time locating participants, scheduling interviews, and conducting them, would I have gathered data? Yes. Would that data have led to the completion of the project? Yes. Was completing the project valuable to me? Yes. So why didn't I spend those two days per week on the project?

To the drawing board again.

I then came across Professors James G. Clawson and Mark E. Haskins's measurement for quiet quitting (which they called *career blues*) in a 2000 edition of *Academy of Management Perspectives*.[2] When I saw this survey item: "This person seems to gather energy from work," it hit me: just thinking about this project completely drained my energy. That's the reason I chose anything and everything else instead of this task, even when had I blocked off time for it.

I returned to Vroom's expectancy theory and realized a piece was missing: Commitment Capital.

Commitment, whether to a goal, a career, an investment, or even a life partnership, means willingly restricting what you will dedicate your resources toward and, in turn, eliminating other choices. In buying this house, I cannot buy any other house. If I dedicate my workday to this project, I cannot make progress on other projects that day. We make these either-or choices—whether consciously or subconsciously—based on the resources we have available (such as time, finances, mental energy, emotional energy, etc.) compared to the resources required for the effort. This led me to the formula shown in Figure 10.2.

Figure 10.2   Commitment Capital Formula.

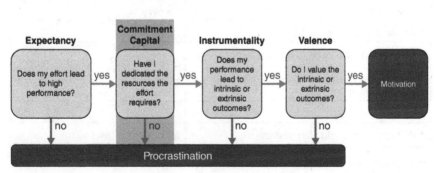

I applied this to my project and discovered that although I had set time aside for the project and I was willing and able to conduct interviews, I hadn't gotten past go because I hadn't dedicated the resources the effort required. But why? Part of the problem was that I was trying to start this project less than a year after finishing the monumental effort of my doctoral dissertation, and I was a bit reluctant to dive back into those waters. But breaking through this roadblock was going to take further examination.

I began by listing the tasks involved in my project. (Sometimes, even this question is enough to reveal the cause of stagnation. Not knowing the tasks involved can stall any effort.) After listing my tasks, I then asked myself again, "Have I dedicated the time and resources that doing this task requires?" I assigned each task a red (no), yellow (somewhat), or green (yes) status. My results are shown in Table 10.1.

Although I was confident in my ability to conduct great interviews, this exercise revealed that I had done virtually nothing to reach that destination. My Commitment Capital was almost nonexistent.

It's tempting to chalk up our lack of progress on an important project as mere busyness, procrastination, or perhaps something worse. But if we want any chance

Table 10.1   Measuring Commitment Capital.

Question: Have I dedicated the time and resources that doing this task requires?	
Project Task	**Commitment Capital**
1. Identify the research purpose.	Somewhat
2. Select the target population and interviewee characteristics.	Somewhat
3. Create the interview script.	No
4. Find, recruit participants, and schedule interviews.	No
5. Conduct the interviews.	Yes[a]
6. Analyze the data.	Somewhat[a]
7. Write the report and plan next steps.	Somewhat[a]

[a]Anticipated but not yet confirmed because previous steps have not been completed.

of moving through our blockages, we must look deeper into the causes of our Commitment Capital shortages.

To diagnosis this, I asked myself three questions about each task:

1. Do I believe I have the competencies (i.e., knowledge, skills, other abilities) I need to complete this task successfully?
2. Am I willing to develop the competencies needed for this task?
3. Am I willing to spend time and energy on this task?

My results are shown in Table 10.2.

My lack of progress was starting to make sense, as I had little confidence in my ability to succeed and availability to do the tasks leading up to interviews. I realized that accomplishing this project was going to require a mixture of skill development, directive coaching, delegation, and efficiency tools. I put together a plan

Table 10.2   Diagnosing Commitment Capital.

Project Tasks	Do I Have the Needed Competencies?	Am I Willing to Develop the Needed Competencies?	Am I Willing to Spend Time and Energy on this Task?
1. Identify the research purpose.	Maybe	Yes	Somewhat
2. Select the target population and interviewee characteristics.	Maybe	Maybe	Maybe
3. Create the interview script.	No	Yes	Maybe
4. Find, recruit participants, and schedule interviews.	No	No	No
5. Conduct the interviews.	Yes	Yes	Yes
6. Analyze the data.	Maybe	Maybe	Maybe
7. Write the report and plan next steps.	Maybe	Maybe	Maybe

and evaluated whether I was prepared to reallocate my scarce resources of knowledge, skills, abilities, time, mental and emotional energy, finances, and more to complete my project. One high achiever I interviewed described this moment as "commitment sticker shock." Reflecting on his own project, he explained to me, "I know that I can technically pay this 'price.' I know I want the 'product.' But it sure looks like it's going to cost *a lot*." In my case, I did decide to proceed, and this book is evidence of that decision. It wasn't easy, but I am glad I did it.

How does all of this apply to your board journey?

EVALUATING YOUR COMMITMENT CAPITAL

Diagnosing Commitment Capital is a critical step for accomplishing important tasks, especially if you have already struggled with procrastination or lack of progress. This process begins with reflection:

1. **Understand the effort.** Take some time to flesh out the tasks and subtasks involved in the project you are delaying. The list does not have to be exhaustive at this point, but enough to begin to gain insights about where progress is breaking down. For me, I knew that figuring out all the project tasks required things like selecting a research question, figuring out whom to interview, writing the interview questions, and more. To prepare for board service and successfully move from an aspiring board member to an actual board member, you will need to do the following:

   • Become a student of the profession of governance. This can be a tall order if you've been out of school for 30 years.
   • Network with others, which can be an unexercised muscle as an executive.
   • Reflect and self-calibrate. Although many executives mean well and intend to do this, few actually block out the time to do this.
   • Enact systems of accountability, which means setting and holding yourself accountable to achieve the goals you said mattered and designating and relying on accountability partners.

- Plan and navigate a strategic career path. If you are like many high achievers who have been tapped for progressive leadership roles all your life, your entire career may have been architected by others. Taking the initiative to do this yourself can require you develop muscles you haven't used before.

2. **Identify the needed resources.** For each task and subtask, consider the resources you need for effective performance. Resources may include time, knowledge, skills, experience, traits, physical energy, mental energy, emotional energy, relationships, financial resources, key decisions, and specialized tools, among others. Similar to the previous step, this list does not have to be exhaustive. The point is to uncover your conscious or near-conscious sticking points. For me, I quickly realized that planning all the excruciating details of the project leading up to the interviews required focus, mental energy, and knowledge of the many options available when conducting research. For example, a 2016–2017 NACD Public Company Governance Survey found that the average director spends 245 hours per year per board seat, allocated to tasks including becoming a student of the profession of governance, networking, reflection and self-calibration, engaging with systems of accountability, and planning and navigating a strategic career path. It is important to assess whether you have the time and related competencies to carry out these tasks effectively.

3. **Assess your ability to commit the needed resources.** For each resource you listed, gauge your willingness and ability to dedicate it. A simply green/yellow/red (yes/maybe/no) convention will be sufficient. In my project, I quickly realized that I was willing to dedicate some but not all the mental energy needed for the planning phases. Dedicating the time and resources may require you to let go of other tasks you are currently performing. Furthermore, some of the muscles you need to exercise in these board-related tasks may be atrophied, meaning you need to find the energy both for rebuilding those abilities and doing the tasks. Each person will need different levels of energy for the same task, depending on their personality, talents, abilities, and attitudes.

4. **Identify the sticking points.** The previous step indicates your project-specific Commitment Capital. Review this scorecard to identify the area

where your progress has stalled. If you have several areas, select the area that feels the most daunting. In my project, fully outlining the methods—which had to occur before recruiting participants or conducting interviews—was my sticking point. Additionally, it will be important to set expectations—both for yourself and for those affected by your decisions. For example, identify any personal or professional commitments that would conflict with preparing yourself for, pursuing, or serving on board opportunities, and be aware that it generally takes three to five years to land a board seat once you decide to do so. Therefore, these commitments need to be able to be sustained over time.

INCREASING YOUR COMMITMENT CAPITAL

Once you understand where and why your progress has stalled, you are able to increase your Commitment Capital. Although the strategies for increasing your Commitment Capital will be as varied as the obstacles getting in your way, here are a few tactics to consider:

- **Change the task.** Most tasks can be accomplished in a variety of ways. Brainstorm alternate methods that use less resources or require different resources that you do have available. For my project, rather than a formal study, I could have opted for casual conversations or administering surveys.

- **Upskill your competencies.** If you lack the knowledge, skill, or expertise needed to carry out the task, brainstorm ways to fill your gaps so you spend less time in learning, trial, and error modes and more time accomplishing the work. In my project, I could have consulted various sources for tips on designing my project.

- **Enlist help.** Consider whether you can outsource or delegate the tasks stalling your progress. Alternatively, you may arrange for a coach to structure and guide your effort or accountability partners to help assure the work gets done. In my project, I enlisted the help of a coach to structure and speed up the initial steps of project planning.

- **Increase task efficiency.** We complete different tasks with different efficiency and effectiveness based on our particular strengths and work preferences. Focus on the tasks that best match your strengths and secure tools and support for less preferred tasks. In my project, I focused on tapping my networks for participants and doing the actual interviews, enlisted help for project planning and leveraged software to aid with scheduling and transcribing.

- **Manage your resources.** Consider the changes you can make to your other projects and demands to make more resources available, such as offloading or changing other tasks. Additionally, build your sense of momentum by organizing and celebrating small wins. In my case, I dedicated Fridays to this work and organized the project into phases to sustain my enthusiasm for the project. Additionally, it is important to consider whether this is the right timing to pursue a board seat. For example, if board service is prohibited due to your corporate role, you need to identify when the right timing would be for this effort.

CASE STUDIES

Although Denise had experience on a prominent gymnastics not-for-profit board, she had little to no exposure to corporate boards at the start of her journey. Although she knew she had some substantial knowledge gaps to fill regarding the profession of governance and the roles that attorneys can play, she had made little progress on closing the gaps. After completing the exercises in this chapter, she realized that she had very limited knowledge, skills, other abilities, time, and energy related to most preparation tasks for securing a board seat. Her self-assessment also revealed she had some openness to increasing her competencies in some ways, but very little time and energy to do so. As a busy law firm partner and mother of two, she felt overwhelmed with the scope of what she needed to learn and develop. After reviewing her activities and schedule, she realized that she could let go of the improv comedy class. The class helped her move beyond her discomfort with not being the smartest or most prepared in the room. Yet, she now needed to take that time and energy and dedicate it toward strengthening her social capital and her board-related knowledge. She used some of her regained time and energy to reach out to existing board members at companies within waste management and logistics industries to gain insight about her intended target of family-owned private boards. From these conversations, she realized she still had substantial distance to cover in terms of being a board-ready director and had to deliberately plan time and bandwidth to seek additional training.

Michele, a tech industry executive at a Fortune 500 company, started her board journey already having experience with her company's internal board as well as with independent director experience on a private and a public board. Through the exercises she completed along the way, she identified her goal of finding two more seats in a growth-oriented private and/or small to mid-cap public board so she could continue providing the strategic advice she most enjoyed as an independent director. As part of the latest exercises, she contemplated her time, energy, and other resources to obtain a specialization certificate in cybersecurity from a board-related professional organization and further develop her general board knowledge as well as her financial acumen. She recognized that her busy professional life left her with limited time and energy to plan and carry out these activities. At the same time, her self-assessment revealed that she had more knowledge, skill, and expertise related to cybersecurity than she had initially realized. This recognition made the idea of pursuing a specialization certificate more conceivable, especially when she cut down on her volunteer activities from weekly to once monthly to create additional space. These efforts created the bandwidth for Michele to proceed with her development.

ACTION ITEMS

Try the following steps to optimize your Commitment Capital:

1. Identify the list of tasks and subtasks involved in securing a board seat. Depending on your current competencies related to this effort, your tasks

may include becoming a student of the profession of governance, networking with those identified in your social capital plan, reflecting and self-calibrating, creating systems of accountability, planning and navigating a strategic career path, and more.

2. Identify the resources you will need to carry out each task you identified in Step 1. Your resources may include time, knowledge, skills, experience, traits, physical energy, mental energy, emotional energy, relationships, financial resources, key decisions, and specialized tools.

3. Gauge your ability to dedicate the needed resources and examine your other commitments. Consult your list of resources from Step 2 and gauge how willing and able you are to dedicate those using a green/ yellow/red or yes/maybe/no scorecard. Where you are lacking in resources, consider your other commitments and whether adjusting your other activities could create the bandwidth you need to complete your board search journey.

4. Identify key areas for development. Identify your top development needs based on your resource analysis. For example, consider any skill and knowledge gaps you have discovered and select the one or two areas to address to best support your board search journey.

5. Organize for success. You may discover challenges with your resources, availability, and commitment. In that event, arrange your support network and approach to the tasks necessary for your success. Consider how you can change the task, enlist help, or become more efficient in your efforts.

SUMMARY

Traveling the path from executive to board member requires a high level of dedication and responsibility. Successfully fulfilling your responsibilities as a director requires significant time each year for board and committee meetings as well as for reviewing the extensive documentation prior to the meetings. In any role, legal exposure is a crucial aspect that must be considered, as it can result in significant consequences if mistakes are made. The recent surge in shareholder activism has made this reality very clear. In addition, board members may be subject to legal action in connection with their service, even long after they have left board service. In other words, board service is far from a walk in the park. In order to succeed in your pursuit of board service and provide exceptional service, it is crucial to have Commitment Capital. This is because, much like other significant endeavors in life, there will never be a perfect time to begin your board journey; yet, at the very same time, it is always the right time. It is your responsibility to ensure that the timing is right by clearly communicating your expectations to yourself and those who will be affected by your efforts, and by investing the necessary resources. This chapter presented the concept of Commitment Capital and guided you through the steps to diagnose and enhance it, enabling you to achieve your board service objectives.

CHAPTER ELEVEN

LEVERAGING YOUR CAPITAL PORTFOLIO

Start where you are. Use what you have. Do what you can.

—Arthur Ashe

Arthur Ashe was born in the 1940s segregated South. Hardship came early with the death of his mother when Ashe was only six years old. Although life had seemed to stack the odds against him, his life began to change when he started playing tennis shortly thereafter. From then until age 18, by taking stock of his unique background, learning the game, showcasing and developing his talent, and exhibiting his commitment, he moved on to form instrumental relationships with coaches like Ron Charity, Richmond's best Black tennis player; Robert Walter Johnson, famed tennis coach of Althea Gibson, one of the first Black athletes to cross the sport's color lines; and tennis coach Richard Hudlin, who hosted Ashe during his senior year of high school. These relationships, in turn, provided Ashe with invaluable mentorship and sponsorship that shaped how he played the game. Ultimately, Ashe took home five Grand Slam titles, was the first Black player selected to the United States Davis Cup team, and the only Black man ever to win the singles titles at Wimbledon, the US Open, and the Australian Open. Ashe is an inspiring example of blending one's own talent, dedication, and hard work with the kind of support that elevates one's vision and opens the doors to possibility.

In the same way, succeeding on your path to the boardroom requires you to understand and leverage your unique skills and strengths; build a supportive network of mentors, peers, and advisors; commit to continuous learning; set clear goals and embrace challenges; seek feedback and adapt; network effectively; and remain committed, persistent, and resilient. This chapter reviews the steps for leveraging your unique sources of capital reviewed in the previous chapters. First, we discuss why being a competent executive is not enough to secure a seat and why, instead, you must leverage your capital and showcase your abilities. Next, we describe how to create your board readiness story and the specific ways to showcase your capital portfolio. The chapter closes with a description of how two of our protagonists leveraged their capital and how you can begin doing so.

IMPORTANCE OF LEVERAGING AND SHOWCASING YOUR ABILITIES

At this point, you may be thinking that it is sufficient to have strong skills and networks and that showcasing them may be unnecessarily self-serving and arrogant. Instead, you must showcase your skills and abilities because doing so demonstrates your expertise and highlights your ability to make meaningful contributions to a board. Demonstrating this helps reduce the sense of ambiguity and risk boards naturally face when seeking a new director. Aparna, an investor and former Fortune 500 CEO who currently serves on two prominent public boards, explained, "You need to have a reputation as having added value and built strong relationships. Once you start to know some of these board members, and once they all know each other, you start to be known."

Showcasing your abilities establishes you as a trustworthy source of expertise, thus inspiring others' confidence about your skills and abilities. Moreover, being able to communicate complex ideas, information, and insights in a clear and understandable manner promotes mutual understanding with fellow board members and stakeholders. Demonstrating critical thinking, problem-solving, and decision-making in conversations highlights your capacity to analyze situations, identify solutions, and make well-informed decisions. Furthermore, highlighting your distinct skills, strengths, and value proposition enables you to set yourself apart in the competitive landscape of board placement and positions you as an exceptional professional with valuable contributions to offer. Aparna added, "Selection committees need to see you as having clear differentiation regarding what you can add to that board. It is important for you to be able to articulate that. Once you can articulate that, others can articulate that about you."

Demonstrating your skills and abilities also can lead to more trusting, open, and meaningful connections with others. When you freely share your expertise, an environment of mutual respect, trust, and collaboration tends to develop. Exhibiting proficiency in discussions cultivates favorable interactions and encourages effective working relationships. Samina, a prolific entrepreneur who was serving on seven boards at the time of this writing, shared a memorable story of how her initiative to share expertise resulted in a board seat:

> The largest board that I have had the honor to serve was due to my efforts to be helpful at any cost. I called one of my friends who was on the board and said: This is crazy. I really love this organization and I wanted to donate. Every time I'm driving, I hear about your fundraising campaign. Then I have to stop somewhere, call you guys, and then send a check or give a credit card. But I have a Donor-Advised Charitable Fund (DACF) and I can easily donate through it. So, I went to your website to see how I can donate to you. There

was no DACF option. So I had to go to my own DACF dashboard. When I found your organization there, I was confronted with literally hundreds of categories of campaigns. I couldn't proceed because I didn't know which is which. That's when I decided to call you.

After talking with my friend, the issue was escalated. By the time this reached the CEO, I had spoken with seven people on the board. This was just motivated by me being helpful and giving advice regarding what they needed to do in terms of digital transformation. After these seven calls and giving them so many additional ideas for this organization I really love, they said, "Why don't you just join our board?"

THE BOARD READINESS STORY

Your board readiness story is a key piece of collateral you will provide to executive recruiters and boards as you seek your first (or subsequent) place at the table, and it also packages your capital portfolio in an easy-to-digest format. This is the time to showcase your board aspirations. Your story consists of your board-related biography, résumé, and narrative of how you came to seek a board seat. It is critical to connect the dots in a cohesive story in this narrative by putting the package together based on central themes. When composing a board readiness story, it is crucial to construct a persuasive narrative that showcases your credentials, background, and preparedness to assume a position on a board of directors. The core elements of your board readiness story are as follows:

1. **Introduction and overarching theme.** Start with a captivating introduction that highlights your experience and enthusiasm for serving on a board. This introduction should convey a persuasive storyline that accentuates your credentials, past involvements, and readiness to assume a position on a board of directors. Essential qualities to highlight include your ability to lead, your strategic foresight, your proficiency in governance, your deep understanding of the sector, and your proven history of achieving outcomes. Be sure to emphasize any prior board experience, committee participation,

or governance training that showcases a solid understanding of board-room dynamics.

2. **Professional journey and core competencies.** Present a concise account of your professional trajectory, highlighting significant accomplishments, pivotal moments, and positions of leadership. Emphasize experiences that demonstrate your ability to make strategic decisions, manage risks, possess financial knowledge, and have industry expertise that is applicable to board responsibilities. Summarize your fundamental abilities and qualities that correspond to the board's criteria. These abilities may encompass strategy planning, corporate governance, regulatory compliance, risk assessment, financial oversight, leadership development, and stakeholder engagement.

3. **Industry insights.** Showcase your comprehension of industry trends, market dynamics, competitive landscapes, and new opportunities or problems. Demonstrate their proficiency in data analysis, evaluation of market risks, and strategic decision-making that leads to the achievement of business objectives.

4. **Experience in governance.** Emphasize any experience in governance, such as participation in advisory boards, nonprofit boards, industry associations, or corporate committees. Examine the contributions you have made in these positions, the governance best practices you adhered to, and the lessons you learned that can be used to prepare for board membership.

5. **Leadership and collaboration.** Evaluate your leadership approach, proficiency in collaborating with others, and aptitude for effectively working with various teams. Present illustrations of pioneering endeavors, spearheading transformation, cultivating novelty, and establishing agreement among interested parties.

6. **Ethical and values alignment.** Highlight your unwavering dedication to upholding ethical standards, maintaining honesty, promoting transparency, and prioritizing corporate social responsibility. Examine the extent to which their values are in line with the organization's mission, vision, and long-term sustainability objectives.

7. **Board contribution.** Clearly state your unique selling points and the valuable contributions they can offer to a board. Emphasize their capacity to offer strategic counsel, present varied viewpoints, question assumptions, manage risks, and improve shareholder value.

8. **Professional development.** Provide details of any current professional development endeavors, board education programs, certificates, or affiliations in governance organizations that showcase a dedication to continual learning and being up-to-date with the most effective methods in boardroom management.

9. **Recommendations and testimonials.** The credibility and comprehensiveness of your board readiness story can be further enhanced by adding recommendations and testimonials from coworkers, mentors, and industry experts who can provide evidence of your readiness and qualifications for a board position. Integrate these endorsements into your narrative of board readiness to enhance your credibility and suitability for board seats.

10. **Summary and request for action.** Provide a concise and persuasive overview of your qualifications, readiness, and passion for serving on the board to conclude the tale. Promote additional dialogues, interviews, or deliberation for board positions based on the robustness of their board readiness narrative.

Once you have written your story, it is important to regularly practice telling it so that you can easily and conversationally share your story. Additionally, you should continually refine your board readiness story as you gain experience and evolve your interests so it communicates why you are the best candidate for the corporate board roles you seek.

SHOWCASING YOUR CAPITAL PORTFOLIO

As outlined in the previous chapters, if you are at the point of searching for a board seat, you have accumulated an impressive set of competencies, including those related to board savviness (director capital); knowledge, skills, and abilities (human capital); relationships and networks (social capital); and fortitude to persist toward goal completion (Commitment Capital). Although you will do your best to capture these in your board readiness story, there are additional steps to take regarding where and when to showcase your full collection of capital, how to showcase it, and how to customize it for the situation at hand. Mastering these elements can greatly increase your likelihood of obtaining a seat at the board.

Where and when to showcase your capital. Many venues are available for sharing your board readiness story and showcasing your capital, including online platforms, networking events, and through board placement services. For example, be sure to optimize your digital presence to increase your visibility as a viable director candidate. Your board readiness story can provide a helpful template for revising your social media profiles and personal branding website. The board members I speak with typically use multiple outlets for communicating their interest and showcasing their abilities. For example, one CFO and director on four corporate boards shared the advice that aspiring directors should "let everyone you know in CPA firms, consulting firms, law firms, and other professional services firms that you are interested in serving on a board because their clients often ask them for recommendations before going to a search firm." This was, in fact, how she secured one of her board seats. She secured another seat by keeping her LinkedIn profile and contacts current so that when one of her neighbors was asked to recommend a candidate with a finance background, she was at the top of the list.

Actively and regularly offering value (e.g., posts, articles, assessments) related to governance topics can further convey the image that you offer insightful and strategic guidance. Networking events, including industry and board association conferences, seminars, workshops, and others, can keep you apprised of the trends and issues of concern related to your desired board target and help expand your governance-related professional network through new or strengthened relationships with board members, governance professionals, and executive recruiters. The resulting interactions are an ideal time to discuss your interest and readiness for board positions. Clara, a retired CEO who serves on multiple boards, highlighted the importance of professional organizations and networking groups in learning about board seats. She mentioned her involvement with the Women's Housing Leadership Society and Extraordinary Women on Boards, noting that these groups provided her with valuable opportunities and connections, as they had recently formed an alliance with Korn Ferry to find seats for women on boards.

Finally, registering with an established board placement service or platform can link you to boards looking for additional directors. Your board readiness story provides the template and content for constructing a captivating profile that gains the interest of board nominating committees, search companies, and organizations in search of competent board members. For example, one director I interviewed found her role through Private Directors Association and another found hers through Nurole. Still others were contacted about open seats through executive search firms and recruiters.

How to showcase your capital. Showcasing your capital means demonstrating your ability to add value and being your own best advocate. Whether you're in the early, mid-, or later stages of your career, if you want to secure a board seat, now is the time to make others aware of your ability to add value. Your goal is to ensure that people see you as someone who can help. To demonstrate your suitability, you need to showcase your ability to have high-level strategic conversations. My rule of thumb here is "It's better to be interested than interesting." Demonstrate your interest through deep and active listening, characterized by seeking information, engaging in dialogue, and challenging others' thought processes. Aiyana, a retired CPA with an extensive track record serving as an independent director on public boards, explained that aspiring directors can do this by "being tuned in and cognizant of what's happening. … It's like being able to pull things out, ask the challenging question, and also encourage management when appropriate. … Good CEOs want to know what you are thinking and be challenged by hearing different ways to think about a topic."

Additionally, you must become a vocal self-advocate. Let your friends, family, colleagues, and acquaintances know that you're interested in serving on corporate boards, which types of boards you would be a great fit for, and why you're interested in serving. For example, use your board readiness story when engaging in networking events and seeking references. Share your story with industry contacts, executive recruiters, board nomination committees, and current board members.

Emphasize your unique selling point and the positive impact you can bring to a board, drawing from your readiness to serve on a board.

Many of the directors I recently interviewed shared that they made a point of mentioning their goals at every opportunity. One director shared that she knew early in her career that she wanted to be on corporate boards outside her company. Her clarity and commitment regarding her post-career vision enabled her to expertly navigate her career so that gaining board experience was part of every hiring conversation, and she selected positions that would optimize her board preparation and service experiences. One new employer even retained an executive search firm to conduct a reverse board search, wherein the firm actively secured external board seats for her and her C-suite colleagues so they could bring back the expertise they gained from their board participation.

The directors I spoke with for this book emphasized that they were extremely deliberate in broadcasting their interest. Victoria, a CEO with 22 years of experience spanning five boards, acknowledged that although it's not advisable to directly ask for a board seat such as "I want to get on the board at [specific company]. Can you help me?" you do need to make your interest known in some way. For example, in response to "What do you do?" you might answer, "I'm [current role] and I serve on several nonprofit boards. I also am looking for opportunities to share my expertise in [specific interests] through corporate board service in [specific sectors and board types]." If you're just getting started with board service, you might say, "I'm [your current role] and I am looking for opportunities to share my expertise in [specific interests] through nonprofit board service." To increase your visibility and opportunities to secure board of director positions, employ a strategic approach. Use your board readiness story to effectively highlight your qualifications, network proficiently, bolster your online presence, actively participate in board-related activities, solicit recommendations, and customize your approach to meet board requirements.

How to customize your capital. When you are presented with a specific opportunity, it is important to customize your narrative and how you are showcasing your capital to correspond with the criteria, anticipations, and difficulties encountered by boards in your desired businesses or sectors. Demonstrate how your expertise, capabilities, and past accomplishments specifically align with the requirements and objectives of the boards you wish to be a part of. Asako, a seasoned executive currently serving on three boards, highlighted her relevant industry expertise and specific technical skills to align with the needs of the boards she joined. For instance, her experience in human capital management was crucial for the board of the small startup on which she is serving. She explained, "They wanted somebody from a large consulting firm in human capital like Accenture, Deloitte, IBM, the Mercers of the world, and I fit that bill." For another board, her extensive background in insurance was a perfect match. "They were specifically looking for somebody [who] had insurance experience. Well, I had 20 years of it before I got to the consulting firm." By communicating her skills and past accomplishments tailored to the specific needs of the board she aimed to join, she demonstrated her value and readiness for board service—and the board's desire to recruit her in turn.

HOW TWO WOMEN LEVERAGED THEIR CAPITAL

Lauren was grateful for learning about board readiness stories when she did. Before that, she had no idea that anything more than a résumé was needed to locate a corporate board seat. She sought advice from her uncle, who emphasized:

> Lauren, never, *never* send a CV to show your expertise. In a sense, the people in charge of finding new board members are volunteering their time. They just don't have time to sift through the résumés of all the people who want to be on a board. Being a badass executive is not enough. You have to distill your expertise to just those things boards care about. It has be something I can read and understand in two minutes.

With that, Lauren got to work carefully going through this chapter. She soon came up with a draft and worked through several versions with her uncle's assistance.

Michele was new to the concept of the board readiness story and even was a bit skeptical, because she was tapped for two board seats before she even really knew what governance was all about. As she got into the exercises, she had difficulty learning to present herself as a board member rather than as an executive. She also realized that she fell into that trap of "the executive mindset" when discussing board opportunities. Since the start of her board journey, she had been invited to a handful of interviews. In her first couple of interviews, when the selection committee asked her something specific about her functional expertise—such as "What do you do related to artificial intelligence (AI)?"—she found herself switching into the autopilot of answering from an expert executive standpoint and responding with, "Well, we have organized our efforts around three pillars: ..." She was proud of the proactive way she led her organization to integrate AI, and she was puzzled about why she hadn't advanced through the selection. After learning about the competencies boards require in their directors, she managed to avoid the executive mindset trap in a recent interview. This time, when asked about AI, she responded with, "There's a lot going on with AI today and how it can be used. What are the board's thoughts about that?" After an engaging discussion, she followed up with "Who on the board today is asking the company about generative AI?" These two strategic questions highlighted her expertise without detailing her résumé. Debriefing this experience with a more seasoned colleague shed even more light on her recent interview. This colleague explained:

> Being a great executive is *not* a differentiator. Responding like an executive and talking about what you did is like looking in the rearview mirror. Your differentiator is showing your ability to look out the windshield. Spark their curiosity and make them think of something new by asking thought-provoking, future-focused questions.

This conversation set Michele on a new path of showcasing her expertise and potential contribution to boards in a new way. She soon found that the resulting conversations were far more stimulating for all involved than those she had had before—*and* she was soon standing out from the crowd in the large pool of potential directors.

ACTION ITEMS

Try the following five steps to begin leveraging your own capital en route to board service:

1. **Review your work.** Review the work you completed for Chapters 3–10. Each contains vital elements of your board readiness story: professional journey and core competencies (Chapter 8), industry insights (Chapters 4 and 5), governance experience (Chapter 7), leadership and collaboration (Chapters 7 and 8), ethical and values alignment (Chapters 3 and 7), board contribution (Chapters 4–7), professional development (Chapters 7, 8, and 10), and recommendations and testimonials (Chapter 9). As you review your work, take notes for each section.

2. **Write your board readiness story.** Using the notes you gathered in Step 1, write the draft of your board readiness story. Share your story with a trusted mentor and ask for feedback, then finalize your draft.

3. **Practice and refine your story.** You need to be able to tell your story coherently and engagingly with board recruitment professionals and boards themselves. Being able to do so comes only with extensive practice. If you are working through this process with colleagues, practice sharing your stories with each other. If you have a trusted mentor, share your story with them. If you are working alone, record and listen to yourself in your effort to refine your story.

4. **Create opportunities to showcase your capital.** Seek and create opportunities to share your board readiness story and showcase your unique knowledge, abilities, and traits. This may occur through creating and sharing thought leadership on social media, delivering talks and participating on panel discussions, taking part in networking events, and engaging with board placement services. The more you demonstrate your abilities, the more effectively you will be able to demonstrate them and describe how they fit specific settings.

5. **Advocate for yourself.** Those who know about open board seats will not be able to refer you for them unless they know of your interest. Take every opportunity to make others aware of your interest and ability to occupy a board seat, from adding "and I'm looking for opportunities to share my expertise in [specific interests] through board service" to your professional introduction, to showcasing your ability to have high-level strategic conversations at an executive level whenever appropriate.

SUMMARY

To achieve success in your journey toward the boardroom, it is crucial to comprehend and use your individual talents and strengths. Additionally, it is important to establish a network of mentors, peers, and advisors who can provide support and guidance. Continuous learning is also essential, as is setting clear goals and embracing challenges. Seeking feedback, adapting, and networking effectively are all key components. Finally, remaining committed, persistent, and resilient is vital to reaching your goals. This chapter reviewed the steps for effectively using your distinct sources of capital, which were discussed in previous chapters. We explored why it's essential to go beyond mere competence as an executive and instead focus on leveraging your capital and highlighting your abilities. We outlined the steps to develop your board readiness narrative and highlight the various methods to present your capital portfolio. Finally, we described how two of our main characters strategically showcased their resources and offered insights on how you, too, can embark on a similar path.

PART III

NAVIGATING THE JOURNEY

As the saying goes, the best-laid plans often go awry. For this reason, we discuss the need and provide tools and techniques for managing yourself, your mindset, and your career. We begin with discussing how to neutralize naysayers (whether yourself or others), and then continue to assembling your support team, picking your battles, and managing your pace.

CHAPTER TWELVE

NEUTRALIZING NAYSAYERS

It is not the critic who counts … . The credit belongs to the man who is actually in the arena, whose face is marred by dust and sweat and blood; who strives valiantly.

—Theodore Roosevelt

On the pathway to success, you will inevitably encounter naysayers of various types. Each poses unique challenges and opportunities, making the journey both more difficult and overcoming them all the more rewarding. Whether you encounter critics trying to boost their own confidence or rivals wanting to win, you need to understand and know how to contend with each opponent. The research I conducted for this book surfaced many stories from directors about the various forms of criticism and opposition they have faced in the boardroom and on their way to the boardroom, from microaggressions to outright hostility. This chapter provides an overview of the typical types of naysayers you are likely to encounter along your path, how these can affect your journey to the boardroom, and how to approach these unique sources of opposition.

YOUR INNER IMPOSTER

The "impostor phenomenon" was first described in the 1980s by Dr. Pauline Clance, based on her work with therapy clients.[1] She noticed that some of her clients had strong feelings that their achievements were undeserved. In their worry about being exposed as a fraud, they experienced severe distress and self-doubt, reduced well-being, and tended to engage in self-sabotaging behavior. She further speculated that people with imposter syndrome tend to exhibit at least two of the following characteristics: (1) a reinforcing cycle of feeling like an imposter, (2) having the need to be special or the very best, (3) feeling they have to be superhuman, (4) having a fear of failure, (5) denying one's abilities and any praise, and (6) feeling afraid or guilt about success. Later researchers suggested that people with imposter syndrome (1) believe they have fooled others that they are competent, (2) feel afraid of being exposed as a fraud, and (3) feel incapable of attributing their success to their competencies.

High achievers from underrepresented backgrounds are at particular risk for imposter syndrome, doubting their own skills and achievements or fearing being exposed as a fraud. According to research by Dr. Cara McGinnis, psychology professor at the University of Calgary, women and people of color may be more likely to feel they don't fit in, they're not welcome, and they don't belong.[2] In my study of Black women who have beaten the odds and made it to corporate boardrooms, one director who was an attorney explained, "I was intimidated for many years in the early part of my board career because I felt underprepared because I didn't have a business degree." Another director, explaining that she "grew up in the shadows of a plantation," reflected, "It's still very much a white male show, so the fact that I was the first African American female on the board was astounding to me."

How Your Inner Imposter Affects Your Board Search

Imposter syndrome also can be crippling mentally and emotionally, drain your energy and attention, and cause you to fall short of the performance you are capable of, thus, feeding the cycle of self-doubt. Perfectionistic ideals further contribute to feelings of inadequacy, increased discomfort, and despair when they believe they are unable to reach the standards they set for themselves or the expectations of their family and others. And even when they succeed, those with imposter syndrome often feel fear, stress, self-doubt, and discomfort rather than happiness. If you experience imposter syndrome, you may explain away your successes by thinking anyone could have done what you did, or thinking you just got lucky, or fearing that others are mistakenly believing that you are talented. As if that isn't bad enough, when you stumble or face challenges, your self-perceived incompetence looms larger than life—increasing your chance of failure and perpetuating the cycle of imposter syndrome. For these reasons, burnout, emotional exhaustion, low motivation, poor achievement, guilt, shame, anxiety, and depression are common experiences for those with imposter syndrome. All of these can affect your board search by making it difficult to broadcast your aspirations, appropriately take credit for your achievements, and enjoy the fruits of your labor once you do reach the boardroom. Helen, who has served on several public boards, as chair of several not-for-profit boards, and chair of many committees, reported many instances of imposter syndrome emerging in the boardroom. She shared, "Sometimes people just don't have the confidence to speak up, or they think that someone already said what they were about to say, or that their question really isn't that great."

Neutralizing Your Inner Imposter

I advise director candidates I work with to harness their moxie to move beyond imposter syndrome. Moxie reflects an intensity of motivation and is related to (but distinct from) traits such as grit, self-control, and the ability to overcome procrastination. In my own research, I've seen that the attributes of moxie—strength of will, self-discipline, and the ability to persist despite challenges—was vital to underrepresented directors' success. One Latina executive I spoke with described moxie in this way: "I noticed my Black colleagues overcoming the obstacles they encountered in their careers. Whenever they set goals, they achieved them. They had a 'refuse to lose' mentality. And once I emulated what I saw in them, I rapidly ascended the corporate ladder myself."

The directors I interviewed explained that they neither internalized the obstacles they encountered as personal failures, nor did they externalize them as irreconcilable systemic barriers. In fact, when I asked them to identify the barriers they faced, it took them a while to recall and identify them because they had transformed their obstacles into sources of motivation. It became apparent that moxie was a response to their childhood experiences of racism, sexism, microaggression, and other difficulties.

In a study by psychology professor Jessica Curtis and colleagues, moxie was found to predict intrinsic and extrinsic motivation more than other motivational constructs like grit or self-control.[3] Moxie also predicted goal achievement—largely because people with moxie invest more resources into their aims. For example, one director I interviewed realized that her career choice of spending years as a consultant and then becoming CEO of a small company created substantial obstacles to her landing a corporate board seat. "Boards still tend to recruit against a checklist of wanting a sitting CEO of a multinational corporation," she explained. "So when I'd approach recruiters, they would push back with, 'Ooo … ah … I'll really have to convince the board that it is worth it for them to speak with you.'" At this point, she could have agreed with others' opinions that she wasn't boardroom material. Instead, she recognized the need to translate her experiences and skills into language a board would understand and find attractive. Now, only a few years into board service, she serves on three publicly traded company boards and three nonprofit boards.

YOUR INNER SUPERSTAR

Your inner superstar is what I call the cognitive bias that is opposite to the imposter syndrome. In this phenomenon, called the *Dunning-Kruger effect*, people with limited competence in a particular domain overestimate their abilities. People who fail to accurately evaluate themselves run the risk of making poor choices, such as pursuing an unhealthy profession or participating in risky activities. Those affected may be less likely to take stock of their weaknesses and work to improve themselves as a result. This bias can be to blame when a sales executive needs to deliver an important pitch and, confident in their "gift of gab," improvises the presentation without adequate preparation. I have witnessed such presentations and can assure you that discerning people recognize their time has been wasted and don't hesitate to walk out of the meeting. Bao experienced a similar consequence when she hastily accepted a board position without fully understanding the implications. She shared:

> I already knew two of the executive directors, and they invited me to attend their board meeting. At the same time, another organization wanted me to serve on their board. In hindsight, I think at that time I was not familiar with each board because I was interviewing with a few other mid-cap and large cap board positions. I made the mistake that when one of them said, "We want you to be on our board," I just agreed. Then the other board was angry, saying, "You didn't tell me you were getting on this board," and they dropped my candidacy.

Bao's experience taught her the importance of thorough consideration and communication before committing to board roles. In this way, inaccurate self-assessment—whether that concerns not fully considering the situation or not having a firm grasp of one's strengths and weaknesses—can lead people to make bad decisions, such as choosing a career for which they are unfit or engaging in dangerous behavior. It may also inhibit the affected from addressing their shortcomings to improve themselves.

How Your Inner Superstar Affects Your Board Search

An unbridled inner superstar can be just as damaging to your board search as an inner imposter. Here's how it works—overconfidence can lead to poor performance and, worse, it can leave you delivering poor outcome after poor outcome without you even realizing you're not hitting the mark. According to *Situational Leadership* (1998, Wiley), Ken Blanchard would call this the state of being an enthusiastic beginner—the state of being wildly confident *and* wildly unskilled. The problem with this is that, at some point, the repeated failures eventually undermine your enthusiasm and confidence, and you slip into disillusionment as you begin to realize how much you don't know or can't do related to the tasks facing you. This disillusionment can turn into a sense of helplessness and self-doubt at the risk of further empowering your inner imposter.

Furthermore, inaccurately gauging your skills can have long-term consequences if it leads you into career paths or board service trajectories for which you are unfit. The result can be missed performance targets, unsatisfying pursuits, and ultimately failure. Short-term poor decisions and project failures also tend to be found in the wake of inner superstars when they go unchecked.

Gabrielle, an accomplished executive and board member, shared an experience of overconfidence leading to frustration in her career when she took on a new executive role with the expectation of advancing quickly. She said, "When I came to the organization, the opportunity was to take on this newly created C-suite role. In essence, I was going to do something we know how to do in a new industry and I would gain the opportunity to run an entire line. For a period of five years, the timeline kept getting pushed out." She added that, in retrospect, had she let go of her eagerness and overconfidence, she could have seen and heeded the signs much earlier that the promises made about the role were not going to come to fruition.

Neutralizing Your Inner Superstar

Overall, being aware that you may have an inner superstar can be a powerful tool in navigating your career path and board service journey. By striving for humility, continuous learning, and a proactive approach to skill development, you can enhance your path to long-term success. In particular, it is helpful to enhance your self-awareness by keeping in mind that you may not know what you don't know and, in turn, actively seeking feedback from peers, mentors, or managers. This feedback can provide valuable insights into your actual competence levels and help you identify areas for growth and development.

Additionally, it can be helpful to keep in mind the 10,000-hour rule popularized by Malcolm Gladwell in *Outliers* (2018, Little, Brown). In other words, building expertise takes most people significant time and effort—and chances are, you are the rule rather than the exception. Therefore, although it is normal to feel a sense of early mastery when you start something new, it is important to continue investing in the ongoing growth of your skills and knowledge.

Related to this is developing a growth mindset, where you view your abilities, intelligence, talents, and skills as attributes to be cultivated through dedication, persistence, learning, and experience. Rather than priding yourself on being a born genius, welcome failure as a stepping stone to success and focus on progressing, improving, and learning over time by looking for new challenges and staying open to feedback and change. Aponi, an independent director and consultant to C-suite women, described her resilience and commitment to continuous learning that was fostered at a very young age:

> I could see the benefits of these when I'd be at school and they would say, "Oh, you're a hard worker!" Or "You're a great student." I fed off of that, and that's what built my thirst for continuous learning and having an impact.

As a result, Aponi has gone on to attain a doctorate and a range of significant professional accomplishments.

YOUR HATERS

When we feel frustrated or disappointed, we sometimes resort to criticism. I've done it, you've done it, and others do it, too. Sometimes we criticize ourselves. Sometimes we criticize others to get a better outcome, or to build our self-confidence and gain a temporary sense of superiority or validation. Other times, we project the traits or emotions we wish we didn't have onto others and then criticize them. Still other times, we may attract attention to others' flaws so we feel less insecure or vulnerable, or to assert dominance and influence, or to win against our rivals. In the following sections, we review two ways we make our own path more difficult, and two ways others obstruct our path, based on my research with women finding their way to the boardroom. According to John Brubaker, who explained in an entire article on *why you need* more haters, "Criticism is self-hate turned outward. I believe hate is often a sign of weakness, envy and fear. Haters hate on you because you're doing what they cannot, will not or are too afraid to attempt."[4]

How Haters Affect Your Board Search

Although haters can affect your board search through direct adverse impacts on your reputation, the more insidious and long-lasting effects are those that land internally. First, the criticism may create a negative emotional impact that can spark not only irritation but also self-doubt, lowered self-esteem, and diminished motivation. These, in turn, can undermine your performance and ability to successfully carry out your board search tasks. You may also shrink back from growth-oriented challenges, help seeking, or calculated risks if you are already feeling overly scrutinized.

Your mentality, resilience, feedback-processing skills, and openness to criticism as a learning opportunity will determine the extent to which criticism from others influences your professional and board service trajectory. Learning to handle criticism well in your professional life by increasing your self-awareness, actively seeking out input, and maintaining an optimistic outlook on the importance of constant progress can help you not only weather criticism but also grow from and welcome it.

Loving the Hate

John Brubaker noted in *Entrepreneur* magazine, "there's a direct correlation between the amount of success you enjoy and the number of haters you have."[5] He added that we need to love the hate, because it's a sign we're on the right track. Everyone from Led Zeppelin to Michael Jordan to Steve Jobs to presidential candidates have had their share of haters. Brubaker explained that haters are a natural part of growing and excelling in your career. It follows that the only way to avoid haters is to sideline your career. If that was something you wanted to do, you would not have gotten to this point in this book. Therefore, the number one rule when you encounter a hater is to recognize it as a sign that you're on the right track.

The second tactic is to receive feedback from trusted mentors or to conduct a low-risk proof of concept. For example, my mentee Marcia came to me for feedback after failing to close an important sale. Since this event, she had played and replayed the scenario in her mind, wondering where she had gone wrong. Moreover, her colleague was quick to criticize, saying, "You didn't handle the objections well and your closing was very weak. If I was the client, I wouldn't have agreed either." Marcia sought me out to gain some clarity and guidance. We reviewed the entire sales interaction step-by-step. I pointed out both where she had done well and where she needed a different approach, such as, "When the client raised concerns about the product's cost, you should have focused on its long-term value and return on investment in relation to their stated outcomes mentioned by their various stakeholders within the company." I offered additional tips for handling the next sales conversation. Marcia used this feedback to create and implement a more successful approach, sparking her growth and improved sales performance.

The third tactic is to reframe any criticism you receive as a hypothesis rather than a statement. Next, identify ways to test the hypothesis, such as by getting feedback from trusted mentors or conducting a low-risk proof of concept. For example, when you agree with the criticism, you also can feed the imposter syndrome. I recently witnessed this in a young and talented mentee of mine who has been spearheading transformative change in her company despite having taken her role only months ago. While her proposed initiative had been blessed by her boss and other executives, another leader above her blocked her with, "Well, your plan is completely unworkable." She slid into a pit of paralyzing self-doubt. Having seen the plan myself, I knew the criticism was unfounded but suspected there was more to the story. Once we debriefed the situation, I realized that she had circulated her plan in a way that inadvertently criticized the leader's work, resulting in a predictable backlash. We then discussed more effective ways to solicit support from the various stakeholders involved—including the leader in question. She then created and implemented a more successful approach, in turn, learning from this experience and strengthening her competencies.

YOUR FRENEMIES

Frenemies are those individuals who are equal parts friends and enemies. At first glance, they seem to be your friend and participate with you in social activities or work experiences. They also might even give you an occasional compliment or offer of support. However, these relationships usually are shallow and lack genuine trust, mutual respect, and strong emotional connection. Under the surface runs a current of resentment, rivalry, jealousy, and even hatred. Competition is the norm as each of you strives for more attention, approval, accomplishment, social standing, or other resources. As a result, you may notice rapid switches between friendly and hostile or passive-aggressive behavior. Jayla, an executive and independent director, shared one memorable experience of dealing with this kind of behavior during a videoconference meeting. She shared, "I made a comment, and another person grimaced and uttered, 'Argh!' I said, 'Stop. I'm sorry—What was with that facial expression and argh?'" Her willingness to confront the behavior head-on ensured that such microaggressions were acknowledged and addressed.

In more extreme circumstances, rivals may engage in covert or overt acts of sabotage to harm each other's success, relationships, or reputation. Frenemies also may participate in gossip, backstabbing, or spreading rumors about one another, often to gain an edge or establish control. Several directors I interviewed had experienced these kinds of covert attacks and betrayals, and these shaped their subsequent experiences. For example, Layla shared a poignant story from her childhood about experiencing betrayal from her best friend. She recounted, "When I was an adolescent, I told a joke about a politician, and my best friend went and reported me to the school principal. The government actually took me for questioning, and I was harassed by school officials the rest of the school years." As Layla's experience shows, frenemies can impose serious and long-term implications.

It follows that complex frenemy relationship is emotionally taxing and unpredictable, with alternating moments of friendship and tension. Individuals in frenemy relationships may feel a mix of camaraderie, competition, animosity, suspicion, and ambivalence toward one another. Frenemy relationships may exhibit boundary violations and problems with trust. Several directors I interviewed for this book expressed their concern about the way that successful professional women too often act as frenemies. Lisa, a retired banking executive and experienced board member, observed, "I've just seen too many other women in business so afraid to support other women. There's some kind of innate feeling that if they support another woman, it's going to take something away from them." She noted that this competitive mentality among women is a significant problem.

How Frenemies Affect Your Board Search

Frenemies can seriously affect your journey to the corporate boardroom by actively or passively obstructing your progress both in your career and in securing board seats. First, frenemies who are passive-aggressive, critical, or competitive can tarnish your confidence and self-esteem. The veiled hostility present in frenemy relationships can produce a sense of constant friction or tension, which can be annoying and distracting. The resulting battles you find yourself in on a regular basis can hamper your ability to focus on work-related tasks and goals.

Frenemies also can affect your relationships and make networking difficult, significant problems given the inherently social process of attracting and securing board seats. For example, they may block you from important events, meetings, or social parties where people meet each other and build relationships. Frenemies also may actively or passively tarnish your image through gossip, backstabbing, and rumors.

Your performance also can be affected when they withhold information, sabotage your projects or efforts, create disagreement related to key decisions, or downplay your accomplishments to stop you from moving up.

Alexandra, an active member of the Black Corporate Board Readiness program, further shared her observations of her own culture: "What I have observed about us as African American people is we are really hard on each other. And we don't advocate and support each other in the ways that I see other ethnic groups doing." She further elaborated on how this lack of support is both visible and detrimental, asking, "Why can't we publicly support each other and then privately have a conversation?"

These various dynamics can be emotionally taxing, in turn, adversely affecting your physical health, productivity, motivation, and achievement. Given the multiple types of attacks you endure, you may find yourself less likely to try new things or reach for challenging opportunities.

Neutralizing Frenemies

Managing frenemy relationships at work can be difficult and requires a complex mix of assertiveness, professionalism, setting limits, and problem-solving. To handle these complicated situations well, you need to put your health first, keep your eye on your goals, and ask for help or support when you need it.

Begin by becoming more aware of your own emotions, motivations, and reactions in the frenemy relationship. Understand why the relationship causes you to feel certain emotions or behave in specific ways.

Be sure to maintain a professional tone and approach and set clear boundaries to protect yourself from harmful interactions. You may need to communicate your expectations and limitations about communication, collaboration, and professional behavior. Aim to concentrate on work-related activities and goals, while avoiding getting involved in personal problems or drama. Avoid gossiping or talking negatively about your frenemy with coworkers. Gossip can exacerbate tensions and foster a toxic workplace atmosphere.

When working together on projects or tasks, prioritize collaboration and professionalism. Maintain straightforward, courteous communication while focusing on mutual goals. If a confrontation arises, handle it calmly, assertively, and constructively. Use *I* expressions to express your views and feelings without criticizing or assaulting the other individual. If feasible, keep your encounters with your frenemy professional and avoid socializing outside of work. Maintaining a certain level of space can help to alleviate conflict and stress.

To buffer the effects of the frenemies in your midst, create a support network of trusted coworkers and mentors who can offer advice, perspective, and emotional support while you deal with the difficulties of a frenemy relationship. In more difficult circumstances, consider getting mediation or conflict resolution assistance from human resources or a professional mediator to encourage open conversation and the development of mutually acceptable solutions.

Remember that handling frenemy relationships involves patience, endurance, and a focus on your personal well-being and professionalism in the workplace. If the relationship becomes too toxic or harmful to your mental health, you may need to reconsider your level of involvement or seek additional help.

CASE STUDIES

Denise found herself shocked as she worked through this chapter and recognized herself in the pages. When Denise started her law career at the boutique firm, she started at the same time as Bette, another new attorney fresh out of law school. Denise and Bette had similar goals for their careers, became fast friends, and respected each other's work—or so Denise thought. A few months in, Denise noticed that Bette had a habit of subtly undercutting Denise. The statements seemed innocent—and even funny—at first. But it wasn't long before the hint of good-natured teasing became strong overtones of criticism and ridicule—both in front of Denise and behind her back. One example was a critical meeting when Denise was assigned to propose the strategy for a key client. Bette quickly expressed concerns that the strategy was "quick, dirty, and irresponsible," pointing out other times Denise proposed ideas that needed workshopping. Ignoring their workplace belief that "a good solution today is better than a great solution tomorrow" and norm of workshopping, Bette's ongoing and vocal criticism planted and watered seeds of doubt in their colleagues' minds about Denise's competence. Denise eventually confronted Bette, who laughed and brushed it off with, "Oh, Denise, you're *so* sensitive. Don't take yourself so seriously! Are you sure you're cut out for this work?" Denise sought guidance from some mentors and made extra effort to build trusting relationships throughout the office—outside of Bette's influence.

Sharon also found herself in the pages of this chapter—particularly related to her inner imposter. As she progressed along her board journey, she was happy to find herself referred by her former independent directors for seats. She was called for interviews, and those went great! She recounted her experiences as a CEO and knocked it out of the park as far as demonstrating her executive prowess. Yet, she never progressed. She was a one-interview wonder. When this started to become a pattern, she contacted her former independent directors to figure out what was going wrong. They referred her to NACD for education. She soon learned that in her role as CEO, although she had generally thought of herself as the boss, she actually had been reporting to the board. As CEO, she had a seat on the board, but she had a whole team of bosses. Further, she lamented, "the only reason I was on that board was because I was the CEO, and the only reason I was the CEO was because my dad founded the company. If none of that were true, I wouldn't have had my career, and I certainly wouldn't be on that board—or *any* board!" She came down with a severe case of imposter syndrome. Through the education she gained, she also realized that all the reasons why she thought she aced her board interviews were the very reasons why she bombed them. She realized she had not made the mental shift from executive to director—and she wasn't sure she had the ability to be an independent director at all. She realized that she had work to do—both on her imposter syndrome and in cultivating her board readiness competencies.

ACTION ITEMS

Try the following steps to begin to identify and neutralize the naysayers you encounter on your journey:

1. To avoid both careless overconfidence and costly overcompensation, when you face challenges along the journey, begin by soberly assessing the situation. Take note of the knowledge, skills, abilities, and resources you need to successfully navigate it.

    If you discover your current competencies are sufficient to tackle the situation: Proceed, taking care to gather evidence of your success to defuse any imposter syndrome.

    If you find significant gaps: Close them through training, guidance from trusted mentors, or expert assistance and resources.

2. To rise to the challenges presented by haters and frenemies, begin by recognizing you wouldn't have these unless you were on the right track, and then seek the support and feedback from trusted mentors to ensure you are staying on the path of growth amid the noise and confusion of criticism.

SUMMARY

You will meet many naysayers on your journey to the boardroom. The adventure becomes increasingly challenging as you encounter new difficulties and chances, but the rewards for achieving them are even greater. You need to be prepared to deal with any kind of opponent, whether they are critics looking to improve their own self-esteem or competitors who are out to win. Identifying the naysayers you are dealing with and outlining your tactics for success are the secrets to finding your way.

CHAPTER THIRTEEN

ASSEMBLING YOUR SUPPORT TEAM

Surround yourself with people who don't just ask how you are doing. Surround yourself with people who make an effort to make sure they are part of the reason you are doing so well.

—Jennae Cecelia

D elivering on a meaningful and compelling vision generally means you have some ground to travel to fulfill it. And to achieve it, it will be important to find those trusted resources who can provide sound guidance as you plan and execute your career to position yourself for your ideal post-career. Many of the directors I interviewed mentioned they relied on mentors and sponsors throughout their careers and board service journeys. These vital sources of support included internal and external contacts, peers, subordinates, managers, and board members, among others. This chapter reviews five sources of support that prove invaluable in crafting a successful career and journey to the boardroom.

ROLE MODELS

Canadian American psychologist and Stanford professor Albert Bandura created social learning theory, which explains the powerful impact of role modeling in learning and development. The essence of the theory is that we can learn how to succeed within a given social context by observing and imitating the behaviors, attitudes, and values demonstrated by the individuals who are already successful within that context.

What this means for our board journey is that we must have successful career role models to observe and emulate if we hope to secure a seat. Ideally, that role model would be someone you could witness firsthand and interact with. However, in the absence of that, you can still gain the benefits of role modeling through indirect methods such as observing from a distance, consuming their thought leadership, and watching their media coverage. Role modeling also can occur by observing fictional characters or symbolic representations of the ideal executive or board member. Once you have selected a role model, the following three elements need to be in place for you to gain the benefits of the relationship.

1. **Observe the role model in context.** Central to learning from a role model is the ability to observe them in action, including witnessing firsthand how they speak, act, respond, and navigate specific challenges. Take care to notice what and how they do things—and take notes to help you later recall what they did. Additionally, it is important to observe them within the desired context because each situation is governed by cultural norms, societal expectations, peer relationships, and environmental circum-stances, and what works in one environment may be less successful (if at all) in another environment. Several directors I interviewed spoke of the powerful effect of witnessing the examples provided by their parents and family members. Sandy reflected on her parents' influence on her career path and work ethic:

My father was a family doctor supporting a family of six. Then he went into the Vietnam War, even with us four children at home. His dedication, his work ethic, and my mother's dedication to raising four children alone during that time was a powerful example for me. And then being the youngest of four helped. I think I have very successful, very smart, and motivated older siblings, which gave me additional role models to follow.

2. **Witness and feel motivated by the outcome.** In addition to observing your role model's behaviors, you also want to see the impacts and outcomes they achieve—and to feel motivated by it. When this occurs, vicarious reinforcement sets in, which consciously and subconsciously motivates you to emulate your role model's behaviors. Kathryn described the inspiration she felt being surrounded by empowered women in her family, particularly her mother, who played a significant role in shaping her perspective and confidence. She explained:

Both my parents were college educated. My mom was a high school math teacher for 30 years who taught at my high school. Both my parents were very active and very community oriented. Candidly, I just always was exposed to empowered women, and that started with my mom.

3. **Practice.** The final step in the process is actually emulating what you observed your role model do. For practice to occur, you need to be able to remember and imitate what your role model did, feel motivated to achieve the result they did, and believe you are capable of carrying out the observed activities. Accordingly, to have effective practice, you may need to gain more observation time, take sufficient notes to recall what they did, and develop your confidence or skills in carrying out the activities. You may need to revisit Part II of this book to boost your knowledge and skills or Chapter 12 to improve your self-confidence. Although Nala shared, "I didn't have a single role model," she instead "followed and modeled the traits and behaviors of people who succeeded."

Overall, what social learning theory tells us is that our abilities, attitudes, and behaviors can be taught, adjusted, and eliminated through our social interactions and exposure to role models. Having role models can help you close any gaps you found in your capital portfolio (see Part II) and help you gain confidence for the journey. This is good news because we find our way to executive roles and the boardroom from a variety of different directions and life experiences. If you have not traveled that path with others or following others who showed you the way, you still can learn how to get there—if you select helpful role models.

Over time, as you observe and emulate them, you begin to internalize their approaches and incorporate them into your own self-concept and identity. In this way, role models provide vital inspiration, guidance, and information that can have a profound impact on your board journey. Shonda described how her role model influenced her own professional decisions and pathway to success. She explained:

> I was drawn to the position because the person who was in it before me was the first woman and the first person of color. She seemed to really thrive at that organization and in that space. So I was drawn to it. I knew it would be a place that I could succeed because I first watched her succeed.

MENTORS

Mentors can be vital sources of personalized guidance who provide support and counsel as you navigate the path to the boardroom. The directors I interviewed during my research for this book described two vital types of mentors: career mentors and board mentors. Career mentors helped them make work-related decisions, navigate organizations and new industries, overcome obstacles and challenges, balance work and life, and prepare for strategic decisions throughout their careers. Board mentors helped them prepare for board service and navigate the transition from C-suite executive to board oversight and governance. One director explained, "If I was worried about public speaking and I saw somebody who was really great at it, I might go to lunch with that person and talk to them about public speaking and ask them to be my mentor." Mentors often support their mentees in the following ways.

- **Competency development.** Mentors provide constructive criticism on their mentees' performance, abilities, and behaviors and encourage their mentees to pursue ongoing learning and development opportunities. They may suggest training programs, certificates, or courses to improve skills and expertise. They assist mentees in identifying areas for improvement and developing action plans to increase their capabilities. They also hold people accountable for their behaviors, goals, and development while offering support and encouragement. "Earlier in my career, I was encountering some steep resistance from some senior leaders when I was trying to launch an initiative. I invited a more seasoned colleague for coffee, as I had seen her navigate these kinds of challenges before, and she ultimately became my mentor."

- **Career navigation.** A mentor additionally can provide guidance on a variety of career- and board-related topics, including search strategies, networking techniques, résumé creation, interview preparation, and competency development. They assist mentees in clarifying their career goals, identifying strengths and areas for improvement, and developing effective success tactics.

- **Network building and exposure.** Mentors assist mentees in broadening their professional network by exposing them to business connections, future mentors or sponsors, and relevant professional associations or events. Tonya described the impact of her mentors at a Fortune 500 company, highlighting the value of having mentors who could provide honest feedback and support her professional growth. She shared, "I had probably two or three really critical mentors. One of them happened to be an African American man who was a director when I started there. As his career progressed, he pulled me along. And he's still a very dear friend."

- **Industry insights.** Mentors impart their knowledge and industry-specific information to mentees, leading to timely and in-depth insights about trends, best practices, and opportunities in the industry. Based on the industry trajectory, mentors can provide keen insights about possible professional routes their mentees may take. Mentors may help the mentee develop a strategic career strategy and set realistic goals consistent with one's aspirations and interests and the industry conditions.

Your mentor's support can help you increase your self-confidence as you get out of your comfort zone by expanding your capabilities and network, taking on new challenges, and achieving more ambitious goals. Through these activities, the mentors of those directors I interviewed helped them prepare for board service and navigate the transition from C-suite executive to board oversight and governance.

In most cases, mentoring relationships form organically. Executive and independent director Cassandra reflected on her long-standing friendship and mentoring relationship with another female executive. She explained how their relationship started and evolved: "She and I met when I had just been hired into a new role. I talked to our CEO about this wonderful woman. He said, 'Oh, can you introduce us?' I introduced her, and soon she came over to our company. She and I have been incredibly close since then."

Although it may feel natural and organic to seek mentoring from peers, it is critical to select a mentor who has already had success in what you're now trying to do. This means expanding beyond your peers to include more experienced colleagues and advisors in your network of mentors. Once you have identified a mentor, decide how often you will meet. You may meet ad hoc as needs arise or on a regular schedule.

Once you have selected an experienced mentor and decided when you will meet, you can convene to discuss your challenges, and they can they confidently tell you what to do and what not to do using their insights forged from their own professional experiences. In this way, mentors bring a unique viewpoint to career issues and decisions. When they have a wealth of experiences you have not yet gained, they can help you see situations from a variety of perspectives, consider alternate solutions, and make educated decisions. Once they impart their wisdom, it is up to you to execute based on the insights you've gained.

ALLIES

Your allies include current and former executives with board experience, current and former board members, coaches, mentors, sponsors, and other potential career enablers. The directors I spoke with in preparation for this book said such individuals were vital sources of support in situations like making work-related decisions, navigating organizations and new industries, overcoming challenges, and preparing for strategic decisions. Although these important allies also are aware of the challenges related to increasing boardroom diversity, you can take several steps to help them help you secure a seat at the table.

The reason you need to mobilize them to help you is that many potential allies may not see themselves as critical members of your support team—although they are. For many allies, the process of architecting one's career to secure board seats has faded from their consciousness, becoming a tacit know-how that evades description. Although they expertly do it themselves, they may not see the need or take the time to explain the steps of how you can secure a board seat. In turn, you miss a vital opportunity to learn from their knowledge and experience.

In my own experience and that of the directors I interviewed, it appears that many diverse directors stumble onto the pathway to board service by accident. As one director described, "I had a lot of one-on-one conversations with board members, really got to see their journey and background, and thought to myself, 'This corporate board service line of work would be a great opportunity.'" Although stumbling onto the pathway is, indeed, one way to get there, you (and the boards you could be serving) risk losing a lot of opportunities in the process.

With the perspective you have gained from this book, you can take three specific steps to mobilize your allies.

1. **Ask them about sponsorship.** To become an active part of improving corporate governance, allies need to be intentional about sponsoring the candidates in their organizations who can be assets to boards. You can help mobilize them to fill that role by asking them about the role they see sponsorship playing in improving their organizations and corporate governance, what recommendations they have for sponsoring others and seeking sponsors, and learning more about their backgrounds. Although this may or may not result in them sponsoring you, it does help stimulate dialogue and awareness about the need for sponsorship.

2. **Understand their framework.** Allies are those individuals who have accumulated corporate achievements and secured more than one board seat along the way. For that reason, navigating the pathway to the boardroom may be an unconscious competence: the process may seem obvious,

and having to articulate just how to go about it can be difficult for them. Help them bring their path and best practices back into consciousness by asking them about their own experiences and identifying the tasks, milestones, and best practices they believe are essential to securing a board seat.

3. **Ask how they connect the dots.** If the allies in your midst have served on one or more boards, the case for navigating toward a board seat may be open-and-shut. It may be so apparent to them that the idea of having to explain why someone should do this may seem ludicrous. However, based on my own experience (as well as that of many of the directors I interviewed), it is not that obvious—even to the most talented high potentials and leaders. Allies have a responsibility to explain the importance of the steps they recommend to those they mentor and sponsor. You can mobilize allies to paint the vision and connect the dots by asking them where they see you potentially going next and asking what questions you should be asking that you haven't asked. It is normal to not know what you don't know, and you need your allies' help to think differently and to think bigger.

SPONSORS

Sponsors play key roles in helping rising professionals gain visibility and advancement opportunities. Sponsors are powerful members of an organization who actively advocate for and assist the progress of others. Unlike mentors, who offer guidance and advice, sponsors take a more aggressive approach to promoting their protégés' professional development and possibilities by opening internal and external doors to help propel those under their wing toward executive and C-suite roles. One of the key purposes of career sponsors is to actively promote their protégés' professional development. This could include campaigning for promotions, raises, leadership positions, and other career advancement milestones. Meanwhile, board sponsors proactively put the protégés in the right places at the right times to help them secure their next board seat. Sponsors exert their impact through several tactics.

- **Advocating for your advancement.** Your sponsor will actively promote and push for opportunities for you within the organization. They will speak positively about your abilities, skills, and potential for progress. Sponsors also can provide opportunities for you to work on tough projects, tasks, or responsibilities that will help you advance your careers and gain visibility within your organization and industry.

- **Expanding your network.** Your sponsor will help you expand your professional network by exposing you to key stakeholders, decision-makers, and powerful individuals both inside and outside the firm. Your sponsor will try to raise your visibility within the organization so that your contributions are recognized and valued by top leaders and stakeholders.

- **Introducing new opportunities.** A career sponsor can have a substantial impact on an individual's career trajectory by introducing them to new opportunities, giving strategic counsel, and increasing exposure and recognition within the firm. Building good relationships with sponsors requires demonstrating value, establishing trust, and aggressively seeking feedback and development opportunities. For example, career sponsors opened internal and external doors to help propel the paths to executive and C-suite roles among the directors I interviewed in my research for this book. As trusted advisors, their board sponsors proactively put them in the right places at the right times to best position them for their next board seat.

- **Providing strategic advice.** Whereas mentors may provide you with daily assistance, sponsors act in a more strategic, periodic way by offering timely comments, insights, and advice for overcoming career problems and capitalizing on opportunities. While sponsors devote time and effort to assisting their protégés, it is frequently a mutually beneficial arrangement. Sponsors can obtain insights, new views, and improved influence by interacting with exceptional persons they support.

As discussed in the mentor section, selection of an appropriate sponsor is essential for reaping the purported results, and in most cases, these relationships form organically. Specifically, your sponsor must have the reputation and leverage in your organization and industry to offer needed support. To vet a sponsor, observe others' reactions to them. If people sit up and lean forward while a certain individual speaks but start fiddling with their phones when another person speaks, you have just discerned between a potentially strong sponsor (the former) and a likely ineffectual one (the latter). Diverse executives I have spoken with shared that the impact of a good sponsor is invaluable and lasting. Not only do effective sponsors provide keen insider insights but also, even after your career paths diverge, these committed sponsors may continue to help you reach progressive leadership positions and support your ongoing career development and advancement.

Given the powerful impact a sponsor can have on you and your career path, you may be wondering what's in it for the sponsor. The answer is that if you have been carrying out the steps in this book and acting on the guidance of your mentors, allies, and sponsors, you will become your sponsor's unicorn and rising star. As a result, their ego-driven altruism kicks in and they want to claim you.

ACCOUNTABILITY PARTNERS

Accountability partners also play an invaluable role along your path to the boardroom, as they commit to supporting your growth and progress, as you commit to supporting theirs. As accountability partners, you help in several specific ways. First, you can help each other establish clearly defined learning goals. By discussing your goals with your partner, you can ensure that they are practical, attainable, and in line with your learning priorities.

Next, set up regular check-ins to monitor progress, discuss and solve difficulties you encounter, and celebrate accomplishments. These check-ins give structure and encouragement to keep you on track with your learning goals. During the check-ins, you also offer each other feedback, advice, support, tools, and support to overcome barriers so that both of you make steady progress.

- **Mutual learning.** Knowing that someone is keeping you accountable might boost your drive and dedication to continue along the lengthy and taxing pathway to the boardroom. Regular check-ins and discussions about your progress can help you stay focused and disciplined. Accountability partnerships frequently include shared learning opportunities in which partners exchange information, skills, and experiences. This collaborative learning strategy can broaden viewpoints and improve comprehension of various topics.

- **Celebrating wins.** A critical aspect of accountability partnerships is celebrating each other's accomplishments and milestones. Recognizing progress and accomplishments promotes morale, reinforces positive behaviors, and encourages continued learning and development. To form an effective accountability relationship for learning and development, it is critical to communicate freely, create clear expectations, prioritize mutual support, and sustain regular participation. Finding a partner with comparable learning goals and values can help the cooperation be more effective and sustainable.

As Suki, a retired executive and board member serving on four corporate boards summarized, "At the end of the day, we're going to need each other to get there. Women helping women, and women helping men, we're stronger together." Suki emphasized the importance of seeking help and building support systems—particularly within a women's initiative in which she has been an active member.

As with every member of your support team, it is important to select a suitable accountability partner, meaning one who can meet regularly with you, work hard on their own goals as you work on yours, and offer the right combination of inspiration, expectation, and understanding. Your accountability partner may be a friend, partner or significant other, or coworker. Above all, it will be important for this relationship to be infused with a heavy dose of mutual trust and respect so that you can be honest with and tough on each other due to the unconditional love, friendship, and support present. This kind of support is invaluable for helping you stay the course when you stumble and lose motivation.

CASE STUDIES

After reading this chapter, Lauren was even more grateful for the support of her uncle in learning about and being inspired to pursue a seat in the corporate boardroom. Lauren's uncle had served on multiple corporate boards; therefore, he not only had a wealth of experience but also a strong network and insights into the dynamics of board appointments. After beginning this book, Lauren decided to become a student of the profession of governance but also continued to seek out her uncle's guidance fueled by her genuine desire to learn. Her uncle continued to be impressed by Lauren's drive and potential for becoming a dynamic independent director. As Lauren completed the exercises in this book, she eagerly shared the results with her uncle. He offered valuable insights about the goals and targets Lauren set for herself, leading her to refine her goals. Second, she shared with him her self-assessment, and he offered valuable feedback and suggestions for how to increase each element of her capital portfolio. Impressed by her ambition and dedication to excel, he introduced Lauren to other board members, executives, and influencers who could provide valuable insights and potential board opportunities. He also advised Lauren on how to strategically position herself as a board candidate. They worked on crafting Lauren's personal brand, updating her résumé and LinkedIn profile, and creating a compelling narrative that highlighted her unique strengths and contributions. Under his advisement, Lauren also completed board readiness programs and workshops, which provided her with deeper insights into boardroom dynamics, governance best practices, regulatory frameworks, and the role of directors. Although Lauren's youth meant that corporate board service likely was still over a decade in the future, her uncle advised her on how to use this time to advance and expand in her expertise. Under his guidance, she set her intentions to obtain promotions from district to regional sales manager or area vice president of sales, and then to regional and vice president roles in operations to gain profit-and-loss experience. He also explained the importance of making a lateral move to operations management to gain actual functional experience across the organization and a robust skill set.

After reading this chapter, Michele realized that although she had gained the benefits of mentors, sponsors, and allies along her path, she had never had an accountability partner since high school cramming for exams with friends. Over the course of the various activities she carried out to pursue her next board seat, she had struck up a friendship with Sarah, who also was attempting to elevate her impact as a board member. They began by setting their respective goals, including what kind of board seat each wanted to secure and by when. Next, each created a project plan complete with dates and details for each task. Based on their goals and timelines, they created a meeting schedule for themselves. At each meeting, they reviewed their respective progress, discussed specific challenges they faced, and brainstormed solutions. They also took time to celebrate achievements and shared with each other the insights and resources they came across as they pursued their goals. Thanks to the benefits of mutual learning and support, both Michele and Sarah were able to move faster and farther toward their goals than they had before they started meeting.

ACTION ITEMS

Try the following steps to assemble your support team:

1. To find potential role models, allies, and sponsors for your board journey, begin by clarifying your values and goals governing the process. Next, brainstorm a list of people in your network or industry who inspire you and learn about successful individuals in your field or interest.
2. Seek to interact with these individuals by attending events they frequent and other opportunities to meet them.
3. As you learn more about each of your potential models, allies, and sponsors, gauge whether you align in terms of values, communication, and principles.
4. Connect with the individuals you identified for the purpose of forging an organic, mutually rewarding relationship. As a friendship unfolds and you continue to learn more about each other, it can be appropriate to ask whether they would be open to mentoring or sponsoring you.
5. To find an accountability partner, start by defining your goals. Look within your network or online platforms for someone with similar goals or interests and ensure that you are equally committed to regular check-ins and clear communication. In your meetings, set clear goals and provide support, encouragement, and constructive feedback to each other. Regularly evaluate the partnership to make sure it's effective and make adjustments if needed.

SUMMARY

A meaningful and compelling vision generally means you have some work to do to fulfill it. To do so, you will need trusted resources who can provide sound guidance as you navigate your primary career to position yourself for your ideal post-career. Your support team can play an invaluable role in smoothing your pathway to the boardroom. Additionally, I have found through my research that women are interested in supporting each other more. However, before you bring someone into your post-career circle of support, it is critical to make sure they are safe individuals. If they are not you may need to find your support outside your organization or even your industry. For example, it could be career limiting to divulge the timing or nature of your post-career plans within your organization. This was the case for Mary, a CEO who reached out to an independent director on her board to say she would leave her role, but only if the independent director would succeed her as CEO. Mary then proposed this plan to the board. Worried about Mary's commitment to the company, the private equity firm that owned the company swiftly removed Mary from her post. If Mary had had mentors, she likely would have avoided this sudden dismissal. By actively seeking and welcoming support but also being discerning about who is providing support, you can accelerate your progress to the boardroom and help ensure that you have all the competencies in place to provide substantial value once you get there.

CHAPTER FOURTEEN

FAIL-PROOFING YOUR JOURNEY

A successful man [or woman!] *is one who can lay a firm foundation with the bricks others have thrown at [them].*

—David Brinkley

The final step in charting your path to the boardroom is fail-proofing your journey, meaning putting in the measures you need to make your progress resilient against the inevitable challenges and pitfalls you will encounter. Your specific fail-proofing plan will be unique to you, but most include tactics such as setting specific short-, mid-, and long-term goals; celebrating small wins; and creating clear action plans yet maintaining flexibility and altering your plan as necessary. Adaptive action planning is necessary because along your journey you will inevitably encounter alluring opportunities. When you do, you will need a framework for discerning career-limiting dead ends from stimulating ventures worth pursuing.

Additionally, it is important to keep in mind that your journey to the corporate boardroom may span several years. You will need to find ways to stay motivated by recognizing your reasons for starting this journey and reminding yourself all along the way of why it is important to you. You will need to view inevitable setbacks as learning opportunities and adapt your strategy as needed. By implementing these tactics, you can boost your chances of success and handle obstacles more efficiently.

The previous chapters in this book have guided you step-by-step through the process of designing both your goals and your detailed project plan for achieving them. You also designed approaches for negotiating the naysayers and assembling your support team. This chapter guides you through the process of fail-proofing your path to the boardroom by navigating opportunities and managing your pace.[a]

THE NEED FOR FAIL-PROOFING

It can be challenging for anyone to secure a board seat; however, the unique challenges described in Parts I and II in this book can make it especially hard for women and people of color. Despite years of perfecting their educational credentials, architecting an impressive résumé of progressive leadership roles, and developing their skills to add exceptional value as a board member, many still lack access to board seats. For that reason, many diverse candidates may believe their difficulties in securing a board seat are due to persistent problems of exclusion, lack of equity, and not being considered viable candidates by recruiters and selection committees. What diverse candidates tend to do in response is doubling or tripling down on their qualifications. Take the case of Simi, who took the following steps to find her way to the boardroom.

1. **Boosted her board-related skills, knowledge, and experience.** Simi assessed her unique strengths, weaknesses, knowledge, skills, experiences, and interests. She explained, "I focused on the current issues in the

---

[a] A portion of this chapter first appeared in Dorsey, Keith D. (2023). From glass ceilings to glass cliffs: A guide to jumping, not falling. *MIT Sloan Management Review* (March 13). https://sloanreview.mit .edu/article/from-glass-ceilings-to-glass-cliffs-a-guide-to-jumping-not-falling/

boardroom and figured out what fit my profile." She also was careful to figure out and fill her board-specific competency gaps so she could become a serious candidate. She joined external board-related groups including Private Directors Association, National Association of Corporate Directors, and 50/50 Women on Boards, and read board and governance-related magazines including *Directors & Boards*, *Private Company Director*, and *Directorship*.

2. **Cultivated her board-related network.** Simi understood that finding a seat was most likely to happen through the existing board members she knew. As she strengthened these relationships, some of these blossomed into mutually rewarding friendships, with some individuals evolving into allies, mentors, and sponsors. As she reconnected with past colleagues, she rekindled a friendship with Aparna who also had been trying to find her way to the boardroom. The women multiplied their learning through goal setting and regular meetings.

3. **Showcased her board aspirations.** While building her competencies and rekindling and strengthening her relationships, Simi also made a point of showcasing her board aspirations to all those who had any potential connection to the recruiting process, including current and former executives, current and former board members, and board search firms. She became proficient in casually expressing her interest in securing a board seat, why she wants to serve, and the types of boards where she would best add value. As another director I interviewed put it, "When you meet with your contacts, tell them you're interested in serving on a board, because those of us who are on boards often are asked if we know anybody."

Given all of her hard work and accomplishments, imagine her surprise when she continued to face resistance from many executive recruiting firms. Simi, like other candidates from underrepresented groups, had exemplary academic credentials and experience, making her more qualified than some of her boardroom peers. Responding to resistance like Simi experienced by doubling down and working even harder can have diminishing and counterproductive results. For that reason, it is important to carefully select your path by picking your battles and setting and monitoring your pace on your personal marathon to the boardroom.

PICKING YOUR BATTLES

As your career progresses and you seek to accumulate the achievements befitting a corporate director, you will face various challenges and tough experiences. Whether these originate from increasing job complexity and leadership expectations; needs for strategic decision-making, organizational change, disputes, or management issues; or competing pressures and priorities, you will need to rise to the occasion by deciding which battles to fight and which hills to surrender. Higher-level positions mean increasing duties, decision-making authority, and participation in complicated projects or initiatives. Managing the resulting complexity can be difficult but can lead to invaluable skill development and experience that will benefit you in the boardroom.

One type of battle you particularly need to understand is the glass cliff assignment, in which women and other minorities are preferentially selected for leadership positions in times of crisis, placing them at increased risk for failure. This phenomenon occurs across industries and geographies, and for women and ethnic minorities alike. Poorly performing Fortune 500 companies were found more likely to appoint a female CEO than those performing well. Another study found that boards were more likely to recruit female directors following decreased stock performance.

In times of crisis, leaders—no matter who they are—tend to be seen as ineffective and part of the problem. When the leader is an occupational minority, any failure or lack of improvement tends to be blamed on their personal failings rather than on the situation. In a phenomenon called the *savior effect*, the minority leader is then replaced by a more prototypical leader who "saves the day." This both perpetuates leadership stereotypes in the organization and constricts diverse candidates' future opportunities.

How Glass Cliff Battles Can Affect Your Board Search

The allure of a very challenging assignment can be intoxicating, especially if you are a diverse candidate and feel you have limited opportunities to rise in the organization. Although you can use this assignment to establish yourself as an exceptional leader and turnaround expert, you must resist the urge to simply accept the assignment and jump in.

Why? Because exceptional leaders hit their performance targets and do so under budget and on time. The opportunity being offered has become a glass cliff assignment precisely because no one in the organization has the capacity or sufficient information to do that yet. Although the assignment is neither intended to be impossible nor a setup for failure, you do need to take specific steps to mitigate your risk and position yourself for success. This begins with asking the right questions—a lot of them, and *before* you accept the assignment. If you wait to discover risks and problems as you go, you risk ending up overdue and overbudget. If you realize the problems only after the dust settles, you may even have difficulty recovering professionally at your organization.

The common feature across all glass cliffs is that they are challenging problems for anyone to solve: no one person or team has the answers or a plan for solving them. Although this means it's unlikely you are maliciously being set up to fail, the downside is that the hiring manager and others in the organization might have trouble helping you explore this cliff and deciding the right course of action.

To have a chance of achieving your performance goals on time and within budget, you must take the initiative and invest time to fully explore the cliff—usually, you will be allowed two to four weeks to evaluate the opportunity.

Exploring and Negotiating the Glass Cliff

Deciding how to navigate a glass cliff begins with recognizing you are facing one. Glass cliff assignments tend to emerge within organizations that are in crisis. Whether the crisis is due to a natural disaster, industrial accident, product failure, negative public perception, management scandal, financial underperformance, or another cause, the defining criterion is that key organizational goals are threatened and a quick response is needed. If people like you are significantly underrepresented in leadership positions and if you are demographically unlike your predecessor, it is possible that you are being offered up as a symbol of change—or, at worst, a sacrificial lamb.

When you realize you are facing a glass cliff, start exploring it by asking the hiring manager to outline the expected performance targets, deadlines, and budget (see Figure 14.1). Next, identify all the additional parties surrounding the problem, such as executive sponsors, individual contributors and their managers, collaborating internal business units, and strategic partners. You may also consult trusted advisors within your network who provide a customer or supplier perspective related to the problem at hand. Then schedule conversations with the hiring manager and each stakeholder group to help you carefully consider the situation relative to its past, present, and future.

You must understand what happened in the past if you are to improve on what your predecessor did. You also need to gauge whether the new performance goals are realistic in the future and what obstacles threaten achievement. Finally, you need to soberly assess whether success is possible, given the resources and stakeholder commitments available to you in the present.

There are no right or wrong answers to these questions: each stakeholder will have different perspectives, and some stakeholders may not be able to answer all

Figure 14.1   Questions for Stakeholders When Evaluating a Glass Cliff Opportunity.

Exploring the Past
What were the goals in this situation?
In what ways was the target reached?
In what ways was the target missed?
Why do you think the goal wasn't achieved?
What do you think was done well?
What could have been done better?
What would you do differently?

Envisioning the Future
What liabilities and threats, both internal and external, could threaten goal achievement?
What competencies and resources are needed to hit the target on schedule and within budget?

Assessing the Present
Which needed competencies and resources are available now?
Which are lacking? What support is available for acquiring or developing these?
What would you do to minimize the risk of failure?
What are you prepared to do differently to achieve the goal and get what you want from this project?
What else could obstruct goal achievement?

of them. Your aim through these conversations is to uncover the patterns of responses across the stakeholders so you can begin to detect the core issues that resulted in the glass cliff, such as problems with organizational processes, structures, or culture.

Once the core issues underlying the problem are identified, you are far better equipped to comprehend the parameters of the opportunity being offered to you. For example, if you discover that the organization's culture is unintentionally hampering achievement of the goal, you need to identify the existing practices and processes that are obstructing success. Once identified, determine what you need from the organization to support change, such as vocal executive sponsorship, revisions to organizational and reporting structures, or additional incentives and rewards.

Planning and Deciding Whether to Jump

Based on the information you gained from your exploration, create a detailed plan for the assignment, including your short-, medium-, and long-term goals; the mentors, sponsors, and allies you will call on for support and guidance; and your plans for knowledge and skill building, if needed. At the same time, be ready to justify your requests, and realize that you are not going to get everything you ask for. You must also distinguish your must-haves from your nice-to-haves, identify workarounds for must-haves, and outline your plans for negotiating for and securing additional time, resources, and headcount, if needed.

After creating the plan, seek feedback from trusted advisors. Helpful questions to ask during their review include, "What am I not asking? What am I not negotiating for that I need to? Is my plan realistic?" Their perspectives and guidance can be vital ingredients to your success. At the same time, do not be dissuaded if they respond with "This will never work" or "We tried this before," because they are subject to biases and assumptions, as is anyone. Instead, test their response further by asking questions such as "What did you try? Why didn't it work? What is the business climate now, and would it work now given current business conditions?"

If you have carefully conducted your due diligence, crafted a plan that your trusted advisors agree is credible, and the organization has agreed to the plan, you may decide to proceed with the opportunity. Implement your plan and celebrate your early wins to build momentum. Monitor and ensure that the organization provides the support you negotiated for by involving your sponsors as needed. Throughout implementation, seek guidance from your mentors to optimize your chance of success.

However, if you discover through your due diligence that you are not the right fit for the opportunity, you cannot devise a realistic plan for the situation, or the organization does not agree to the plan you have outlined, the chance for success may be too low to warrant risking your career. In these cases, it may be wiser to decline the position and watch for the next opportunity.

SET AND MONITOR YOUR PACE

Traveling the path to the boardroom is a marathon—and, for some, an ultramarathon—rather than a sprint. Long-term success relies heavily on consistency. For that reason, managing your pace is critical for both making steady progress and preventing burnout. By contrast, pushing yourself too hard for an extended period can cause physical and mental tiredness, poor productivity, and a general lack of well-being. By controlling your speed, you can work toward your goals without suffering drastic variations in energy or productivity. I often remind myself and my mentees of this truism by saying, "Just because you can doesn't mean you should." Although refraining from a compelling opportunity may feel against your nature as a high achiever, I cannot emphasize enough that declining opportunities—your no—is what gives meaning to your yes.

Achieving the correct balance of work and rest improves your performance. Working at a manageable pace enables you to focus, think critically, and consistently deliver high-quality results. Rushing—or conversely—working too slowly can hamper your decision-making skills. Managing your pace enables you to devote the time and clarity required to make sound judgments. Jacqueline reflected on her own wellness epiphany and turning point when she had to start balancing work commitments and personal health:

> I had to learn a hard lesson in my late 40s when I had just worked myself into a place where I was starting to not be a healthy individual. ... Now, all my decisions center [on] "Is that going to leave you where you don't have any gas in your own tank?" Sometimes you have gas left, and sometimes you really do have to go all the way down to empty. But in those situations, it better be worth it. You don't do it unless it's 100% worth it.

Creativity develops when you give yourself time to ponder, reflect, and explore ideas. This includes caring for your physical and mental health, which in turn are critical for maintaining productivity, happiness, and creating the conditions for spontaneous inspiration and creativity to emerge. Managing your pace entails prioritizing self-care activities like getting enough sleep, exercising, and taking breaks as needed. When you honor these practices, you develop the resilience to respond to obstacles, setbacks, and workload changes without becoming overwhelmed or agitated. Many of the directors I spoke with know these principles because they made the mistake of rushing through life. Miranda urged aspiring executives and directors to take time to enjoy life and avoid racing through their education and careers, explaining the long-term nature of professional life. She elaborated:

> Absolutely do not rush to finish college. I actually finished early, and I really wish I hadn't done that. Obviously, it's turned out fine. But when you rush to grow up, you rush into the business world, and you're going to be working for a long, long time. Take your time to get there.

Balancing our activity and speed also enables us to maintain the strong connections with coworkers, friends, and family we need to support our personal and professional well-being. In turn, we can be present, alert, and actively involved in social encounters. Finance executive and board member Sumar highlighted the balance between personal and professional life and the importance of enjoying both. She advised:

> Be sure to enjoy and gather professional experiences, and be sure to really enjoy your family life as well as your corporate life. Inevitably, those two

things are never in balance. At times, they'll swing more in one direction than the other. But make sure you always have a sense of your bank account and that it does balance out over time.

Managing your speed enables you to establish realistic expectations for yourself and others. It prevents overcommitting and guarantees that you can efficiently carry out your responsibilities. It also helps up remain interested, passionate, and committed to your goals in the long run. To achieve balance, deliberately set aside time for reflection, rejuvenation, and self-care. As an executive, I made a rule of not sending emails between Friday at 6:30 p.m. and Monday at 6:30 a.m. to protect my employees' and my own time for relaxation and recovery.

Although I set boundaries around my work activities, other diverse executives I have spoken with opted to shift their roles to create more balance. One described exchanging full-time for part-time consulting to create more predictability and personal time for herself. Another moved from a CFO role to financial consulting. Regardless of the details, the bottom line is that rest, self-care, and balance are critical to artfully surviving and navigating the corporate jungle and your career.

CASE STUDIES

Denise had built a successful career as partner of a boutique environmental law firm, advocating for sustainable practices and legal compliance in the corporate world. She was known for her expertise, integrity, and commitment to environmental justice. One day, Denise received an unexpected offer: to lead a high-profile case representing a major corporation accused of environmental violations. At first, Denise hesitated. The case was complex, high-stakes, and highly visible. It presented significant challenges, including public scrutiny, legal complexities, and potential backlash from environmental activists and the media. After reading this chapter, Denise realized she was facing a glass cliff opportunity. Denise carefully vetted the situation and, after sufficiently examining the risks and opportunities, negotiated for the resources she needed so that she would have a sufficient chance of success. As she proceeded with the case, she faced numerous obstacles and pressures. The media scrutinized her every move, environmental groups protested outside the courthouse, and public opinion was divided. However, Denise remained steadfast in her principles, conducting thorough research, collaborating with experts, and presenting compelling arguments based on facts and evidence. Despite the challenges, Denise's leadership and dedication paid off. The case resulted in a landmark settlement that not only addressed the environmental violations but also implemented sustainable practices and contributed to environmental conservation efforts. Denise's role in achieving this outcome earned her recognition as a leading advocate for environmental justice and corporate responsibility.

Sharon had a reputation during much of her work life as driving herself and her staff incredibly hard. Every day was a work day and everyone was expected to be available at any hour. This caused tremendous strain for her staff, and Sharon's own health took the toll. After she had a heart attack, work-life balance no longer was an option. She made time for exercise, rest, and relaxation. She began to practice mindfulness. Therefore, when she read about managing her pace, she knew all too well that this was not an option either. As thrilling as it was to return to a semblance of work tasks and challenging goals, she knew better than to fill her days from dawn to dusk with activities to move her faster toward the boardroom. She made sure to leave room in her schedule for time with her children and grandchildren, time for her friends, and time for her favorite hobbies of pleasure reading, tennis, and swimming. When she was tempted to stay up late researching some board and industry trends, she fought the urge to make sure she got adequate rest every night. In this way, she was able to stay relaxed and refreshed, without dampening her excitement about her board search or her efficiency and effectiveness in securing a seat. She felt she had really figured out how to manage her pace and how to find a board seat in an ambitious yet responsible way.

ACTION ITEMS

Try the following steps to fail-proof your own journey to the boardroom:

1. Assess your opportunities before proceeding. When you find yourself facing a glass cliff or other compelling but challenging opportunities,

carefully evaluate and negotiate the situation using the exercises in this chapter. Take time to assess the competencies, energy, and passion you would need to overcome it, and then soberly evaluate whether you want to invest your resources in this way. For example, if you discover that success requires knowledge or skills you don't have and cannot realistically develop in the needed time frame, or when you cannot get the mentoring or advocacy you need to succeed, it may be wiser to walk away. When you deliberately evaluate the obstacles facing you, you will either take on the challenges fully informed or reallocate your abilities in more suitable environments.

2. Create bandwidth by pruning your commitments. Our lives, like trees, must be regularly pruned if we are to produce our healthiest outcomes. Decide what to prune by using your personal vision, mission, and values as your guide. For example, early in my career, I was pursuing several important goals at once, including finishing my college degree, training for the British Tang Soo Do championships, and pursuing my next military rank. At that time, I found that pruning other activities was critical to focusing and being disciplined to achieve these milestones.

3. Plan and celebrate early wins and milestones. Securing a seat at the table requires hard work, sacrifice, and sometimes pain. For that reason, you must nourish yourself along the way by building in meaningful rewards that compensate for the pain and sacrifice involved in persisting on the path.

4. Manage your energy through rest, recovery, and self-care. Although the convention in Western culture is to push ourselves to the point of exhaustion and even destruction, growth and restoration only happens with adequate rest. For example, metabolic waste builds up in our brains during waking time; we need sufficient sleep to flush out this waste. In this way, self-care—rather than a luxury—is a necessity for performing at our best. As a corporate executive, I established the practice in all my teams of keeping weekends for personal time. I considered this downtime essential for myself and my direct reports to gain adequate rest and separation from work—after all, it is during rest when strength, resilience, and well-being is forged. Schedule your time for rest and rejuvenation as you would for any other meeting.

SUMMARY

Fail-proofing your journey means taking the necessary precautions to protect your progress from the inevitable problems and pitfalls that will arise on your path to the boardroom. The precise strategy may differ from one aspiring director to another; however, most incorporate tactics such as identifying defined short-, mid-, and long-term goals; celebrating modest triumphs; and developing clear action plans while being flexible and adjusting your plan as needed. Additionally, you must be adept at distinguishing the enticing but career-limiting dead end from the challenging endeavor worth pursuing. Additionally, because it may take several years to reach the boardroom, you will need to discover strategies to stay motivated by recognizing your reasons for embarking on this journey and reminding yourself of their importance along the route. You also will need to consider inevitable setbacks as learning opportunities and adjust your strategy accordingly. By applying these strategies, you can increase your chances of success and deal with challenges more effectively.

CHAPTER FIFTEEN

CONCLUSION

Prosperity is temporary, adversity is inevitable, and effort is essential.
—Pastor Mont Mitchell, Westbrook Christian Church

Only a small percentage of people seeking a board seat actually go on to become a director. Having read this book, you now understand that if you want a board seat, you are going to have to work hard to get it. My research has indicated that, for the few who actually make it, they take three to five years from the point of saying "I want to get on a board" to actually landing a seat, and those three to five years are filled with deliberate actions that make that board seat a reality.

This book guided you through the process and steps of finding your route to meaningful board service. First, we got oriented to the board landscape and the benefits of holding a board position. Then, we learned the process of self-evaluation and mobilization for the journey. Finally, we gained tools and tactics for managing ourselves along the way in order to achieve the best possible board service results. In each chapter, we also revisited our protagonists to see how they were navigating each step of the journey and gained practical action steps to implement on the journey. In this chapter, we review the most critical action steps for you to take next before revisiting where each of our main characters are now.

WHAT'S NEXT

Although this book is full of action items, a few points bear repeating. First, you should become a vocal advocate for yourself by letting anyone and everyone know you are interested in serving on corporate boards and by continuing to network with recruiters. This is crucial because it will help you increase your visibility, access board opportunities, gain valuable insights, receive referrals and recommendations, enhance your professional development, build relationships, and stay informed about market trends. It presents you as a proactive and strategic board candidate prepared to make a significant impact in the boardroom.

Second, be sure to lift others up along the way. You can do so by recommending others for open positions when you are invited to fill a position that doesn't match your availability, interests, or competencies. Nominating others for positions you cannot fill yourself can be both strategic and beneficial because it contributes to the board's diversity and inclusion, strengthens your relationships and professional network, enhances your reputation, and promotes reciprocity and collegiality within your network. Moreover, nominating others can increase the likelihood that they include you in their professional networks and recommend you for opportunities in the future.

Third, the opportunities you seek and create for yourself need to be customized to your specific competencies, needs, and aspirations. For example, your plan may include seeking positions that develop needed competencies (e.g., profit-and-loss experience) and contributing to your own company's board by helping its committees or presenting to the board regarding your function. It is particularly important to gain these experiences if you work for a public company, as that can pave the way to a public corporate seat of your own in the future. As you progress through your career, carefully selecting the opportunities you take is crucial to ensure alignment with your goals and needed development of your skills and professional reputation. Each career experience has a cost, so it's essential to carefully invest time, energy, and resources in the most impactful experiences. Ultimately, selectively choosing career experiences results in higher levels of personal fulfillment and satisfaction, because it enables you to pursue work that aligns with your passions, interests, and values.

Fourth, start immediately. None of this is easy to do if you begin after you have left your corporate career or even a couple of months before you leave. Some of the directors I spoke with started on their road to a meaningful post-career in their 20s because they had role models within their families who were board members and advised them to secure progressive management roles throughout their careers. It takes significant time to cultivate new competencies, build relationships, and create the opportunities you need to achieve a fulfilling post-career; therefore, beginning early is a must.

HELPFUL RESOURCES

You've covered a lot of ground in the preceding pages and gained valuable insights and strategies to travel the path toward securing a seat at the corporate board table. To ensure you remain on the path to the boardroom, it's crucial to leverage additional resources that can further enhance your skills, expand your network, and deepen your understanding of corporate governance. Following is a curated list of helpful resources, from educational programs and professional organizations to mentorship opportunities and research tools, all designed to support your continued growth and success in securing a board position.

Board readiness programs and networking groups. A variety of online and in-person courses are available that cover the essentials of being a board member. These programs provide a robust mix of education, practical insights, and networking opportunities to help individuals prepare for and excel in corporate board roles. Several reputable programs that can help prepare individuals for corporate board positions include the following:

Global
- **50/50 Women on Boards Workshops** provides workshops focusing on board readiness and effective governance practices, aimed at increasing the number of women on corporate boards.
- **ECGI (European Corporate Governance Institute)** is an international scientific nonprofit organization offering research and policy advice on corporate governance. It serves as a forum for academics and practitioners to share knowledge and best practices in governance.

- **Executive Leadership Council (ELC) Corporate Board Navigator** is a membership program that offers resources, networking, and guidance for executives aiming to secure board positions, with a focus on diversity and inclusion.
- **Harvard Business School's Women on Boards** is specifically designed for women executives to prepare for board roles through leadership development and networking opportunities.
- **INSEAD International Directors Programme** offers a comprehensive approach to corporate governance and board effectiveness, tailored for current and aspiring board members.
- **International Center for Corporate Governance** provides research, education, and training programs to enhance board effectiveness and governance practices globally, helping directors improve their performance in corporate governance roles.
- **National Association of Corporate Directors (NACD)** provides networking opportunities, educational resources, and events for corporate directors across various industries.
- **Stanford Women on Boards Initiative** provides resources, training, and networking opportunities to prepare women for board service, emphasizing strategic governance and leadership.
- **Women Corporate Directors Foundation (WCD)** offers forums, events, and resources to connect and empower women who serve on corporate boards.

Europe, Middle East, and Africa
- **The Boardroom** is a Switzerland-based exclusive club for women executives preparing for board roles. It offers tailored education, networking opportunities, and expert support to enhance board readiness. With a focus on empowering women leaders, The Boardroom fosters growth, collaboration, and confidence, helping members achieve their goals and succeed in corporate governance.
- **deb** (Diverse Executive Boards) is a Swedish organization dedicated to enhancing corporate governance by increasing diversity in boardrooms.

They offer board training programs and recruitment services to equip boards with the necessary competencies and perspectives for future challenges.

- **Diversity on Board** is an organization that focuses on advancing diversity in corporate leadership through training, mentorship, and advocacy, helping executives from underrepresented groups gain access to board opportunities.
- **European Women on Boards Network** provides training, networking, and advocacy designed to enhance the presence of women on corporate boards in Europe.
- **Inclusive Capitalism European Women on Boards** offers education and support for women aspiring to board positions with the aim to improve gender diversity in boardrooms across Europe.
- **Institute of Directors (IoD)** offers networking, professional development, and resources for directors across multiple sectors in the UK.
- **The Institute of Directors in South Africa (IoDSA)** provides comprehensive training, development, and certification programs for directors and aspiring board members across various sectors. The institute focuses on enhancing governance standards and promoting ethical leadership through networking events, educational resources, and board-level certifications.
- **Strathmore Business School Board Readiness Forum** offers training and resources for executives to prepare for board roles, with a focus on governance and leadership.
- **Women on International Boards Program** was launched by the UAE's Gender Balance Council, and aims to equip women with the skills and knowledge needed for board service on international corporate boards. It focuses on leadership development, governance training, and fostering global networking opportunities to increase female representation in top decision-making roles.

The Americas

- **Ascend Board of Directors Program** provides resources, training, networking, and continuing education designed to help Asian directors secure and succeed in board roles.

- **Athena Alliance** provides executive coaching, mentorship, and board placement services, particularly aimed at increasing women's representation in corporate boardrooms. The platform helps executives expand their leadership skills and board readiness through networking and personalized learning.
- **Black Corporate Board Readiness (BCBR)** is housed at Santa Clara University's Leavey Executive Center. Becoming Corporate Board Ready prepares executives for board service, highlighting the importance of governance, leadership, and strategic oversight.
- **Corporate Directors Forum** is a premier platform offering valuable resources and educational programs designed to enhance the effectiveness of corporate directors. It provides insights, networking opportunities, and tools for best practices in corporate governance, fostering excellence in boardroom leadership.
- **Extraordinary Women on Boards (EWOB)** is a private network of experienced female board directors dedicated to advancing boardroom excellence and modernizing governance. With over 700 members representing more than 2,400 corporate boards, EWOB provides cutting-edge knowledge, valuable resources, and powerful connections to amplify women's influence in boardrooms and beyond.
- **illumyn Impact** offers events and networking designed to accelerate diversity on corporate boards by connecting women leaders with board opportunities.
- **Institute of Corporate Directors** is a leading organization dedicated to advancing boardroom effectiveness and corporate governance excellence in Canada through rigorous education, certification, and thought leadership.
- **Kellogg School of Management Women's Director Development Program** prepares senior women executives for board service, with a strong emphasis on corporate governance and networking.
- **Latino Corporate Directors Association (LCDA)** offers networking and professional development opportunities for Latino directors, designed to increase the number of US Latinos on corporate boards.

- **OnBoarding Women** provides training, mentorship, and networking designed to prepare women for corporate board service and increase female representation on boards.
- **OnBoard** provides educational resources and networking opportunities for women seeking to join corporate boards, focusing on governance, leadership, and board dynamics.
- **Private Directors Association (PDA)** offers networking and educational opportunities specifically for directors of private companies, including webinars and virtual events, covering a wide range of governance topics.
- **Stanford Directors' College** located within Stanford Law School is a premier executive education program offering insights into boardroom dynamics, regulatory updates, and strategic oversight.
- **University of North Carolina Director Diversity Initiative** provides training and networking opportunities to increase the diversity of corporate boards by preparing women and minorities for board service.

Asia-Pacific

- **Board Academy Asia** offers specialized training programs for aspiring and current board members, with a focus on corporate governance, leadership, and strategic oversight in the Asia-Pacific region. The academy provides workshops and networking opportunities designed to prepare leaders for board roles in diverse industries.
- **EY ISB Executive Program on Board Effectiveness** offers specialized training for board members, focusing on governance, strategy, leadership, and diversity. The program includes workshops and expert insights to enhance boardroom effectiveness and impact.
- **Get on Board Australia Boardroom Bootcamp** is a comprehensive bootcamp for aspiring board members, covering governance, board dynamics, and strategic oversight.
- **SID (Singapore Institute of Directors)** is a national association for company directors, offering a wide range of professional development programs, certifications, and networking opportunities aimed at enhancing board effectiveness and corporate governance standards. SID provides

resources for directors to stay informed on best practices and regulatory changes in governance.

- **University of Queensland MBA Becoming Board Ready** prepares MBA graduates for board service with a focus on governance, strategy, and leadership.

Corporate governance certifications. The following certifications are recognized globally and provide valuable knowledge and skills for those seeking to enhance their expertise in corporate governance:

- **Chartered Director (C.Dir) by The Directors College** provides comprehensive training in corporate governance, strategy, and ethical decision-making.
- **Harvard Business School Corporate Governance Program** provides an in-depth understanding of corporate governance, including board responsibilities, financial oversight, and strategic leadership.
- **ICSA: The Chartered Governance Institute** offers the Chartered Governance Qualifying Program (CGQP), which covers a wide range of governance topics, including corporate law, risk management, and compliance.
- **INSEAD Certificate in Corporate Governance:** is tailored for board members and aspiring directors, focusing on best practices in governance, board dynamics, and leadership.
- **Institute of Corporate Directors (ICD)** offers various certification programs, including the ICD.D Designation and the ICD-Rotman Directors Education Program (DEP), designed to enhance governance competencies and board effectiveness.
- **NACD Directorship Certification°** is a comprehensive certification program designed to enhance board members' governance knowledge and skills and covers key areas such as governance, risk management, and financial acumen.

- **Private Directors Association Certificate in Private Company Governance** provides comprehensive training on governance principles for private company boards, focusing on best practices and director responsibilities.

Board-related publications. Your director capital will be greatly enhanced by subscribing to journals that have authoritative content and insights into corporate governance, leadership, and boardroom dynamics essential reading for aspiring board directors. These sources will help you stay informed about the latest governance trends, best practices, and regulatory changes.

- *Agenda* offers expert insights into corporate governance, boardroom dynamics, and leadership trends. The publication covers key issues affecting directors of public and private companies, including regulatory changes, risk management, and strategic oversight, making it an essential resource for board members.
- *Directors & Boards Magazine* is a leading publication focused specifically on corporate governance, providing in-depth articles, interviews, and analysis on boardroom issues and trends.
- **European Corporate Governance Institute publications** provide resources and research on corporate governance practices in Brazil that are useful for understanding international governance standards.
- *NACD Directorship Magazine* is published by the National Association of Corporate Directors, and provides comprehensive coverage of boardroom issues, best practices, and regulatory updates.
- *Private Company Director* covers unique challenges faced by private company boards, offering guidance on improving board effectiveness and navigating governance complexities. It also provides valuable insights on governance, best practices, and strategic leadership.

Publications for keeping pace for changing business dynamics. Staying updated on publications in business and corporate governance can provide invaluable insights into leadership trends, emerging strategies, and global market dynamics. These resources can help you navigate challenges, foster innovation, and maintain a competitive edge. Following is a list of publications to explore:

- *The Economist* provides global coverage of economic trends, corporate governance, and leadership challenges. It offers a macro perspective on business, politics, and economics, giving corporate directors insights into global market dynamics and governance challenges.
- *Fast Company* highlights innovation, leadership, and creative business strategies that drive success in the modern corporate environment. It offers articles on governance, corporate culture, and the trends shaping business and leadership today.
- *Forbes* delivers in-depth articles on corporate governance, leadership, and strategy from top business leaders and experts. Its coverage includes insights on board practices, risk management, and innovations shaping modern business governance.
- *Fortune* provides comprehensive coverage of business leadership, corporate governance, and industry trends. It offers insights into how top companies and leaders are navigating challenges and shaping the future of business, making it a must-read for corporate directors.
- *Harvard Business Review (HBR)* is renowned for its articles on leadership, strategy, and management and provides valuable insights and research on corporate governance and board practices.
- *Inc.* focuses on entrepreneurial leadership and innovation, offering valuable insights on governance, management, and scaling businesses. It covers trends in business strategy, leadership, and emerging technologies, making it an essential resource for growing companies.
- *McKinsey Quarterly* is published by McKinsey & Company and includes articles on corporate strategy, governance, and performance, with insights from global business leaders.

- *MIT Sloan Management Review* focuses on how management and technology intersect, offering insights into business strategy, innovation, and leadership. It provides research and thought leadership on governance and management practices in a rapidly evolving business landscape.

Events for building general and specialized director capital. General networking events also can offer excellent opportunities for you to network with current board members and executives, gain insights from industry leaders, and stay updated on the latest trends and challenges in corporate governance and leadership. Following is a list of some of these events:

- **World Economic Forum (WEF) Annual Meeting in Davos** gathers global leaders from various sectors, including business, politics, and academia, providing unparalleled networking opportunities with top executives and board members.
- **Fortune Global Forum** is organized by *Fortune* magazine and brings together CEOs of the world's largest corporations, offering opportunities to network with high-level executives and board members.
- **The Conference Board's CEO Council** offers a series of events designed for CEOs and senior executives, providing a platform for networking and discussing corporate governance and leadership challenges.
- **NACD Global Directors Summit** is hosted by the National Association of Corporate Directors and is the largest and most comprehensive event for board directors, featuring networking opportunities with board members and top executives.
- **Milken Institute Global Conference** is an annual event that gathers leaders from finance, health, education, and technology sectors, facilitating high-level networking and discussions on critical global issues.

Mentorship and coaching. In Chapter 13, we reviewed the importance of having trusted mentors and coaches to help you navigate your primary career and position yourself for a board role. By discerningly seeking support, you can accelerate your progress and ensure you possess the competencies needed to add substantial value as a board member. You may find the mentoring and coaching you need from organizations such as following:

- **Chief** provides executive coaching and peer mentoring opportunities designed specifically for women in leadership roles. Its network fosters a supportive environment where members can enhance leadership skills and strategically prepare for board positions.
- **Athena Alliance** offers personalized coaching, networking, and educational resources tailored to women aspiring to board roles. Members gain access to board readiness programs and mentors who provide guidance on governance, leadership, and career strategy.
- **Lean In** focuses on building communities where women can find mentorship and support for leadership and boardroom aspirations. It provides tools and peer circles designed to strengthen leadership abilities and help members prepare for board responsibilities.

Research and insights. In Chapter 7, we discussed the need for generalized and specialized knowledge and how that contributes to the director capital that will enable you to set yourself apart as a prospective board member. The following resources can help you stay informed on industry trends, governance best practices, and emerging risks. This knowledge can enhance your decision-making and strategic oversight capabilities, helping you in providing substantial value to the board and effectively navigate complex business environments.

Market research tools. The following tools offer valuable insights and data that can significantly enhance the strategic decision-making capabilities of corporate board members:

- **Gartner** provides in-depth research and analysis on various industries and technologies, helping board members make informed strategic decisions.
- **IBISWorld** offers comprehensive industry reports and data, giving insights into market conditions, trends, and forecasts that are crucial for strategic planning and risk management.
- **Statista** is a robust platform for statistics, market data, and industry reports, enabling board members to access critical data for making evidence-based decisions.

- **Bloomberg Terminal** provides real-time financial data, news, and analytics, essential for board members to understand market movements, company performance, and economic trends.
- **PitchBook** delivers data on private and public markets, including information on venture capital, private equity, and mergers and acquisitions, which is vital for strategic growth and investment decisions.

Company analysis reports. Subscriptions to resources can provide you with access to detailed company financials and analyses. These resources can help equip you with critical insights and detailed analysis essential for making well-informed strategic decisions:

- **Bloomberg Intelligence** provides comprehensive research reports on companies, including financial performance, market position, and strategic initiatives. It is widely used for its detailed and timely information.
- **Bloomberg Terminal** provides real-time financial data, news, and analytics, essential for board members to understand market movements, company performance, and economic trends.
- **Diligent** provides governance-focused insights and tools, offering comprehensive data on board performance, risk oversight, and compliance trends. Diligent's analyses are pivotal for understanding digital transformation and environmental, social, and governance (ESG) integration in board practices.
- **Equilar** delivers data-driven insights on executive compensation, board composition, and shareholder engagement. Equilar's analyses equip directors and executives with key metrics and benchmarking tools essential for making informed governance and leadership decisions.
- **Gartner** provides in-depth research and analysis on various industries and technologies, helping board members make informed strategic decisions.
- **IBISWorld** offers comprehensive industry reports and data, giving insights into market conditions, trends, and forecasts that are crucial for strategic planning and risk management.
- **Moody's Investors Service** delivers credit ratings, research, and risk analysis on companies, providing insights into their financial stability and creditworthiness.

- **Morningstar** offers in-depth company reports focusing on financial health, competitive positioning, and market analysis. It is well regarded for its unbiased and thorough evaluations.
- **S&P Global Market Intelligence** features detailed company profiles, financial data, and strategic analysis, helping board members make informed decisions based on robust data.
- **Statista** is a robust platform for statistics, market data, and industry reports, enabling board members to access critical data for making evidence-based decisions.
- **LSEG Data & Analytics** offers comprehensive financial analysis, company reports, and market data, enabling board members to assess company performance and industry trends effectively.

Books and reports. Understanding the boardroom landscape (Chapter 2) and building the board-related knowledge (Chapter 7) is greatly enhanced by reading books, articles, and subscribing to journals. In fact, I consider this essential for staying informed about the latest governance trends, best practices, and regulatory changes. These resources provide in-depth knowledge, practical advice, and insights from experienced directors, enhancing your ability to contribute effectively and strategically in board roles.

Recommended reading list. Books can provide valuable insights and practical advice on various aspects of board governance, making them essential reads for both aspiring and current board directors. Here are some of my favorites:

- *The Board Book: An Insider's Guide for Directors and Trustees* by **William G. Bowen.** This book provides insights from a seasoned board member, offering practical advice on governance, decision-making, and board dynamics.
- *Boards That Lead: When to Take Charge, When to Partner, and When to Stay Out of the Way* by **Ram Charan, Dennis Carey, and Michael Useem.** This book offers practical guidance on how boards can lead effectively, balance their roles, and work in partnership with CEOs.
- *The Corporate Director's Guidebook* by **American Bar Association.** A comprehensive guidebook that covers legal responsibilities, best practices, and emerging trends for corporate directors.

- *Corporate Governance Matters: A Closer Look at Organizational Choices and Their Consequences* by **David Larcker and Brian Tayan.** This book examines the intricacies of corporate governance, providing evidence-based insights and practical advice for board members.
- *The Effective Board of Trustees* by **Richard P. Chait, William P. Ryan, and Barbara E. Taylor.** Although aimed at nonprofit boards, this book also is highly relevant for corporate boards. The authors discuss the roles, responsibilities, and best practices for effective board governance.
- *To the Top: How Women in Corporate Leadership Are Rewriting the Rules for Success* by **Jenna C. Fisher.** This book serves as a practical guide for women in corporate leadership, offering strategies to navigate board dynamics and succeed.
- *Startup Boards: A Field Guide to Building and Leading an Effective Board of Directors* (2nd ed.) by **Brad Feld, Matt Blumberg, and Mahendra Ramsinghani.** This guide offers actionable advice for entrepreneurs on building, managing, and leveraging effective startup boards for success.
- *Winning the Board Game: How Women Corporate Directors Make THE Difference* by **Betsy Berkhemer-Credaire.** Berkhemer-Credaire offers a compelling exploration of how women on corporate boards drive better decision-making and improve organizational performance.

Annual governance trends. Annual governance trend reports offer comprehensive insights into current board governance practices and emerging trends across industries. The following list provides some of the leading reports:

- **Deloitte's Annual Board Agenda** outlines the critical governance issues for boards in 2024, focusing on enterprise risk management, cybersecurity, and the impact of generative artificial intelligence. It offers insights on how boards can navigate these challenges and opportunities.
- **Diligent's Annual Board Governance Insights Report** highlights key governance trends, such as digital transformation, risk oversight, and the role of ESG in shaping board agendas.

- **Equilar's Annual Corporate Governance Outlook** examines trends in executive compensation, board composition, and shareholder engagement, offering data-driven insights for corporate directors.
- **Ernst & Young's Global Corporate Governance Annual Reports** explore governance priorities, including board accountability, risk oversight, and emerging trends in digital transformation and sustainability.
- **Harvard Law School's Corporate Governance Annual Report** provides a comprehensive overview of governance trends, including shareholder activism, board diversity, and legal responsibilities of directors.
- **KPMG's Private Company Board Survey** highlights trends in board composition, leadership, and priorities for private companies, emphasizing governance practices and engagement with stakeholders like employees and customers.
- **NACD's Annual Key Insights for Boards** highlights key trends for 2024, including geopolitical risks, economic uncertainty, digital innovation, and regulatory changes. It provides survey data from over 500 directors, detailing how these trends will shape boardroom decision-making.
- **PwC's Annual Corporate Directors Survey** focuses on board diversity, technology governance, and how directors are addressing economic uncertainty and ESG concerns.

Online resources and communities. Webinars, podcasts, and online communities can be another invaluable source for you to conveniently access practical knowledge, leadership insights, and governance strategies, while providing you with opportunities to network and stay informed about the latest trends and best practices in corporate governance.

Webinars. Webinars can provide a convenient way for you to gain valuable knowledge and practical insights as you prepare for and sharpen your ability to contribute in corporate board roles. Some webinars you might find helpful include the following:

- **NACD webinar series** offers a variety of webinars focused on boardroom basics, governance trends, and best practices.

- **Deloitte's Board Governance webcasts** provides insights on board governance, risk management, and regulatory updates.
- **Stanford Graduate School of Business—Directors' Consortium webinars** feature discussions on strategic board governance, risk oversight, and board effectiveness.
- **PwC Governance Insights Center webcasts** cover various topics including boardroom effectiveness, ESG issues, and governance challenges.
- **Harvard Business School—Corporate Director Webinar series** focuses on enhancing the effectiveness of board members through insights on governance, strategy, and leadership.

Podcasts. Podcasts can be another source of valuable insights into leadership, governance, and business strategy. The following podcasts provide insights on effective board practices, scaling businesses, gender diversity, and executive effectiveness, enhancing your capability to contribute meaningfully in board roles:

- **"HBR IdeaCast" by *Harvard Business Review*** provides weekly discussions on business and management topics.
- **"Masters of Scale" by Reid Hoffman** provides interviews with entrepreneurs and business leaders on scaling businesses.
- **"The Corporate Director Podcast" by Diligent Corporation** discusses corporate governance issues and insights for board members.
- **"The Boardroom Governance Podcast" by Evan Epstein** features discussions on corporate governance, including interviews with directors and governance experts.
- **"The Corporate Director Podcast" by Dottie Schindlinger and Meghan Day** explores corporate governance, strategy, and boardroom best practices, featuring interviews with industry leaders.
- **"Strategic Advisor Board Podcast"** by Jason Miller delivers insights from business leaders across various industries, sharing stories, challenges, and successes in governance and strategy.
- **"Board Shorts Podcast"** by Get on Board Australia offers education and development for new and aspiring company directors and board members, focusing on governance and leadership.

- **"C-Suite Perspectives"** by The Conference Board provides weekly conversations on pressing business issues, offering insights for C-suite executives and board members.
- **"The Look & Sound of Leadership" by Tom Henschel** focuses on executive coaching and leadership development. https://essentialcomm.com/podcast/

Online communities. Online communities provide valuable opportunities for networking, learning, and staying informed about the latest trends and best practices in corporate governance. Consider the following forums and online communities as you progress down your path to the boardroom:

- **NACD Connect** is a platform for NACD members to engage in discussions, share insights, and network with other board members. It offers a wealth of resources on governance best practices and boardroom trends.
- **BoardProspects** is an online community for board members and boardroom prospects to connect, share knowledge, and access educational resources. It features board opportunities, networking events, and forums.
- **International Corporate Governance Network on LinkedIn** is another LinkedIn group focused on corporate governance. Members include board directors, governance professionals, and industry experts who share insights and discuss the latest in boardroom practices.
- **Women Corporate Directors Foundation (WCD)** is a global membership organization dedicated to connecting and empowering women who serve on corporate boards. WCD offers forums, events, and resources to support board members and aspiring directors.

Legal and compliance resources. Accepting a seat on a corporate board comes with significant a legal and ethical responsibility that should not be underestimated. Take the time to review legal responsibility guides and compliance training to understand these legal obligations and best practices and ensure you are well-versed in ethics, risk management, and governance, all of which are crucial for effective board service.

Guides on legal responsibilities. The following guides offer essential information and practical advice on the legal responsibilities of corporate board members.

This can be helpful as you are learning about how to navigate complex governance issues to fulfill your fiduciary duties as a board member:

- **"The Corporate Director's Guidebook" by American Bar Association** is a comprehensive guide that provides detailed information on the legal responsibilities, fiduciary duties, and best practices for corporate directors.
- **"Directors' Responsibilities in Canada" by Osler, Hoskin & Harcourt LLP** is a guide that offers an in-depth look at the legal duties and liabilities of directors in Canada, including governance, compliance, and risk management.
- **"The Duty of Care of Corporate Directors and Officers" by Harvard Law School Forum on Corporate Governance** is a resource that provides a scholarly overview of the duty of care expected from corporate directors and officers, discussing legal standards and case law.
- **"Corporate Governance Principles for U.S. Listed Companies" by The Business Roundtable** is a document that outlines the key governance principles and legal responsibilities for directors of publicly traded companies in the United States.
- **"Directors' Duties: Navigating the Boardroom" by The Institute of Directors (IoD)** is a guide from the IoD that provides practical advice on the legal duties and responsibilities of directors, with a focus on governance and compliance.

Compliance training. The following providers offer programs that help corporate board members stay informed and compliant with the latest regulations and best practices in governance and ethics:

- **Society of Corporate Compliance and Ethics (SCCE)** offers a wide range of compliance and ethics training programs, including webinars, workshops, and certification programs tailored for corporate board members.
- **Harvard Business School Online** provides comprehensive online courses on corporate governance, compliance, and ethics, designed to enhance the knowledge and skills of board members.
- **Thomson Reuters Compliance Learning** delivers a variety of online compliance training courses covering key areas such as regulatory compliance, risk management, and corporate governance.

- **MIT Sloan School of Management Executive Education** offers specialized executive education programs focusing on compliance, corporate governance, and risk management, providing in-depth training for board members.
- **Deloitte Learning Academy** provides customized compliance and governance training programs for board members and executives, covering topics such as regulatory updates, ethics, and risk management.

THE ONE THING
TO DO NOW

I have hundreds of meetings with aspiring board directors and a consistent percentage, when asked "What type of board do you want to get on and why," answer, "I don't care, Keith, as long as you can get me on a paid board." Unfortunately, that mindset will not get you on a corporate board. Any lack of preparation or cavalier attitude will be detected during board interviews, likely disqualifying you from the process. Therefore, what you do need now is careful self-reflection and consideration of what corporate boards need and how and why you can fill those needs.

Therefore, if this is your first pass through the book, the most important thing to do now is to go back to the beginning and carefully work through the exercises presented in each chapter. Don't just skim through the content. Actively do the work by ensuring you complete all assignments and reflections thoroughly. Dot your I's and cross your T's. As you do so, you will notice yourself developing the qualities and mindset suitable for a board member, and making the deliberate transition from an unconsciously competent executive to a consciously competent governance professional.

Here are my top five tips to help you along this journey:

1. **Understand your motivation.** Reflect deeply on why you want to join a board. This clarity will keep you motivated and focused, especially during challenging times.

2. **Adopt a board member mindset.** Shift your thinking from being a leader who directs to a servant leader who collaborates and supports. This mindset is crucial for board roles where governance and oversight are key.

3. **Create a concrete plan.** Develop a clear, actionable plan outlining the steps you need to take. Include milestones and timelines to track your progress.

4. **Build a support system.** Engage with mentors, peers, and accountability partners who can provide guidance, support, and feedback. They will help you stay on track and make necessary adjustments.

5. **Reflect and adapt.** After every step you complete, take time to reflect on what you've learned and how you can improve. This mindset of continuous improvement will help you stay aligned with your goals and adapt to new challenges.

By following these steps and maintaining a disciplined approach, you will significantly increase your chances of securing a board seat and excelling in that role. Remember, this journey is about growth and transformation. It's about preparing you to make a meaningful contribution to the boards you aspire to join.

WHERE THEY ARE NOW

Over the course of this book we have been following our four protagonists, and each has progressed in substantial ways.

Lauren's interest in corporate boards began in high school when her uncle mentioned firing a CEO and searching for a replacement. Awestruck by the idea that CEOs could have bosses, the seeds of her curiosity about board service were planted. Over the years, spirited discussions with her uncle about corporate scandals, social unrest, and board responsibilities deepened her interest. Although she still has much to learn about corporate board practices and membership, her early career success and mentorship from her uncle have positione her well to bridge those knowledge gaps. As her story comes to a close, she has found several additional mentors who serve on corporate boards thanks to her nonprofit board service. With their insights and guidance, she is continuing to build her own human and social capital. She also is beginning to be known by other board members who are gaining firsthand knowledge of her service in governance roles. Lauren also now has a stronger vision for her career pathway forward. She is currently building relationships with her peers in operations so that, eventually, she could move into one of their roles, thus, gaining the breadth of expertise she needs to be a competent corporate board member.

Denise's background, education, and legal career provided minimal exposure to corporate boards. Her initial introduction occurred unexpectedly when she received an invitation to join the board of a gymnastics not-for-profit. Intrigued, she consented to attend a meeting, anticipating a gathering of seasoned professionals in a rustic lodge environment. She found herself pleasantly surprised by the diversity of the members and the vibrant, club-like atmosphere. With a keen interest, she joined the board and fulfilled the membership fee, despite her limited understanding of corporate governance. During fitness evaluations, Denise conducted thorough research on waste management and logistics companies while strategically networking with board members in those sectors, establishing robust relationships with individuals who acknowledged her contributions. Although these connections did not result in board appointments, a few facilitated interviews with other boards in the industry. Denise spent considerable time cultivating these new relationships and focused on being more interested in her new connections than in trying to be interesting to them. She found she had to call on the tenacity she built through her cultural capital to be able to hang in there until she finally got her first referral for a board seat after 18 long months. As her story comes to a close, she has just landed her first corporate board seat as an independent director with a second-generation family-owned metal recycling company.

Michele had been completely immersed in advancing her career into leadership positions, leaving little room for thinking about board service, apart from her internal board responsibilities tied to her professional roles. This shifted several years back when two executives from her leadership team independently brought up the importance of obtaining board positions. Although she might not have fully grasped the implications, her curiosity was piqued, and she determined, "When the opportunity arises, I will conduct my research and take action." Then California Senate Bill 826 was enacted, and the social unrest of 2020 unfolded. That fall, she was selected for two boards: one associated with private equity and another with a large cap public entity. With confidence stemming from her robust experience and contributions to internal boards, she accepted the opportunity. With that, she boldly entered the realm of corporate board service. Michele engaged in numerous reflection exercises to identify her purpose, ultimately realizing that her greatest fulfillment comes from serving on private corporate boards for growth-oriented companies seeking digital transformation. As her story comes to a close, Michele makes the tough decisions to retire from her corporate executive role and resign from the public company board role at the end of her first term. Realizing that life is short, she considered it vital to focus on governance in this phase of life, serving on boards where she could add the most value while maximizing what most warms her heart. Although she was highly competent in all three areas of board service, she realized she most liked the service and advisory part of her board service duties. Michelle now has a portfolio career serving on four private company boards: one 60-year-old family-owned manufacturing company owned and operated by the family's third generation, which had just brought on its first independent directors; two private equity-backed firms that hope to be acquired over the next three to five years; and one mid-sized private company looking to go public.

Sharon held the position of CEO on her company's internal board for 12 years. Although independent directors were present on her board, she had not previously held a position on any other board and had not considered it at all. It was only when the allure of retirement diminished that she recognized her desire to contribute to corporate boards as a key element of her post-career strategy. Sharon had to shift not only from being an executive and inside board director at her own company to being an independent director on someone else's board, she also had to learn new skills to build her social capital, repair strained past relationships, and conquer her imposter syndrome. Sharon has always been a hard worker, taking on these challenges in a "classic Sharon" way. She secured two private company boards through interesting channels. The first came about when she walked her dog (like she does every morning) and started a conversation with a neighbor who asked what type of things she was doing during her retirement. She decided to include in her list of activities that she is looking to serve on a private company board that could benefit from her decades of experience running a successful manufacturing business. Her neighbor responded, "My son, a recruiter for a search firm, just mentioned at a family function last week that he was looking for someone with your background." As they say, the rest was history because Sharon knew how to show up and present her skill sets in a way that her future board members could envision her adding value to their board. The second board role came about when Sharon commented on a LinkedIn post from a former colleague who left her company on unfavorable terms due to the way Sharon had treated him. After briefly exchanging pleasantries via LinkedIn, Sharon and the former employee agreed to meet in person. She learned he is now an executive advisor working with two different private equity firms. He reiterated to Sharon that he always appreciated her business acumen and heard from several of his former colleagues that she made many positive changes after her health scare. He introduced Sharon to several partners at the private equity firms, and Sharon eventually was placed on one of their portfolio company boards.

SUMMARY

This book has outlined the challenging path to the boardroom, what you need to do to get there, and who you need to become to reach it. The road to securing a board seat is long and challenging, but the rewards are immensely fulfilling. The journey requires sustained effort, continuous learning, and the ability to adapt and grow. This isn't for those seeking quick wins. It's for those committed to long-term success and making a meaningful impact.

Although I have used the metaphors of trails and pathways to describe the journey, corporate life—and the boardroom, by extension—more often is referred to as a jungle. This is not a mistake. Life in the jungle can threaten everything you know and believe about yourself and how to survive. Corporate life and board service, at their worst—and sometimes, even on a daily basis—can feel the same way.

Tahir Shah (2004, John Murray) wrote in *House of the Tiger King*, "The situation was different in the jungle. Every inch of ground had to be earned and was done so through much exertion…" (p. 11). Although the corporate and boardroom jungle requires equally significant exertion to earn ground, especially for women and people of color, if you survey the landscape, gear up for the trek, and effectively navigate the journey, you can not only survive this jungle but also achieve success. I wish you well on your journey.

NOTES

CHAPTER ONE

1. Paul, H.J. (2013). *The South Sea bubble: An economic history of its origins and conse-quences.* Routledge.
2. Zimbardo, P. ((2008)). *The Lucifer effect: Understanding how good people turn evil.* Random House Philip Zimbardo: The psychology of evil. (2015). YouTube. Retrieved November 4, 2015.
3. Booth-Bell, D. (2018). Social capital as a new board diversity rationale for enhanced corporate governance. *Corporate Governance: The International Journal of Business in Society 18*: https://doi.org/10.1108/CG-02-2017-0035.; Brammer, S., Millington, A., and Rayton, B. (2007). The contribution of corporate social responsibility to organiza-tional commitment. *International Journal of Human Resource Management 18*: 1701–1719. https://doi.org/10.1080/09585190701570866.
4. Cook, A. and Glass, C. (2018). Women on corporate boards: Do they advance corpo-rate social responsibility? *Human Relations 71* (7): 897–924. https://doi.org/10.1177/0018726717729207.; Zweigenhaft, R.L. and Domhoff, G.W. ((2014)). *The new CEOs: Women, African American, Latino, and Asian American leaders of Fortune 500 compa-nies.* Rowman & Littlefield..
5. Brammer et al., 2007; Carter, David A., Simkins, Betty J., and Simpson, W. Gary. (2003). Corporate governance, board diversity, and firm value. *The Financial Review 38*: 33–53. https://doi.org/10.1111/1540-6288.00034.; Kirsch, A. (2018). The gender composition of corporate boards: A review and research agenda. *The Leadership Quarterly 29*: 346–364.

https://doi.org/10.1016/j.leaqua.2017.06.001.; Nielsen, S. and Huse, M. (2010). Women directors' contribution to board decision-making and strategic involvement: The role of equality perception. *European Management Review 7*: https://doi.org/10.1057/emr .2009.27.

6. Carter et al., 2003; Kirsch, 2018; Post, C. and Byron, K. (2015). Women on boards and firm financial performance: A meta-analysis. *The Academy of Management Journal 58*: https://doi.org/10.5465/amj.2013.0319.; Terjesen, S., Sealy, R., and Singh, V. (2009). Women directors on corporate boards: A review and research agenda. *Corporate Governance: An International Review 17*: 320–337. https://doi.org/10.1111/j.1467-8683 .2009.00742.x..

7. Konrad, A., Kramer, V., and Erkut, S. (2008). Critical mass: The impact of three or more women on corporate boards. *Organizational Dynamics 37*: 145–164. https://doi .org/10.1016/j.orgdyn.2008.02.005.; Torchia, M., Calabrò, A., and Huse, M. (2011). Women directors on corporate boards: From tokenism to critical mass. *Journal of Business Ethics 102*: 299–317. https://doi.org/10.1007/s10551-011-0815-z.; Wiley, C. and Monllor-Tormos, M. (2018). Board gender diversity in the STEM&F sectors: The critical mass required to drive firm performance. *Journal of Leadership & Organizational Studies 25* (3): 290–308. https://doi.org/10.1177/1548051817750535.

8. Adams, Renée B., & Ferreira, Daniel. (2008). Women in the boardroom and their impact on governance and performance. European Corporate Governance Institute (ECGI) Finance Working Paper No. 57/2004. https://ssrn.com/abstract=1107721; Kirsch, 2018; Nielsen & Huse, 2010; Sidhu, J.S., Feng, Y., Volberda, H.W., and Van Den Bosch, F.A.J. (2021). In the shadow of social stereotypes: Gender diversity on corporate boards, board chair's gender and strategic change. *Organization Studies 42* (11): 1677–1698. https://doi.org/10.1177/0170840620944560.; Terjesen et al., 2009; Torchia et al., 2011.

9. Adams & Ferreira, 2008; Grosvold, J., Rayton, B., and Brammer, S. (2016). Women on corporate boards: A comparative institutional analysis. *Business & Society 55* (8): 1157–1196. https://doi.org/10.1177/0007650315613980.; Pathan, S. and Faff, R. (2012). Does board structure in banks really affect their performance? *Journal of Banking & Finance 37*: https://doi.org/10.1016/j.jbankfin.2012.12.016.; Terjesen et al., 2009.

10. Adams & Ferreira, 2008; Kirsch, 2018; Nielsen & Huse, 2010; Sidhu et al., 2021.

11. Brammer et al., 2007; Carter et al., 2003; Sinclair-Desgagné, B., Francoeur, C., and Labelle, R. (2008). Gender diversity in corporate governance and top management. *Journal of Business Ethics 81*: 83–95. https://doi.org/10.1007/s10551-007-9482-5.; Kirsch, 2018; Nielsen & Huse, 2010; Post & Byron, 2015.

12. Adams & Ferreira, 2008;Amorelli, María-Florencia, & García-Sánchez, Isabel-María. (2020). Critical mass of female directors, human capital, and stakeholder engagement by corporate social reporting. *Corporate Social Responsibility and Environmental Management, 27*(1), 204–221. 10.1002/csr.1793; Kirsch, 2018.

13. Nielsen & Huse, 2010; Post & Byron, 2015; Terjesen, S., Couto, E., and Francisco, P. (2015). Does the presence of independent and female directors impact firm performance? A multi-country study of board diversity. *Journal of Management & Governance* 20: https://doi.org/10.1007/s10997-014-9307-8.

14. Creary, Stephanie J., McDonnell, Mary-Hunter ("Mae"), Ghai, Sakshi, & Scruggs Jared. (2019). When and why diversity improves your board's performance. *Harvard Business Review* (March 2). https://hbr.org/2019/03/when-and-why-diversity-improves-your-boards-performance; Dominguez, C., & Lyles, L. (2019). *Fit for the future: An urgent imperative for board leadership*. NACD Blue Ribbon Commission; Nielsen & Huse, 2010; Post & Byron, 2015.

15. Guest, P.M. (2019). Does board ethnic diversity impact board monitoring outcomes? *British Journal of Management* 30 (1): 53–74. https://doi.org/10.1111/1467-8551 .12299.

16. Adams & Ferreira, 2008; Grosvold et al., 2016; Guest, 2019; Hekman, D.R., Johnson, S.K., Foo, M.-W., and Yang, W. (2017). Does diversity-valuing behavior result in diminished performance ratings for non-white and female leaders? *Academy of Management Journal* 60 (2): 771–797. https://doi.org/10.5465/amj.2014.0538.; Kirsch, 2018; Post & Byron, 2015; Terjesen et al., 2009, 2015.

17. Adams & Ferreira, 2008; Bosworth, W. and Lee, S. (2017). Mandated or spontaneous board diversity? Does it matter? *Journal of Business and Behavioral Sciences* 29 (1): 45–56.; Byron & Post, 2016; Del Carmen Triana, M., Miller, T.L., and Trzebiatowski, T.M. (2014). The double-edged nature of board gender diversity: diversity, firm performance, and the power of women directors as predictors of strategic change. *Organization Science* 25 (2): 609–632. https://doi.org/10.1287/orsc.2013.0842.; Kirsch, 2018; Rasmussen, C.C., Ladegård, G., and Korhonen-Sande, S. (2018). Growth intentions and board composition in high-growth firms. *Journal of Small Business Management* 56 (4): 601–617. https://doi.org/10.1111/jsbm.12307.

18. Crenshaw, K. (1989). Demarginalizing the intersection of race and sex: A black feminist critique of antidiscrimination doctrine, feminist theory and antiracist politics. *University of Chicago Legal Forum 1989* (1): https://chicagounbound.uchicago.edu/ uclf/vol1989/iss1/8.; DeHaas, D., Akutagawa, L., & Spriggs, S. (2019). Missing pieces report: The 2018 board diversity census of women and minorities on Fortune 500 boards alliance for board diversity. Deloitte. https://www2.deloitte.com/content/dam/ Deloitte/us/Documents/center-for-board-effectiveness/us-cbe-missing-pieces-report-2018-board-diversity-census.pdf; Glass, C. and Cook, A. (2017). Appointment of racial/ethnic minority directors: ethnic matching or visibility threat? *Social Science Research 61*: 1–10. https://doi.org/10.1016/j.ssresearch.2016.07.004.; Sanchez-Hucles, J. and Davis, D.D. (2010). Women and women of color in leadership: Complexity, identity, and intersectionality. *The American Psychologist* 65 (3): 171–181. https://doi .org/10.1037/a0017459.; Schäpers, P., Windscheid, L., Mazei, J. et al. (2021). "Like will to like" or "opposites attract"? Management board diversity affects employer attractiveness. *Gender in Management 36* (5): 569–590. https://doi.org/10.1108/GM-10-2019-0182.

19. Deloitte, 2022. Missing pieces report (7th ed.). https://www2.deloitte.com/us/en/pages/center-for-board-effectiveness/articles/missing-pieces-report-board-diversity.html

20. Castañón Moats, M., DeNicola, P., and Malone, L. (2020). *Insights from PwC's 2020 Annual Corporate Directors Survey*. PwC's Governance Insights Center https://www.pwc.com/us/en/services/governance-insights-center/library/annual-corporate-directors-survey.html.

CHAPTER TWO

1. New York State. (2011). The statute law of the state of New York: Comprising the revised statutes and all other laws of general interests, in force January 1, 1881. (Vol. II). George S. Diossy.

2. Gevurtz, F.A. (2004). The historical and political origins of the corporate board of directors. *Hofstra Law Review 33* (1)): Article 3. http://scholarlycommons.law.hofstra.edu/hlr/vol33/iss1/3.

3. Heaslip, Emily. (2023). Nonprofit vs. not-for-profit vs. for-profit: What's the difference? https://www.uschamber.com/co/start/strategy/nonprofit-vs-not-for-profit-vs-for-profit

4. Heaslip, 2023.

5. NACD. (2023). 2022 Inside the public company boardroom. https://www.nacdonline.org/about/NACD-in-the-news/press-release/nacd-inside-the-public-company-boardroom-survey-report-finds-gender-diversity-ticking-upward/

6. Bolster. (2021). A declaration of independents: The important role independent directors play on diversifying & strengthening private company boards. https://bolster.com/resources/benchmark/

7. Rassart, C., & Miller, H. (2015). Through the eyes of the board: Key governance issues for 2015. *Directors' Alert* (p. 4). Retrieved from www2.deloitte.com/content/dam/../gx-ccg-directors-alert-2015.pdf

CHAPTER THREE

1. Erikson, Erik. (1950). *Childhood and society*. W. W. Norton.

2. Sinek, S. (2009). *Start with why*. Portfolio.; Sinek, Simon. (2009). How great leaders inspire action. TED Talk. https://www.ted.com/talks/simon_sinek_how_great_leaders_inspire_action?language=en

3. Dorsey, Keith. (2023, April 11). Designing a career of board service (Part I). *Forbes*. https://www.forbes.com/sites/forbesbusinesscouncil/2023/04/11/designing-a-post-career-of-board-service-part-i/; Dorsey, Keith. (2023, May 15). Designing a career of board service (Part II). *Forbes*. https://www.forbes.com/sites/forbesbusinesscouncil/2023/05/15/designing-a-post-career-of-board-service-part-ii/

CHAPTER FOUR

1. Locke, E.A. (1968). Toward a theory of task motivation and incentives. *Organizational behavior and human performance* 3 (2): 157–189. https://doi.org/10.1016/0030-5073 (68)90004-4.
2. Caspar, C., Dias, A.K., and Elstrodt, H.-P. (2010). *The five attributes of enduring family businesses*. McKinsey & Company https://www.mckinsey.com/capabilities/people-and-organizational-performance/our-insights/the-five-attributes-of-enduring-family-businesses.
3. https://globalnetwork.io/perspectives/2017/12/examining-family-businesses
4. https://eqvista.com/industries-sectors-received-vc-funding/
5. https://www.cib.barclays/our-insights/5-trends-in-shareholder-activism-that-have-emerged-in-2023.html
6. https://investor.bankofamerica.com/corporate-governance/management-team-and-directors
7. https://www.webuysg.com/Investor/corporate.html
8. Hurst, D.K. (1995). Crisis and renewal: Ethical anarchy in mature organizations. *Business Quarterly* (Winter), 33–40. http://www.davidkhurst.com/wp-content/uploads/2012/01/Crisis-and-Renewal-Ethical-Anarchy-in-Mature-Organizations-1995.pdf
9. https://ccsenet.org/journal/index.php/ijbm/article/view/57687

CHAPTER FIVE

1. https://www.forbes.com/sites/forbescoachescouncil/2020/02/06/how-can-you-assess-your-career-fitness/?sh=11b43d492fc7
2. https://www.sec.gov/edgar/search-and-access
3. KPMG. (2023). Private company board survey insights. https://boardleadership.kpmg.us/relevant-topics/articles/2023/private-company-board-trends.html
4. Spencer Stuart. (2023). 2023 U.S. Spencer Stuart board index. https://www.spencerstuart.com/research-and-insight/us-board-index

5. Deloitte. (2022). Missing pieces report (7th edition). https://www2.deloitte.com/us/en/pages/center-for-board-effectiveness/articles/missing-pieces-report-board-diversity.html
6. EgonZehnder. (2023). 2022/2023 Global board diversity tracker report. https://www.egonzehnder.com/global-board-diversity-tracker

CHAPTER SIX

1. Bourdieu, P. (1990)). Structures, habitus, practices. In: *The logic of practice*, 52–79). Stanford University Press.
2. https://www.rmmagazine.com/articles/article//2018/09/04/-Pale-Stale-Male-Does-Board-Diversity-Matter-
3. https://papers.ssrn.com/sol3/papers.cfm?abstract_id=835406
4. https://experientiallearninginstitute.org/what-is-experiential-learning/

CHAPTER NINE

1. Johnson, M. (2020). Playing the "long game" of networking to earn a board seat. *CIO* (February 13). https://www.cio.com/article/202180/playing-the-long-game-of-networking-to-earn-a-board-seat.html
2. Missing pieces report: Board diversity census. (2021, June 8). Catalyst. https://www.catalyst.org/research/missing-pieces-report-board-diversity-census

CHAPTER TEN

1. Sinek, S. (2009). *Start with why: How great leaders inspire everyone to take action.* Portfolio.
2. https://journals.aom.org/doi/10.5465/ame.2000.4468069

CHAPTER TWELVE

1. Clance, P.R. (1985). *The impostor phenomenon: Overcoming the fear that haunts your success.* Peachtree.

2. University of Calgary (2020, February 12). *Impostor syndrome as a diversity, equity & inclusion issue.* https://www.ucalgary.ca/news/impostor-syndrome-diversity-equity-inclusion-issue

3. Curtis, J., Hatvany, T., Barber, K.E., and Burkley, E. (2022). Moxie: Individual variability in motivation intensity. *Current Psychology 42*: 22226–22238.

4. https://www.entrepreneur.com/leadership/why-the-most-successful-people-have-the-most-haters/254282

5. Ibid.

INDEX

Note: Page references in *italics* refer to figures and tables.